DEAD OF WINTER™

GOOD GOOD DOG

AN ONI PRESS PUBLICATION

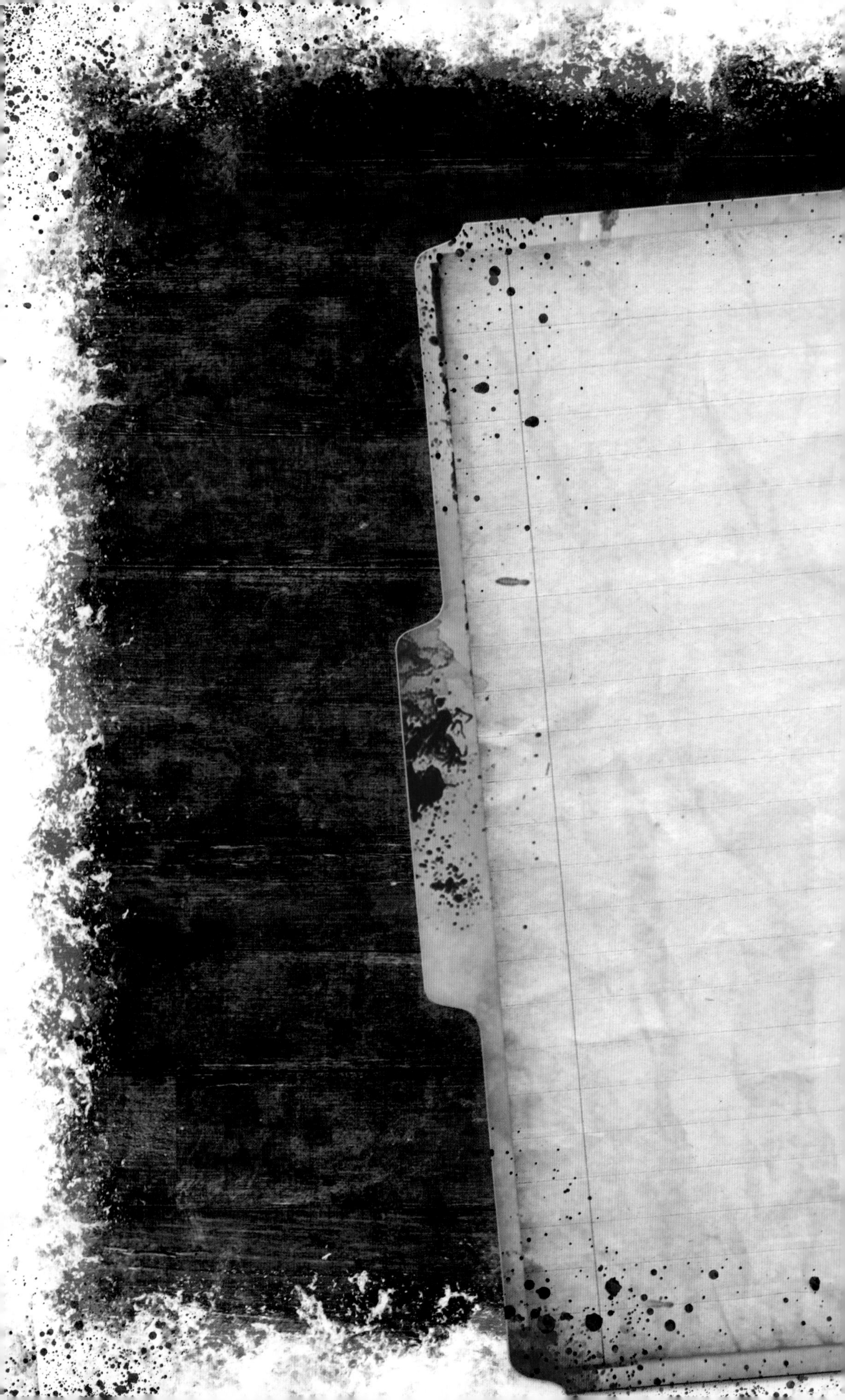

DEAD OF WINTER™

GOOD GOOD DOG

WRITTEN BY KYLE STARKS
ILLUSTRATED AND COLORED BY GABO
LETTERED BY CRANK!

RETAIL COVER ILLUSTRATED BY BRIAN HURTT & COLORED BY BILL CRABTREE
EXCLUSIVE COVER BY FERNANDA SUAREZ

Designed by Kate Z. Stone
Edited by Desiree Wilson with Charlie Chu

Dedicated to my best friend Stella, a Very Good Dog and to all the good dogs everywhere. —Kyle Starks

Dedicated to all the pups that have ever saved lives, whether it be physically or mentally. To all you humans, please remember to consider adopting! Specially the old puppers, they still have a lot of love to give! XOXO. —Gabo

PUBLISHED BY ONI PRESS, INC.

Joe Nozemack founder & chief financial officer

James Lucas Jones publisher

Charlie Chu v.p. of creative & business development

Brad Rooks director of operations

Rachel Reed marketing manager

Melissa Meszaros publicity manager

Troy Look director of design and production

Hilary Thompson senior graphic designer

Kate Z. Stone junior graphic designer

Angie Knowles digital prepress lead

Ari Yarwood executive editor

Robin Herrera senior editor

Desiree Wilson associate editor

Alissa Sallah administrative assistant

Jung Lee logistics associate

onipress.com
facebook.com/onipress
twitter.com/onipress
onipress.tumblr.com
instagram.com/onipress

Based on the game by

This volume collects issues #1-4 of the Oni Press series *Dead of Winter*™: *Good Good Dog*.

First Edition: April 2018
Retail ISBN 978-1-62010-483-5
Exclusive ISBN 978-1-62010-554-2
eISBN 978-1-62010-484-2

Printed in China.

Library of Congress Control Number: 2017952713

1 3 5 7 9 10 8 6 4 2

CHAPTER ONE

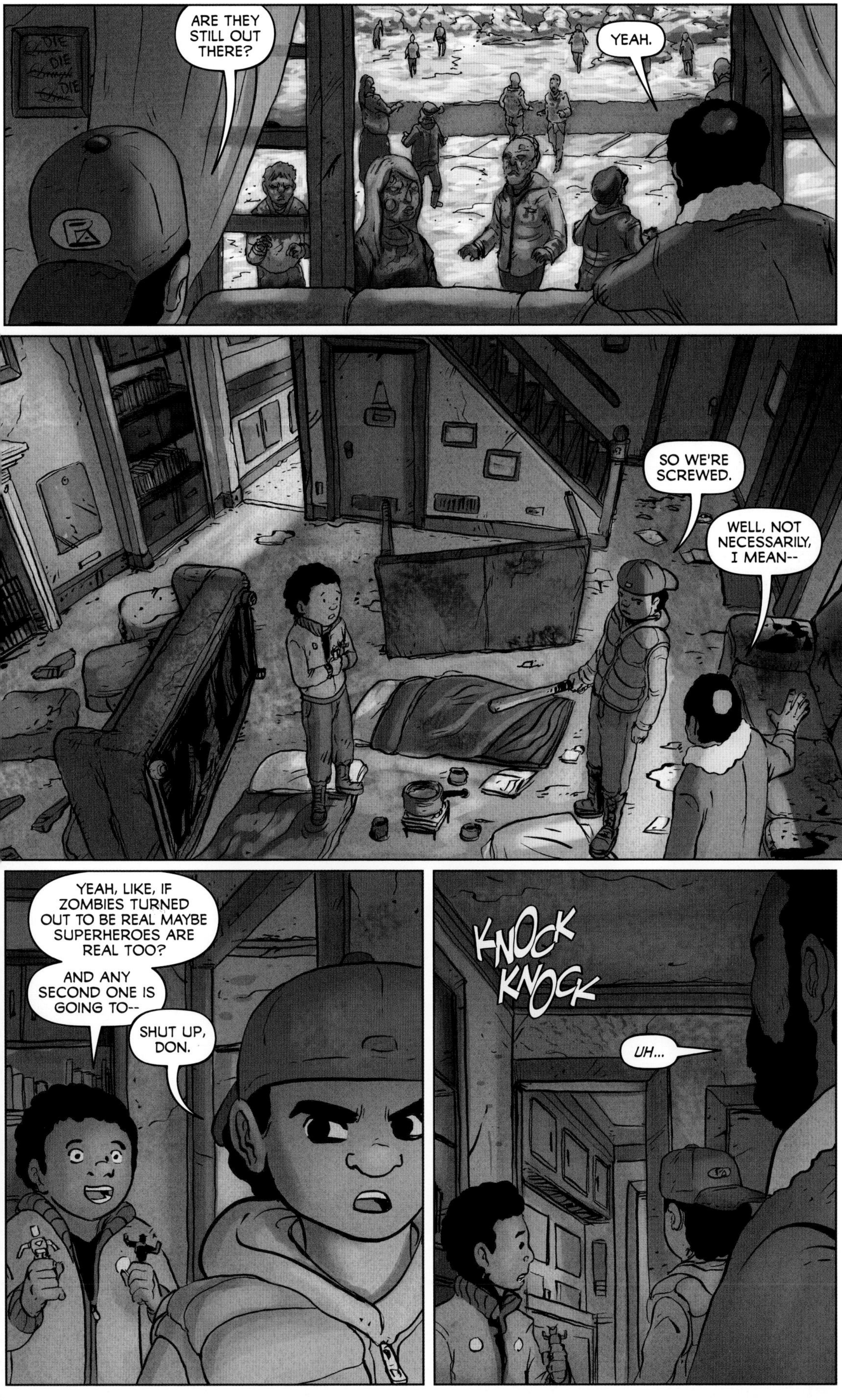
DIE
DIE
DIE
ARE THEY STILL OUT THERE?
YEAH.
SO WE'RE SCREWED.
WELL, NOT NECESSARILY, I MEAN--
YEAH, LIKE, IF ZOMBIES TURNED OUT TO BE REAL MAYBE SUPERHEROES ARE REAL TOO?
AND ANY SECOND ONE IS GOING TO--
SHUT UP, DON.
KNOCK KNOCK
UH...

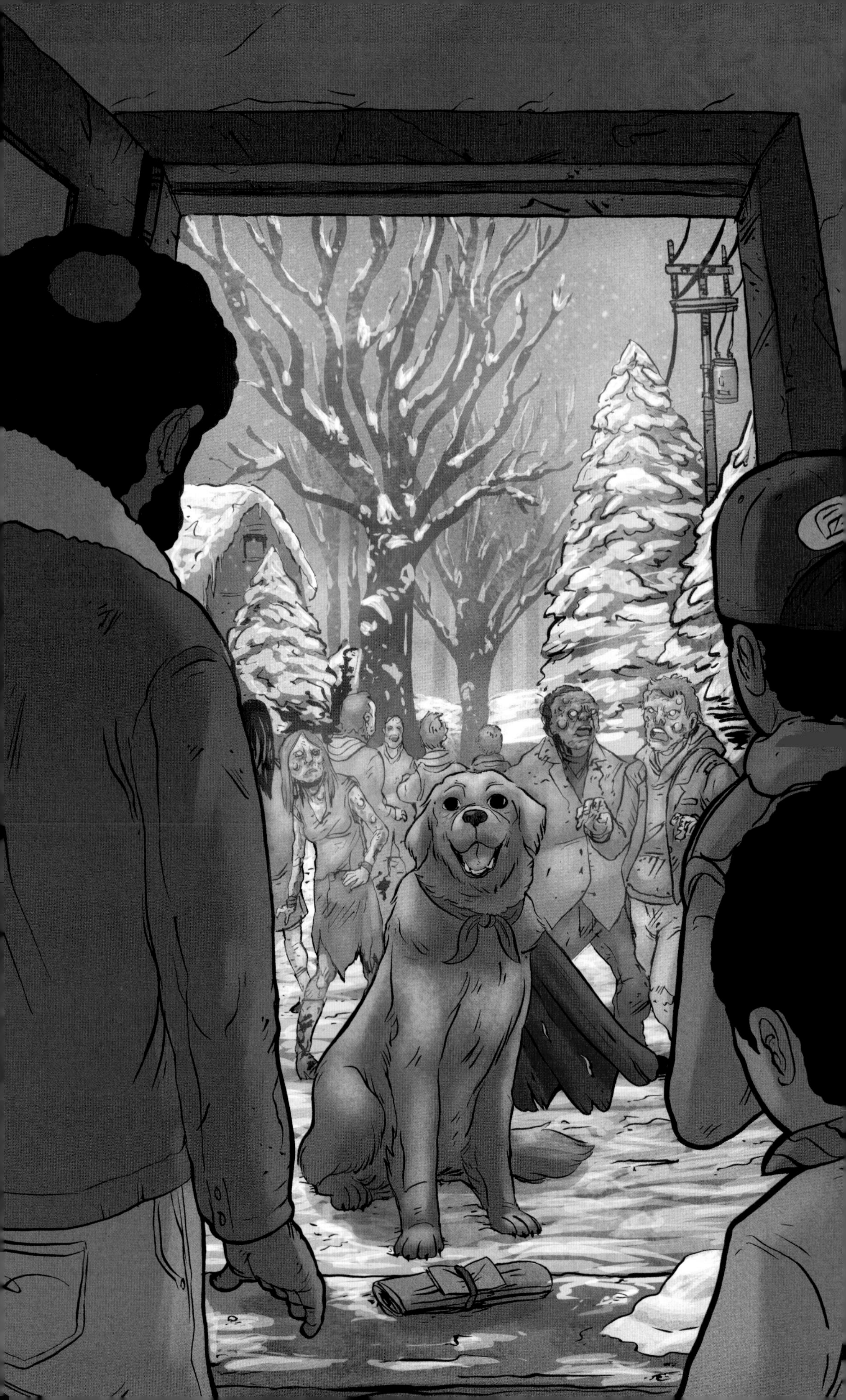

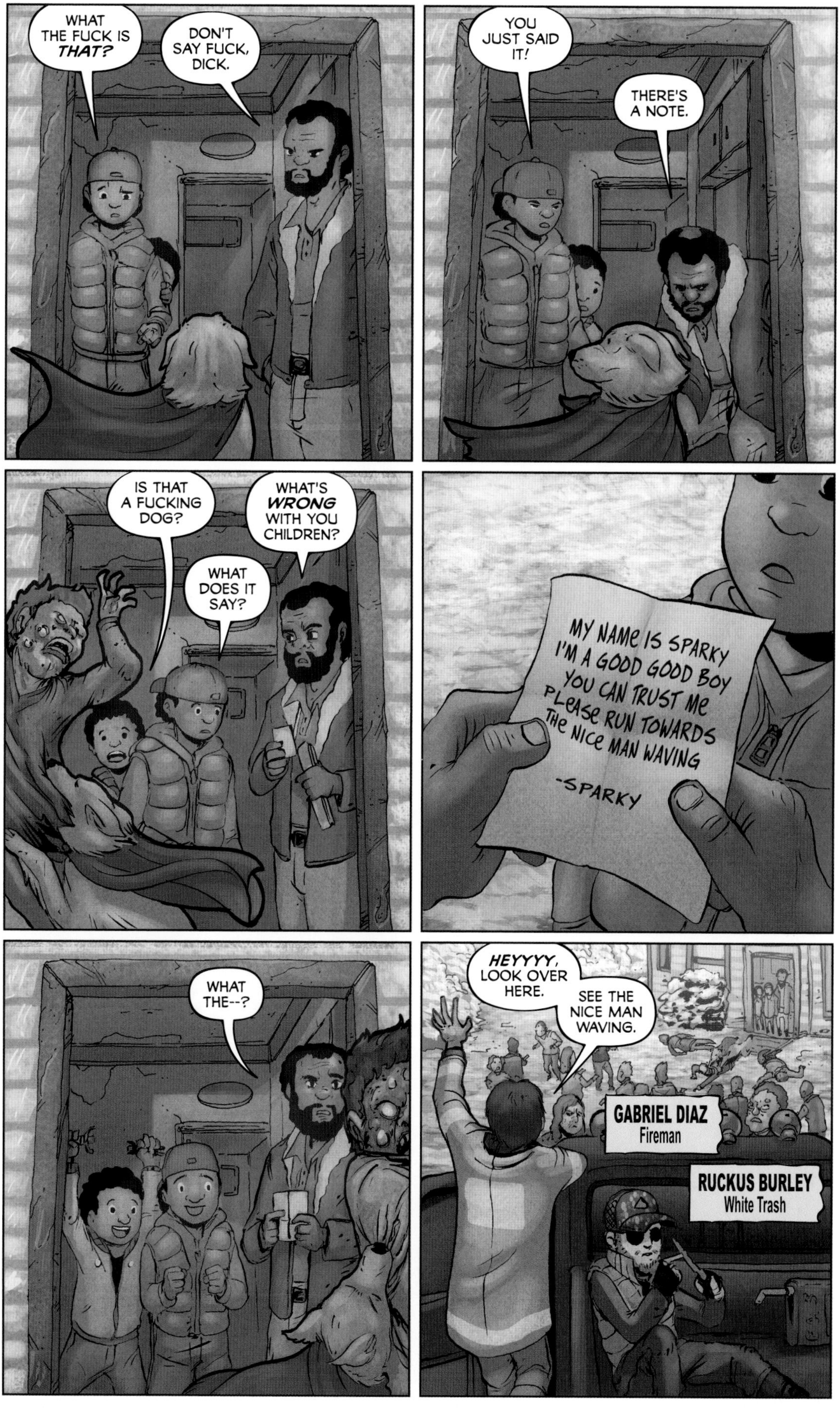
WHAT THE FUCK IS *THAT?*
DON'T SAY FUCK, DICK.
YOU JUST SAID IT!
THERE'S A NOTE.
IS THAT A FUCKING DOG?
WHAT'S *WRONG* WITH YOU CHILDREN?
WHAT DOES IT SAY?
MY NAME IS SPARKY
I'M A GOOD GOOD BOY
YOU CAN TRUST ME
PLEASE RUN TOWARDS
THE NICE MAN WAVING
-SPARKY
WHAT THE--?
HEYYYY, LOOK OVER HERE.
SEE THE NICE MAN WAVING.
GABRIEL DIAZ
Fireman
RUCKUS BURLEY
White Trash

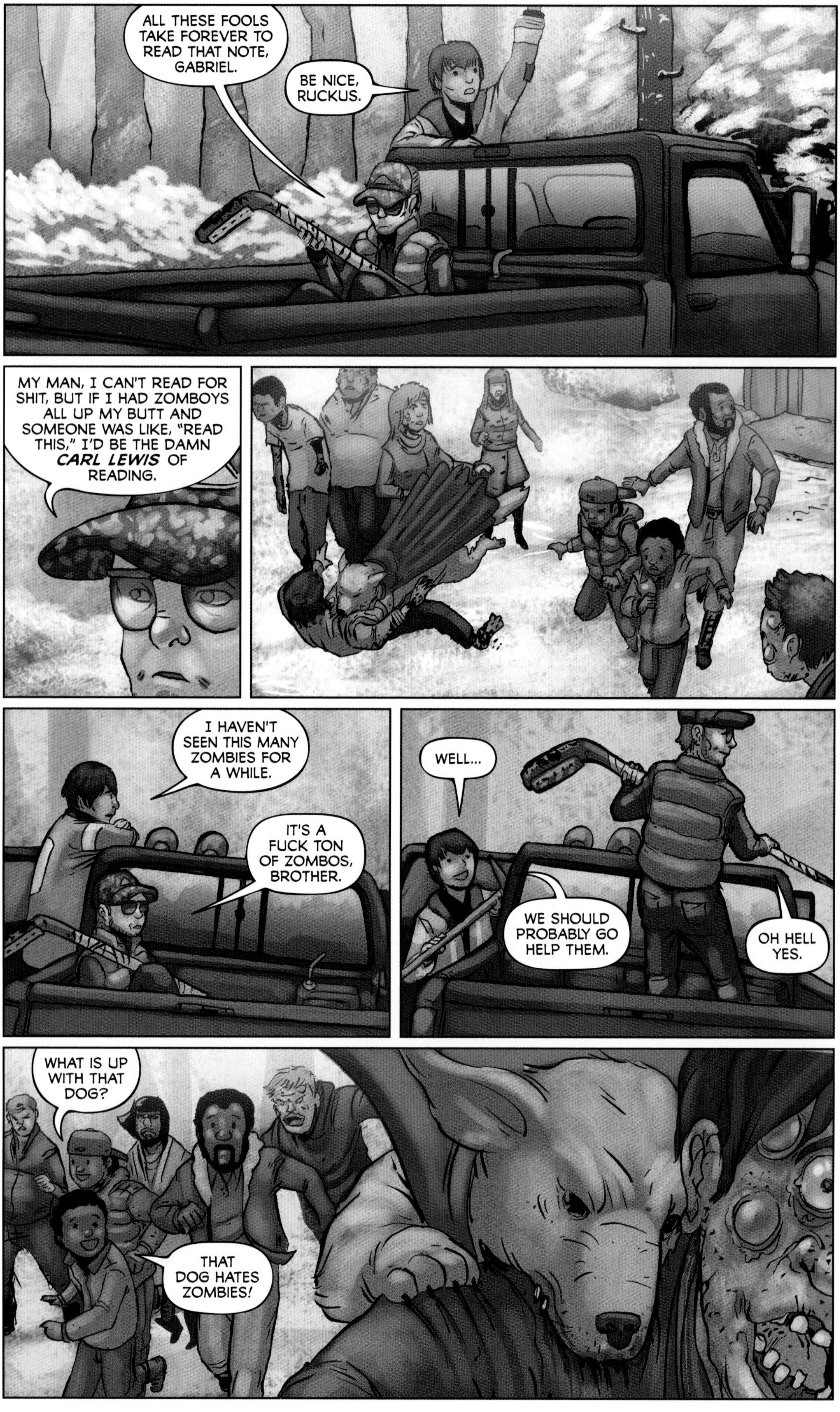
ALL THESE FOOLS TAKE FOREVER TO READ THAT NOTE, GABRIEL.
BE NICE, RUCKUS.
MY MAN, I CAN'T READ FOR SHIT, BUT IF I HAD ZOMBOYS ALL UP MY BUTT AND SOMEONE WAS LIKE, "READ THIS," I'D BE THE DAMN *CARL LEWIS* OF READING.
I HAVEN'T SEEN THIS MANY ZOMBIES FOR A WHILE.
IT'S A FUCK TON OF ZOMBOS, BROTHER.
WELL...
WE SHOULD PROBABLY GO HELP THEM.
OH HELL YES.
WHAT IS UP WITH THAT DOG?
THAT DOG HATES ZOMBIES!

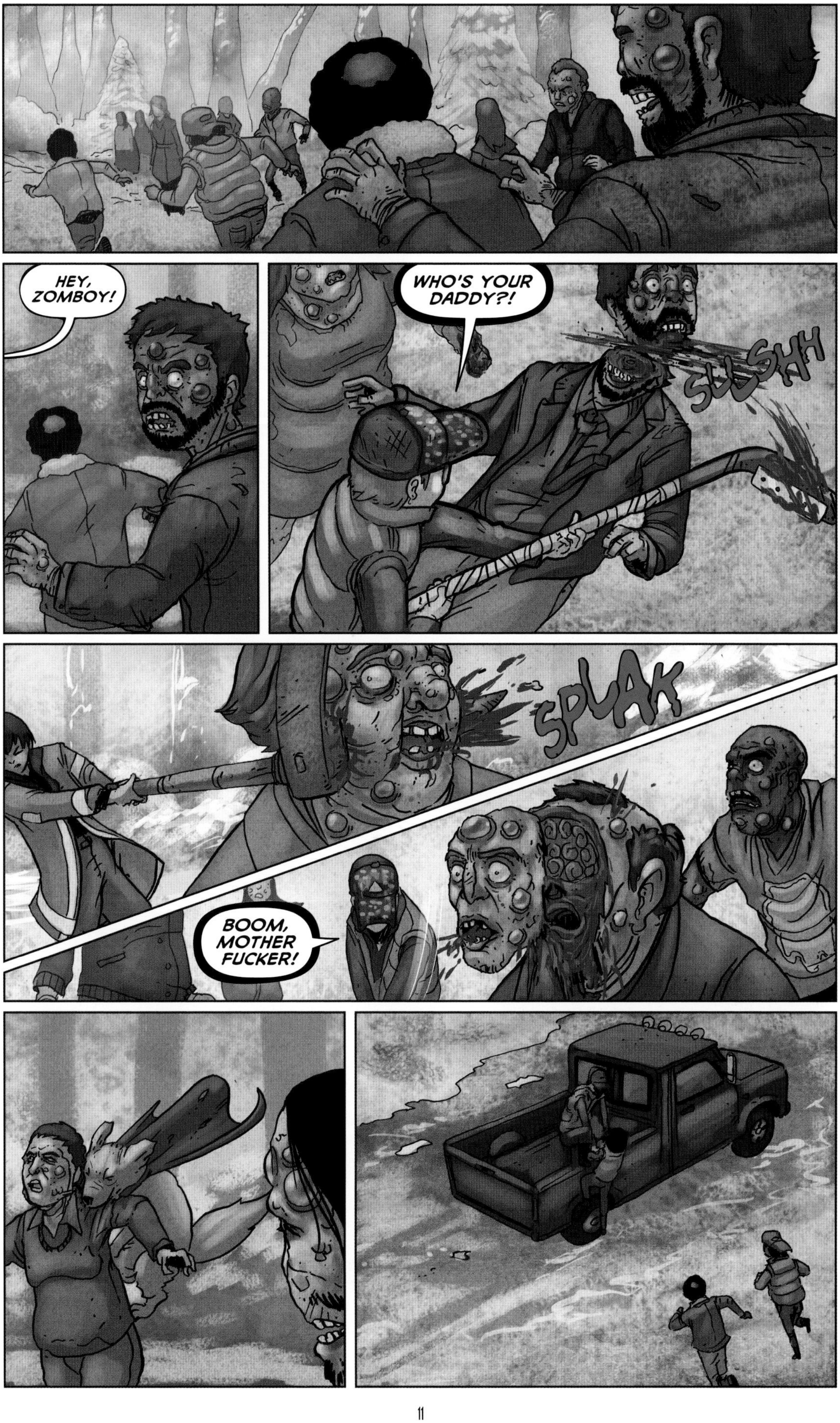
HEY, ZOMBOY!
WHO'S YOUR DADDY?!
SLSHH
SPLAK
BOOM, MOTHER FUCKER!

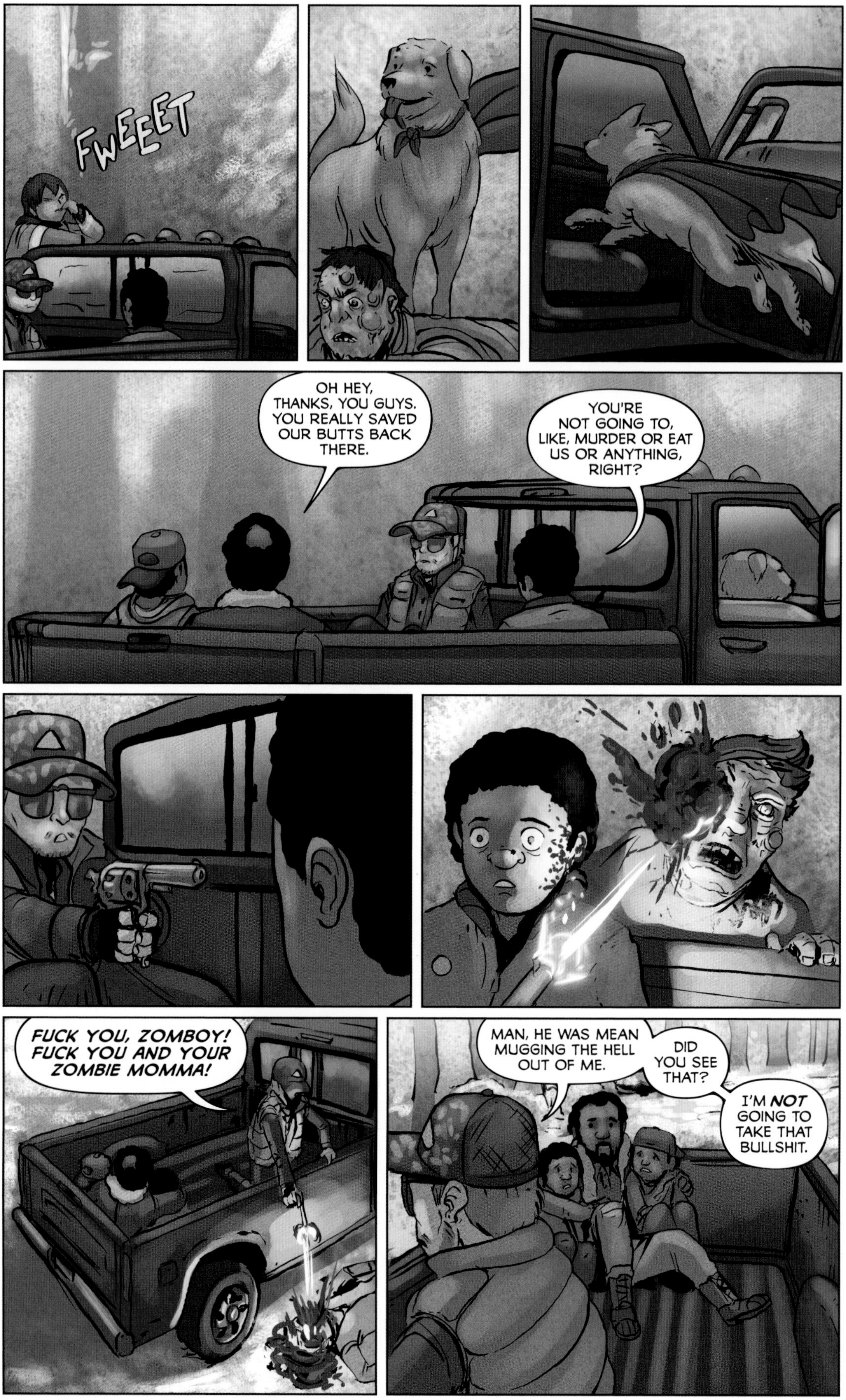
FWEEET
OH HEY, THANKS, YOU GUYS. YOU REALLY SAVED OUR BUTTS BACK THERE.
YOU'RE NOT GOING TO, LIKE, MURDER OR EAT US OR ANYTHING, RIGHT?
FUCK YOU, ZOMBOY! FUCK YOU AND YOUR ZOMBIE MOMMA!
MAN, HE WAS MEAN MUGGING THE HELL OUT OF ME.
DID YOU SEE THAT?
I'M **NOT** GOING TO TAKE THAT BULLSHIT.

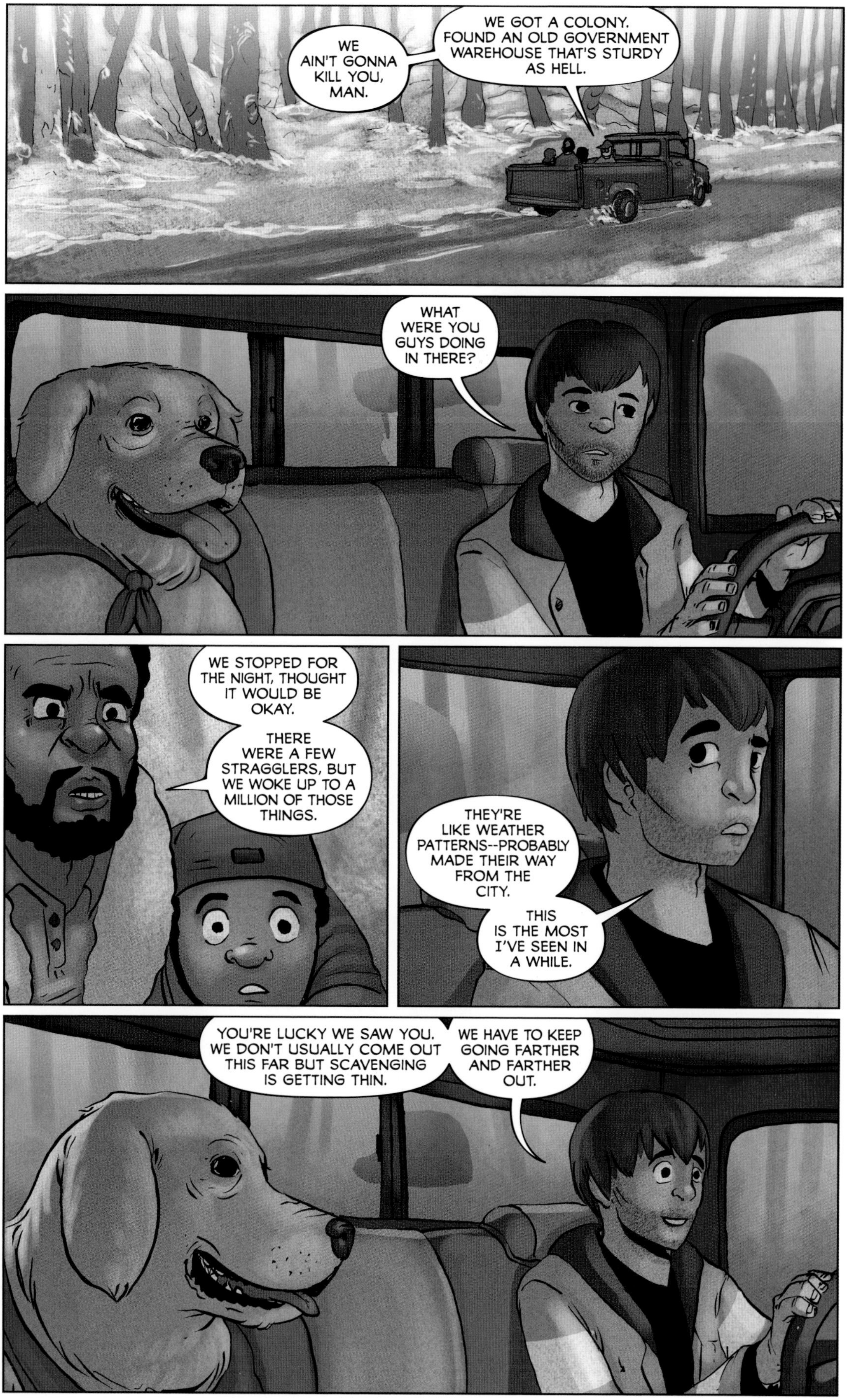
WE AIN'T GONNA KILL YOU, MAN.
WE GOT A COLONY. FOUND AN OLD GOVERNMENT WAREHOUSE THAT'S STURDY AS HELL.
WHAT WERE YOU GUYS DOING IN THERE?
WE STOPPED FOR THE NIGHT, THOUGHT IT WOULD BE OKAY.
THERE WERE A FEW STRAGGLERS, BUT WE WOKE UP TO A MILLION OF THOSE THINGS.
THEY'RE LIKE WEATHER PATTERNS--PROBABLY MADE THEIR WAY FROM THE CITY.
THIS IS THE MOST I'VE SEEN IN A WHILE.
YOU'RE LUCKY WE SAW YOU. WE DON'T USUALLY COME OUT THIS FAR BUT SCAVENGING IS GETTING THIN.
WE HAVE TO KEEP GOING FARTHER AND FARTHER OUT.

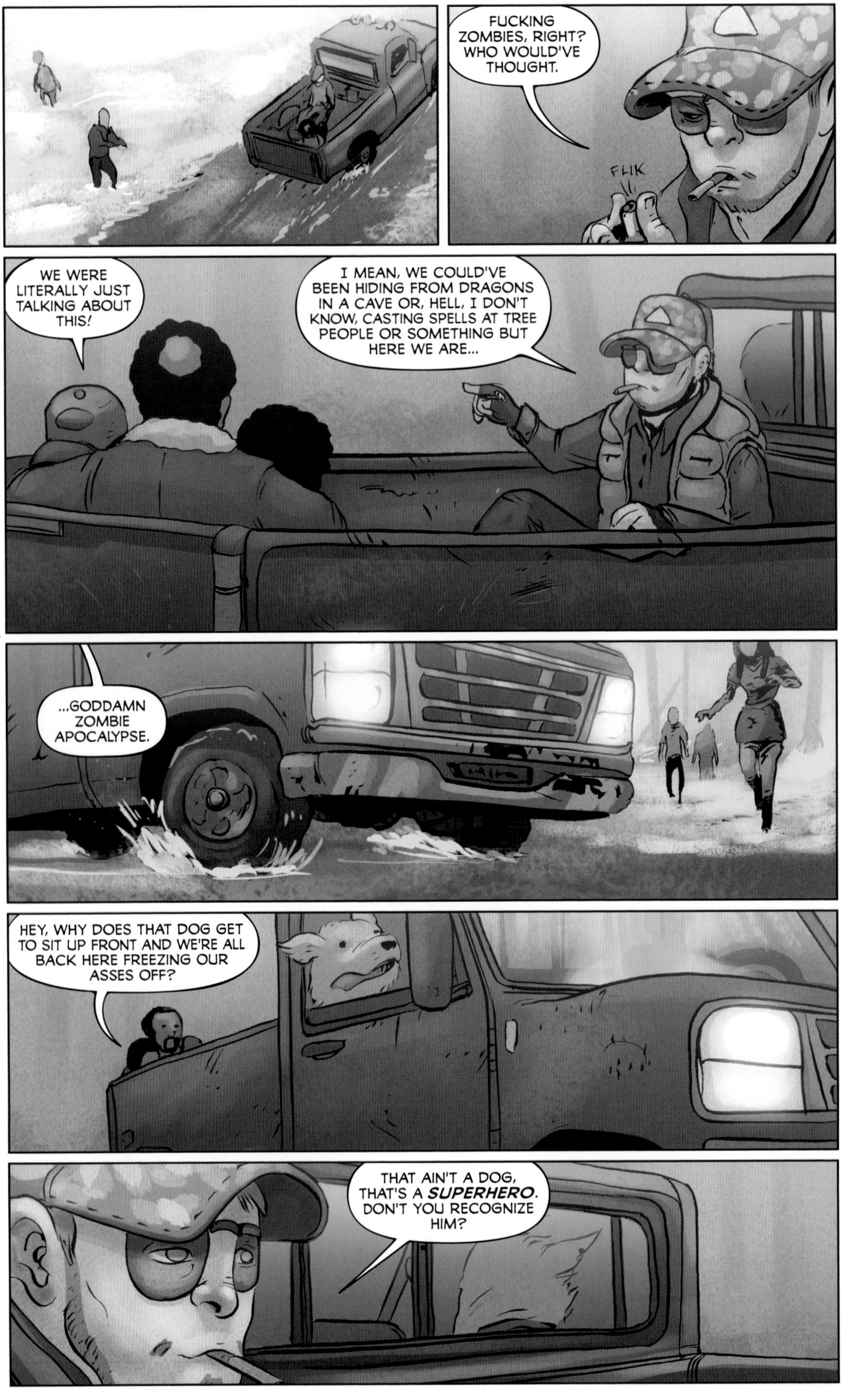
FUCKING ZOMBIES, RIGHT? WHO WOULD'VE THOUGHT.
FLIK
WE WERE LITERALLY JUST TALKING ABOUT THIS!
I MEAN, WE COULD'VE BEEN HIDING FROM DRAGONS IN A CAVE OR, HELL, I DON'T KNOW, CASTING SPELLS AT TREE PEOPLE OR SOMETHING BUT HERE WE ARE...
...GODDAMN ZOMBIE APOCALYPSE.
HEY, WHY DOES THAT DOG GET TO SIT UP FRONT AND WE'RE ALL BACK HERE FREEZING OUR ASSES OFF?
THAT AIN'T A DOG, THAT'S A ***SUPERHERO***. DON'T YOU RECOGNIZE HIM?

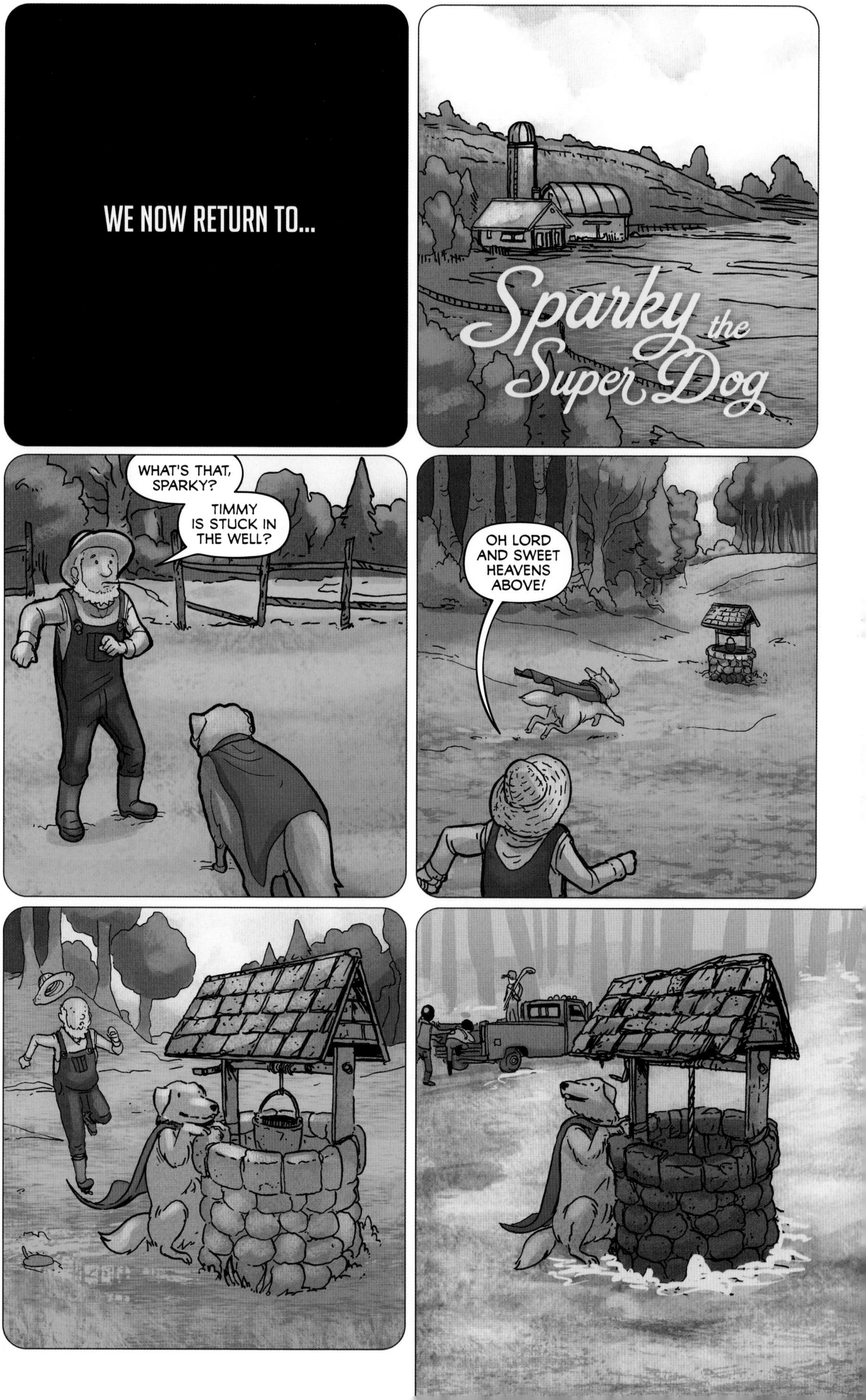
WE NOW RETURN TO...
Sparky the Super Dog
WHAT'S THAT, SPARKY?
TIMMY IS STUCK IN THE WELL?
OH LORD AND SWEET HEAVENS ABOVE!

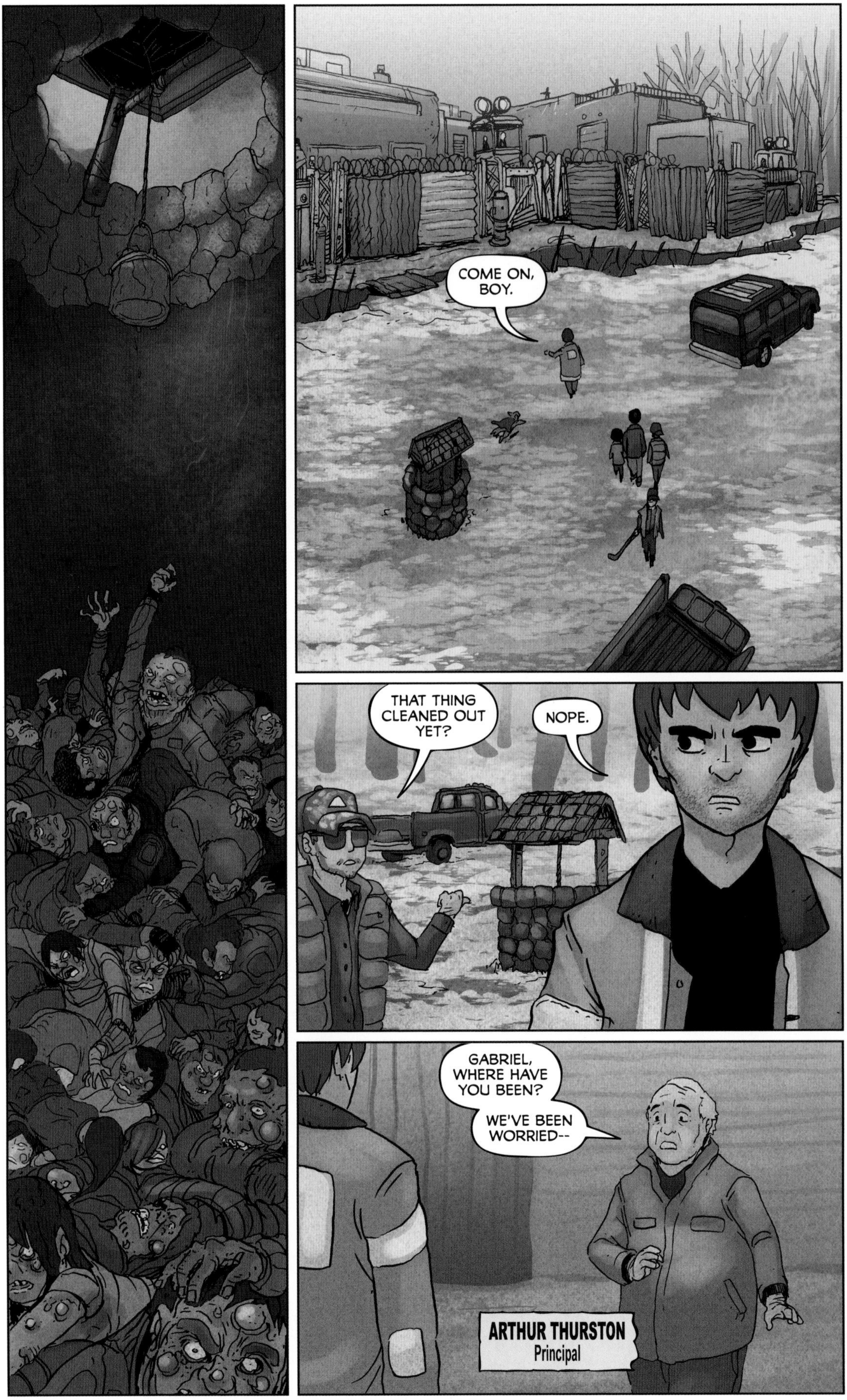
COME ON, BOY.
THAT THING CLEANED OUT YET?
NOPE.
GABRIEL, WHERE HAVE YOU BEEN?
WE'VE BEEN WORRIED--
ARTHUR THURSTON
Principal

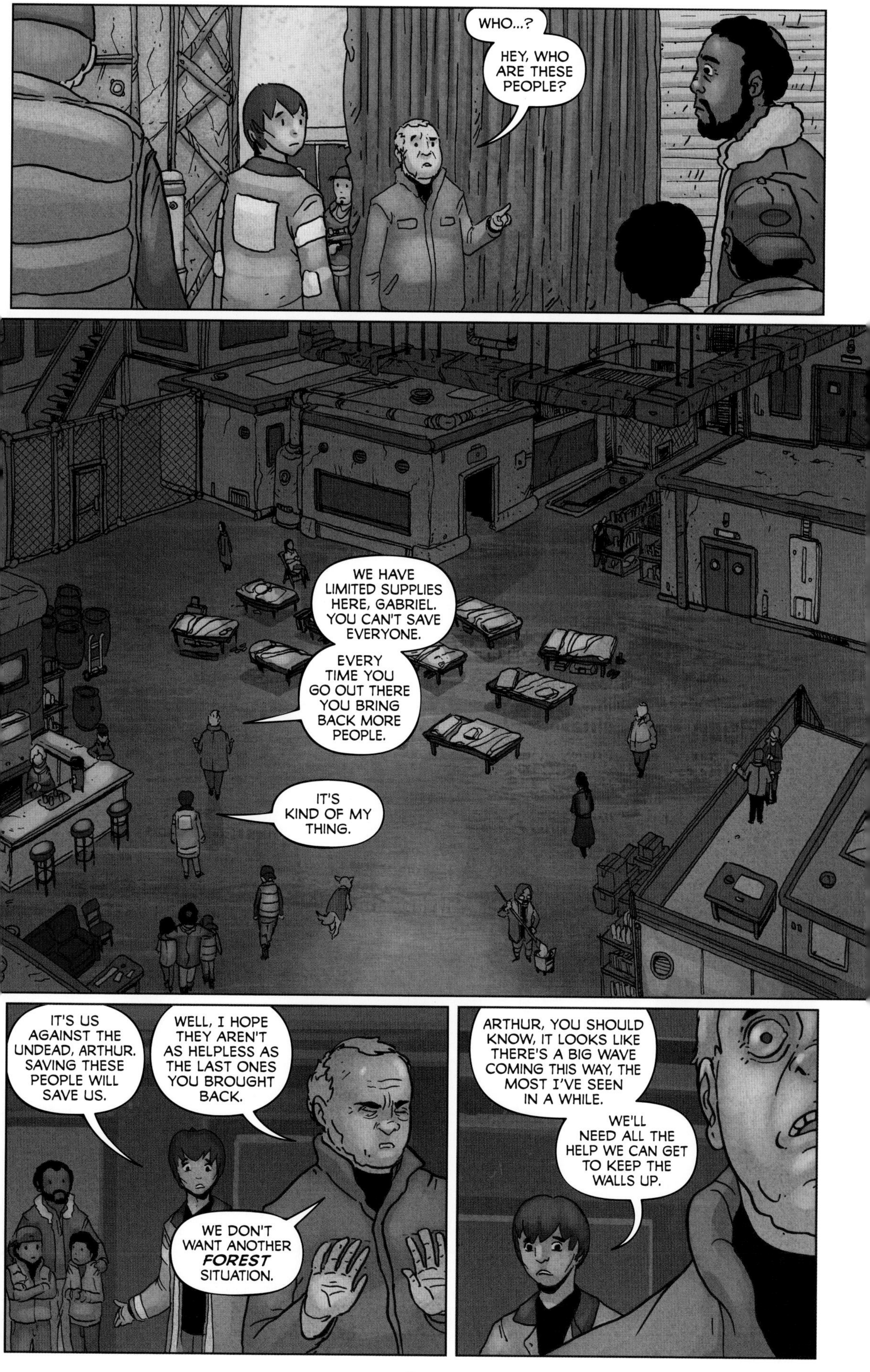
WHO...?
HEY, WHO ARE THESE PEOPLE?
WE HAVE LIMITED SUPPLIES HERE, GABRIEL. YOU CAN'T SAVE EVERYONE.
EVERY TIME YOU GO OUT THERE YOU BRING BACK MORE PEOPLE.
IT'S KIND OF MY THING.
IT'S US AGAINST THE UNDEAD, ARTHUR. SAVING THESE PEOPLE WILL SAVE US.
WELL, I HOPE THEY AREN'T AS HELPLESS AS THE LAST ONES YOU BROUGHT BACK.
WE DON'T WANT ANOTHER ***FOREST*** SITUATION.
ARTHUR, YOU SHOULD KNOW, IT LOOKS LIKE THERE'S A BIG WAVE COMING THIS WAY, THE MOST I'VE SEEN IN A WHILE.
WE'LL NEED ALL THE HELP WE CAN GET TO KEEP THE WALLS UP.

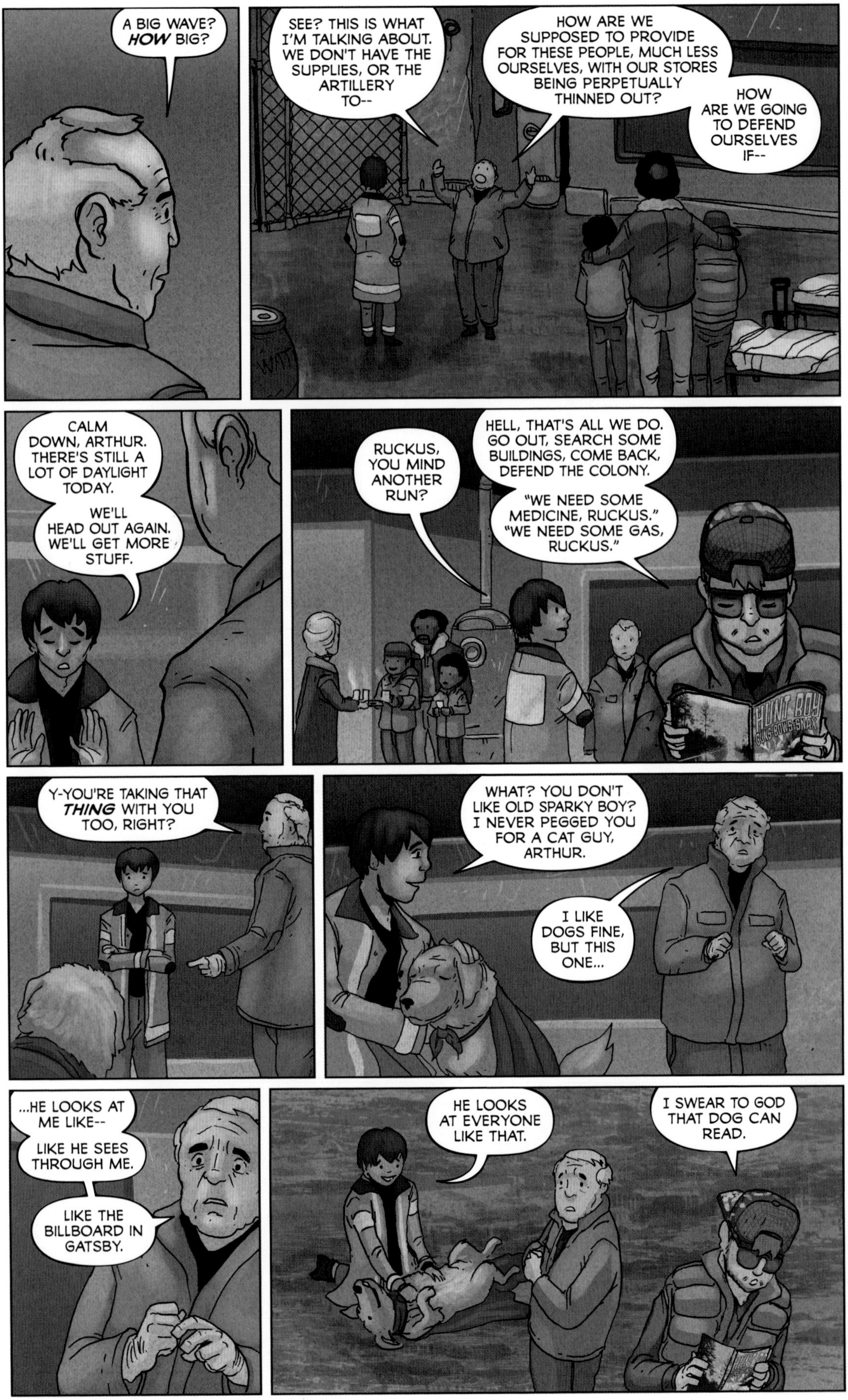
A BIG WAVE? *HOW* BIG?
SEE? THIS IS WHAT I'M TALKING ABOUT. WE DON'T HAVE THE SUPPLIES, OR THE ARTILLERY TO--
HOW ARE WE SUPPOSED TO PROVIDE FOR THESE PEOPLE, MUCH LESS OURSELVES, WITH OUR STORES BEING PERPETUALLY THINNED OUT?
HOW ARE WE GOING TO DEFEND OURSELVES IF--
CALM DOWN, ARTHUR. THERE'S STILL A LOT OF DAYLIGHT TODAY.
WE'LL HEAD OUT AGAIN. WE'LL GET MORE STUFF.
RUCKUS, YOU MIND ANOTHER RUN?
HELL, THAT'S ALL WE DO. GO OUT, SEARCH SOME BUILDINGS, COME BACK, DEFEND THE COLONY.
"WE NEED SOME MEDICINE, RUCKUS." "WE NEED SOME GAS, RUCKUS."
HUNT BOY
Y-YOU'RE TAKING THAT *THING* WITH YOU TOO, RIGHT?
WHAT? YOU DON'T LIKE OLD SPARKY BOY? I NEVER PEGGED YOU FOR A CAT GUY, ARTHUR.
I LIKE DOGS FINE, BUT THIS ONE...
...HE LOOKS AT ME LIKE--
LIKE HE SEES THROUGH ME.
LIKE THE BILLBOARD IN GATSBY.
HE LOOKS AT EVERYONE LIKE THAT.
I SWEAR TO GOD THAT DOG CAN READ.

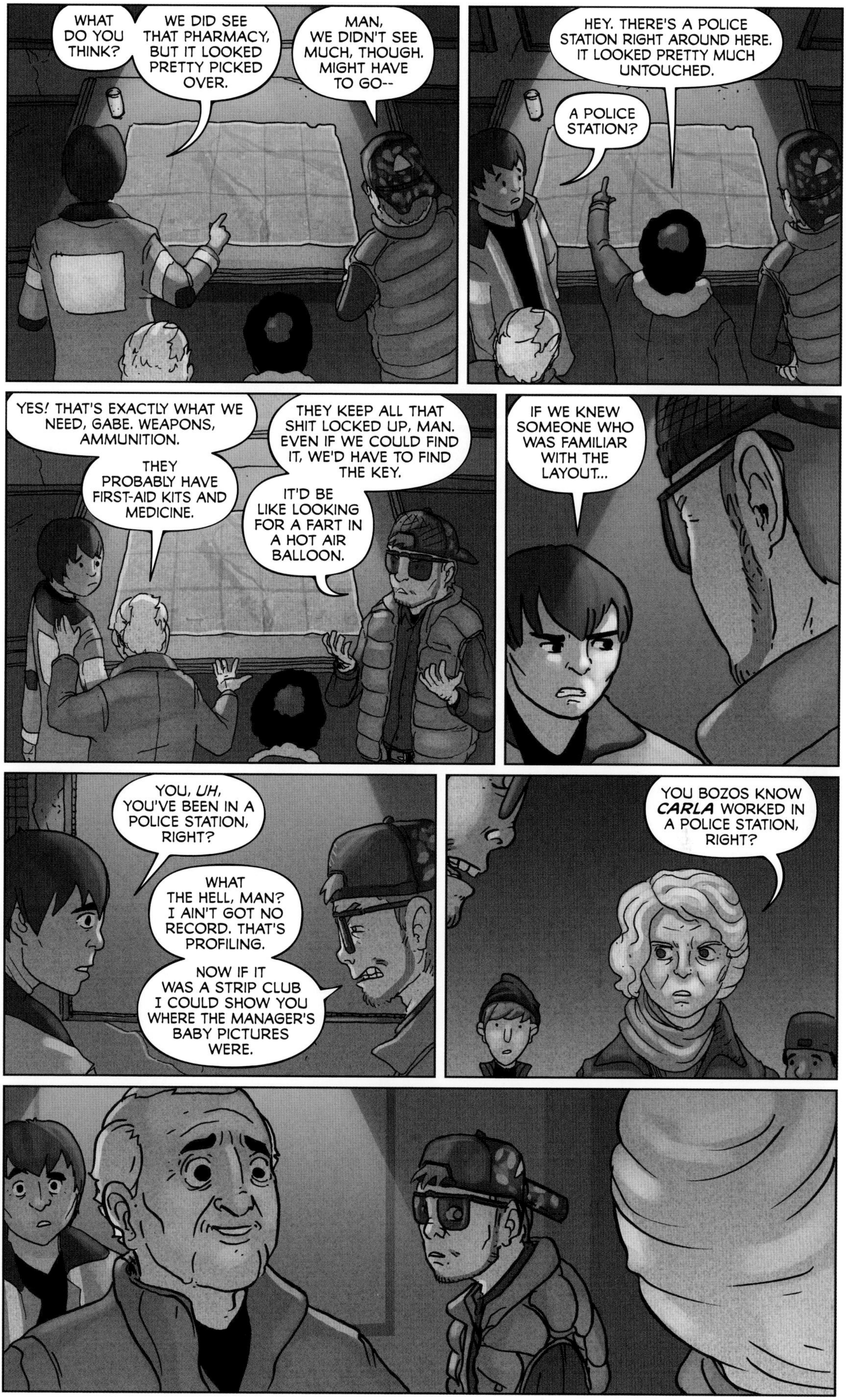
WHAT DO YOU THINK?
WE DID SEE THAT PHARMACY, BUT IT LOOKED PRETTY PICKED OVER.
MAN, WE DIDN'T SEE MUCH, THOUGH. MIGHT HAVE TO GO--
HEY. THERE'S A POLICE STATION RIGHT AROUND HERE. IT LOOKED PRETTY MUCH UNTOUCHED.
A POLICE STATION?
YES! THAT'S EXACTLY WHAT WE NEED, GABE. WEAPONS, AMMUNITION.
THEY PROBABLY HAVE FIRST-AID KITS AND MEDICINE.
THEY KEEP ALL THAT SHIT LOCKED UP, MAN. EVEN IF WE COULD FIND IT, WE'D HAVE TO FIND THE KEY.
IT'D BE LIKE LOOKING FOR A FART IN A HOT AIR BALLOON.
IF WE KNEW SOMEONE WHO WAS FAMILIAR WITH THE LAYOUT...
YOU, *UH*, YOU'VE BEEN IN A POLICE STATION, RIGHT?
WHAT THE HELL, MAN? I AIN'T GOT NO RECORD. THAT'S PROFILING.
NOW IF IT WAS A STRIP CLUB I COULD SHOW YOU WHERE THE MANAGER'S BABY PICTURES WERE.
YOU BOZOS KNOW ***CARLA*** WORKED IN A POLICE STATION, RIGHT?

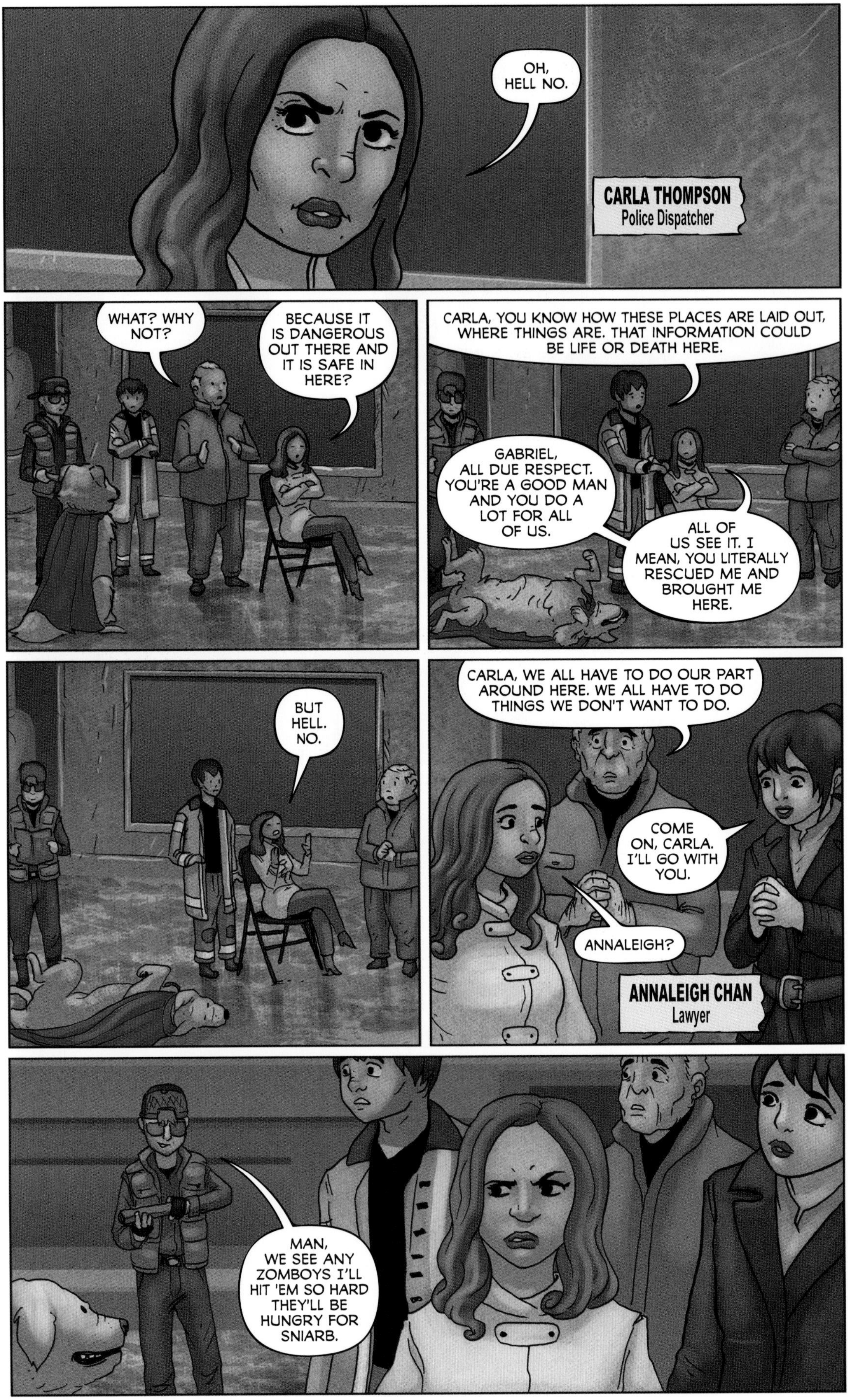
OH, HELL NO.
CARLA THOMPSON
Police Dispatcher
WHAT? WHY NOT?
BECAUSE IT IS DANGEROUS OUT THERE AND IT IS SAFE IN HERE?
CARLA, YOU KNOW HOW THESE PLACES ARE LAID OUT, WHERE THINGS ARE. THAT INFORMATION COULD BE LIFE OR DEATH HERE.
GABRIEL, ALL DUE RESPECT. YOU'RE A GOOD MAN AND YOU DO A LOT FOR ALL OF US.
ALL OF US SEE IT. I MEAN, YOU LITERALLY RESCUED ME AND BROUGHT ME HERE.
BUT HELL. NO.
CARLA, WE ALL HAVE TO DO OUR PART AROUND HERE. WE ALL HAVE TO DO THINGS WE DON'T WANT TO DO.
COME ON, CARLA. I'LL GO WITH YOU.
ANNALEIGH?
ANNALEIGH CHAN
Lawyer
MAN, WE SEE ANY ZOMBOYS I'LL HIT 'EM SO HARD THEY'LL BE HUNGRY FOR SNIARB.

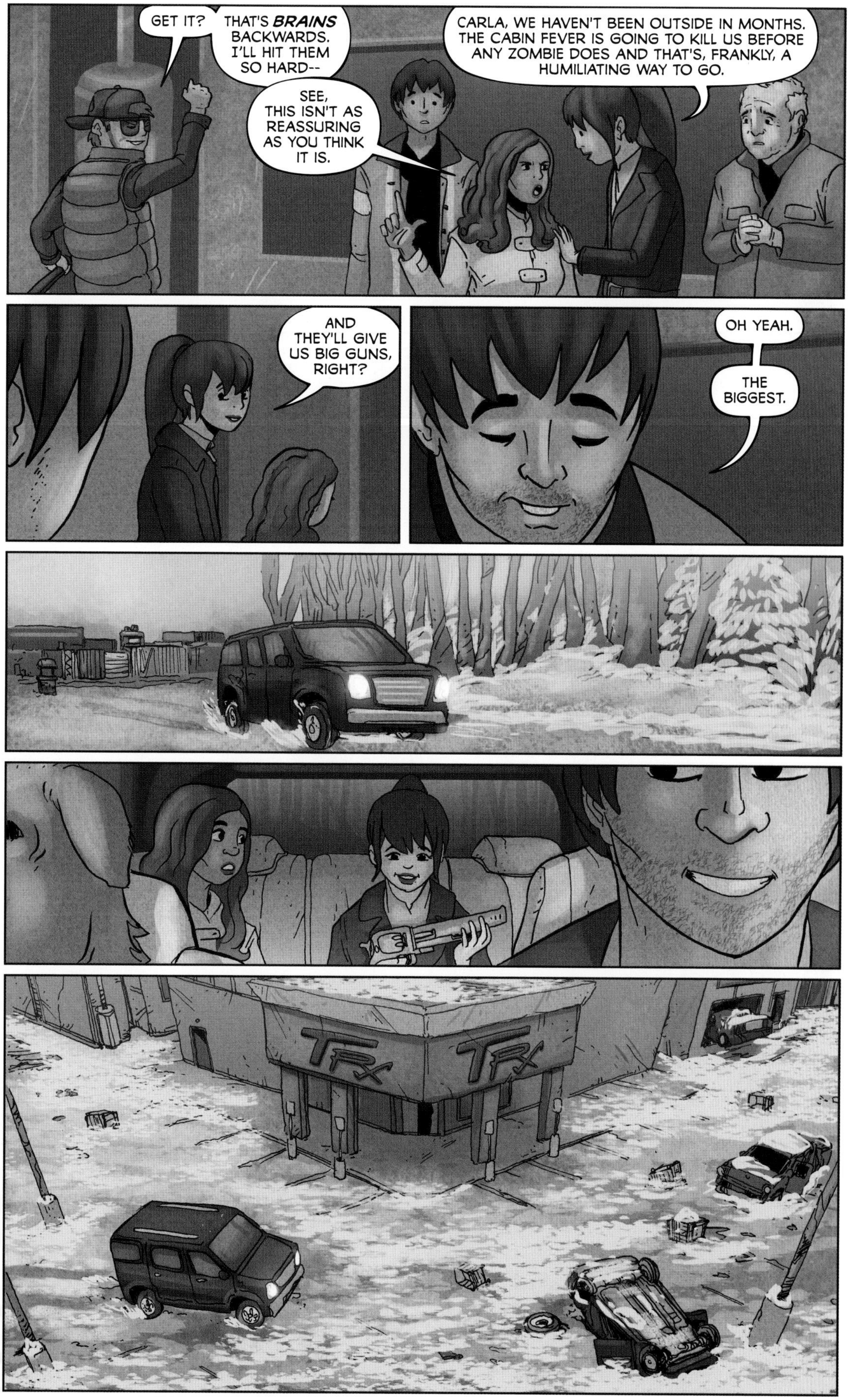
GET IT?
THAT'S BRAINS BACKWARDS. I'LL HIT THEM SO HARD--
SEE, THIS ISN'T AS REASSURING AS YOU THINK IT IS.
CARLA, WE HAVEN'T BEEN OUTSIDE IN MONTHS. THE CABIN FEVER IS GOING TO KILL US BEFORE ANY ZOMBIE DOES AND THAT'S, FRANKLY, A HUMILIATING WAY TO GO.
AND THEY'LL GIVE US BIG GUNS, RIGHT?
OH YEAH.
THE BIGGEST.
TRX
TRX

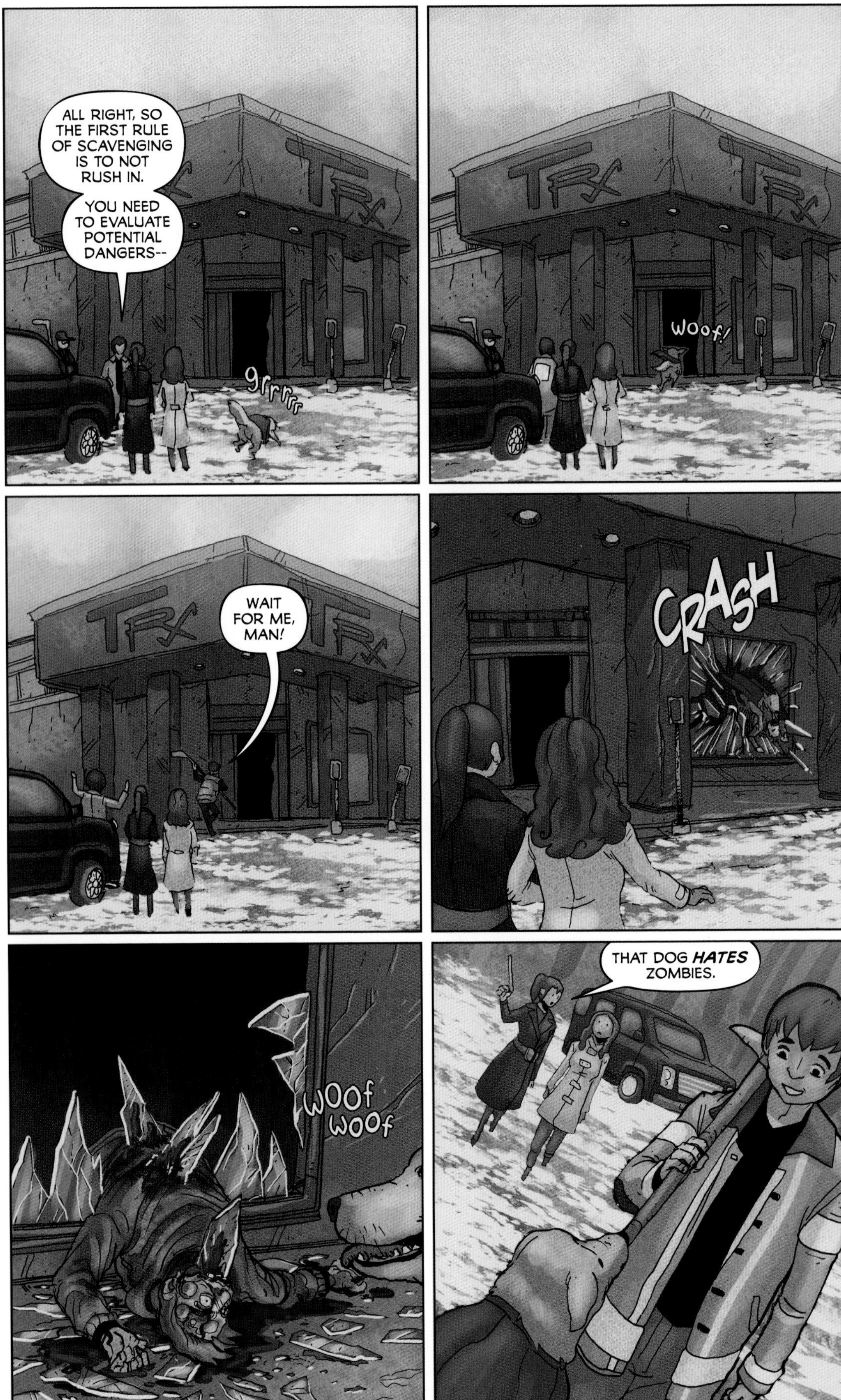
ALL RIGHT, SO THE FIRST RULE OF SCAVENGING IS TO NOT RUSH IN.
YOU NEED TO EVALUATE POTENTIAL DANGERS--
grrrrr
WOOF!
WAIT FOR ME, MAN!
CRASH
WOOF WOOF
THAT DOG **HATES** ZOMBIES.

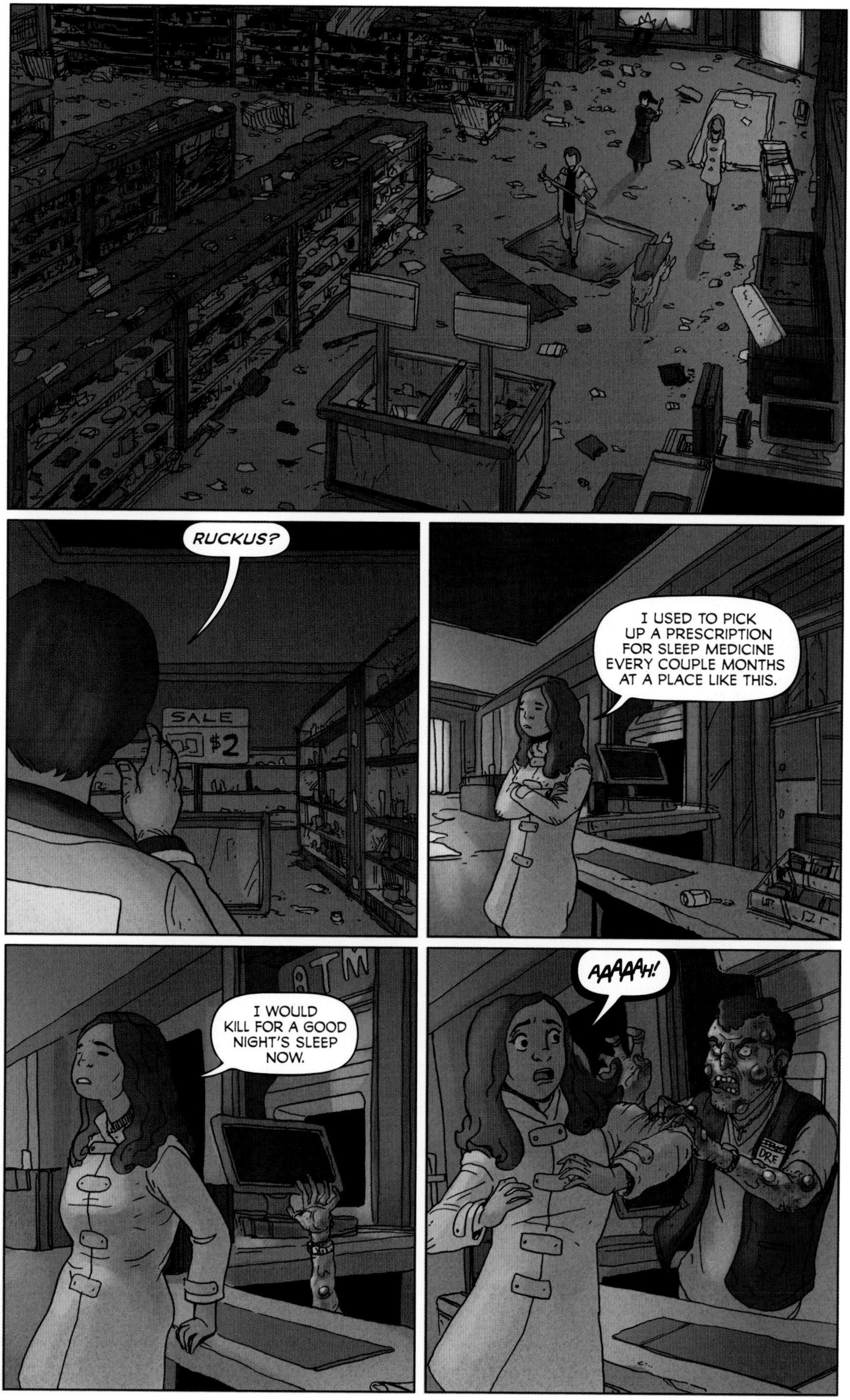
RUCKUS?
SALE
$2
I USED TO PICK UP A PRESCRIPTION FOR SLEEP MEDICINE EVERY COUPLE MONTHS AT A PLACE LIKE THIS.
ATM
I WOULD KILL FOR A GOOD NIGHT'S SLEEP NOW.
AAAAAH!

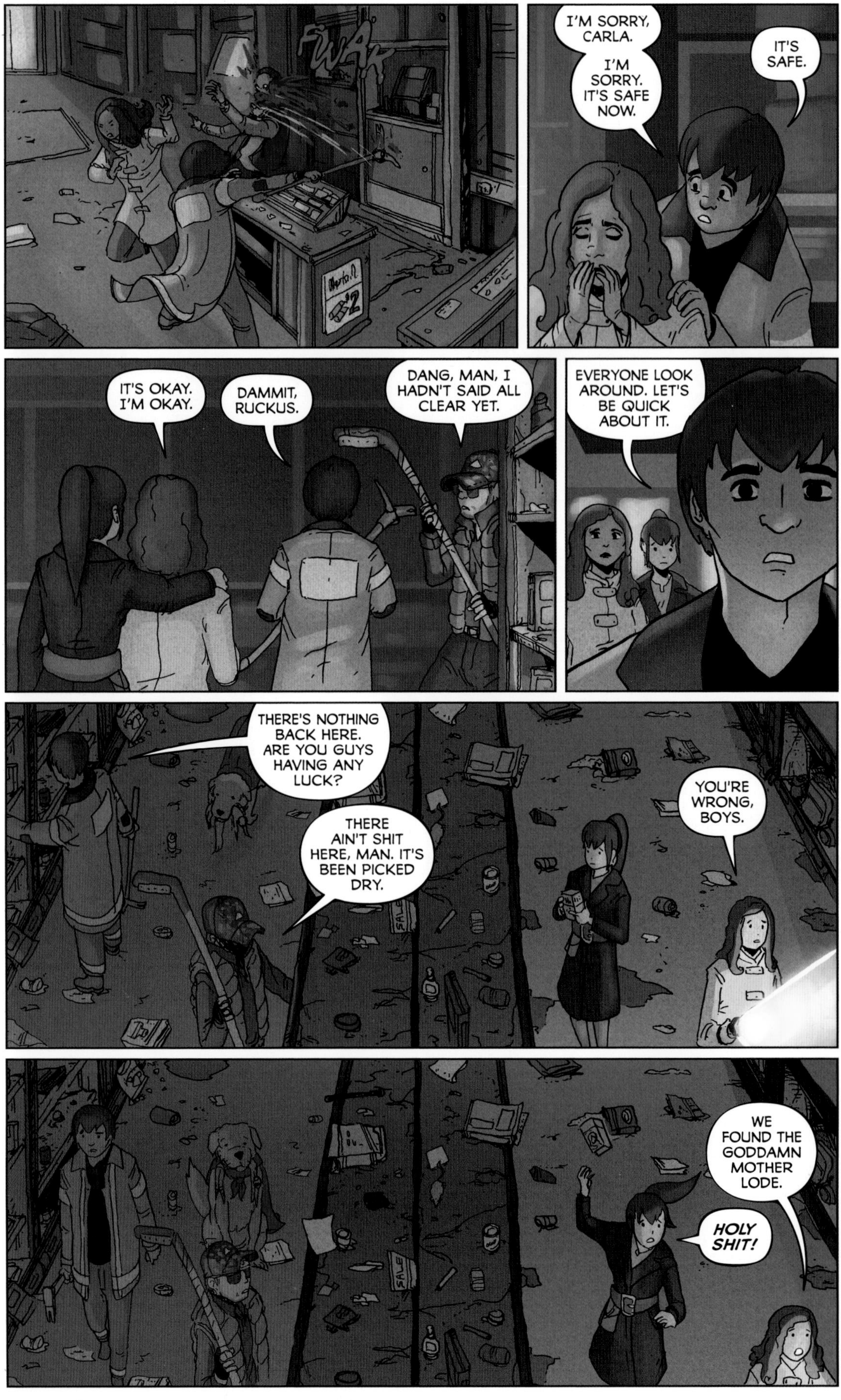
FWAK
I'M SORRY, CARLA.
I'M SORRY. IT'S SAFE NOW.
IT'S SAFE.
IT'S OKAY. I'M OKAY.
DAMMIT, RUCKUS.
DANG, MAN, I HADN'T SAID ALL CLEAR YET.
EVERYONE LOOK AROUND. LET'S BE QUICK ABOUT IT.
THERE'S NOTHING BACK HERE. ARE YOU GUYS HAVING ANY LUCK?
THERE AIN'T SHIT HERE, MAN. IT'S BEEN PICKED DRY.
YOU'RE WRONG, BOYS.
WE FOUND THE GODDAMN MOTHER LODE.
HOLY SHIT!

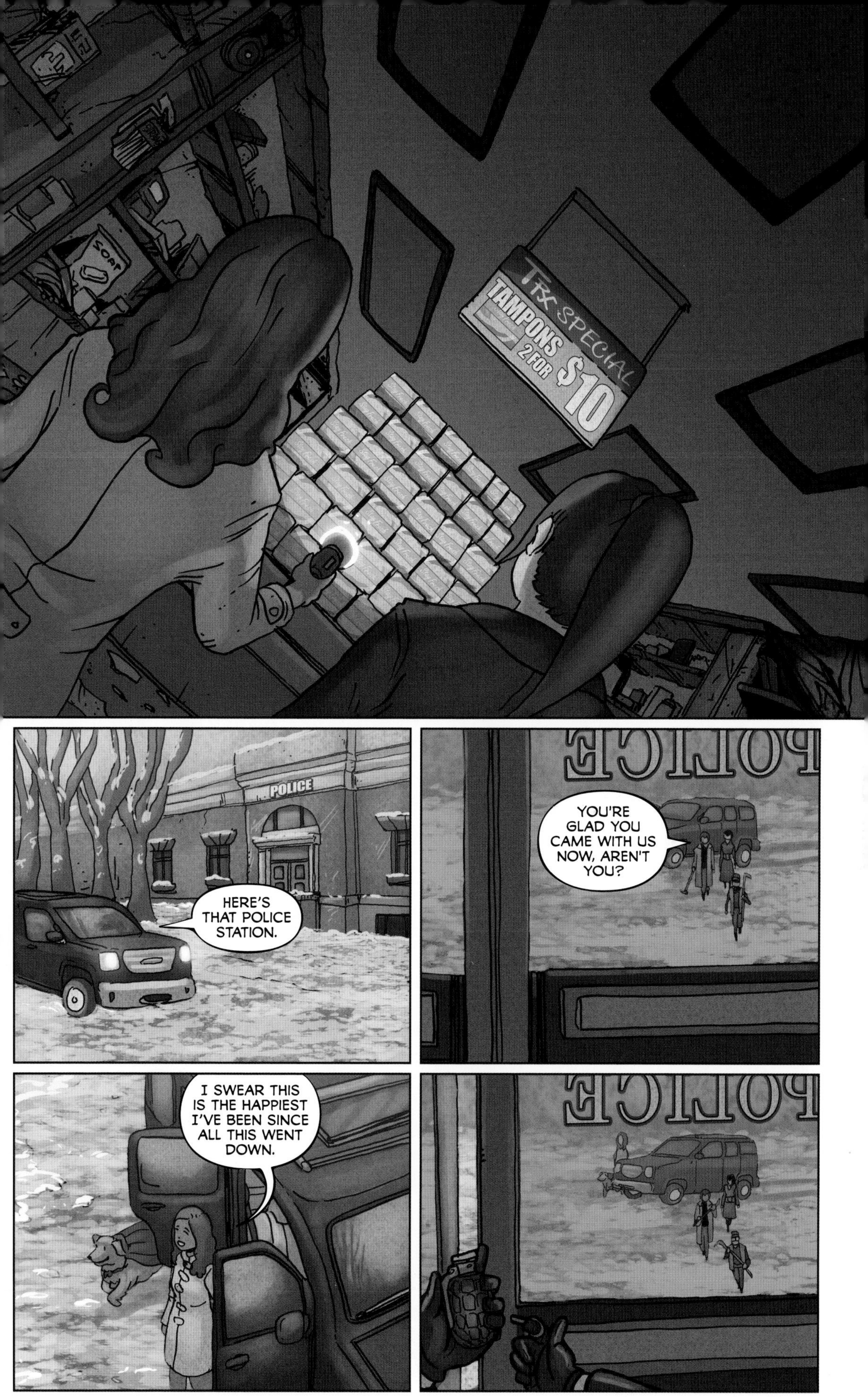
SOAP
TRX SPECIAL
TAMPONS
2 FOR $10
POLICE
HERE'S THAT POLICE STATION.
YOU'RE GLAD YOU CAME WITH US NOW, AREN'T YOU?
I SWEAR THIS IS THE HAPPIEST I'VE BEEN SINCE ALL THIS WENT DOWN.

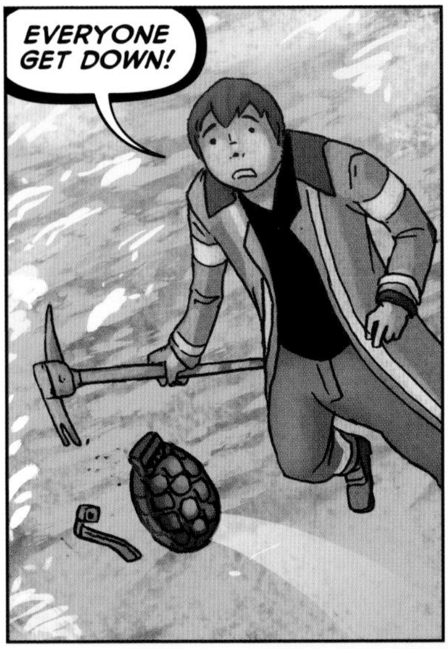
EVERYONE GET DOWN!
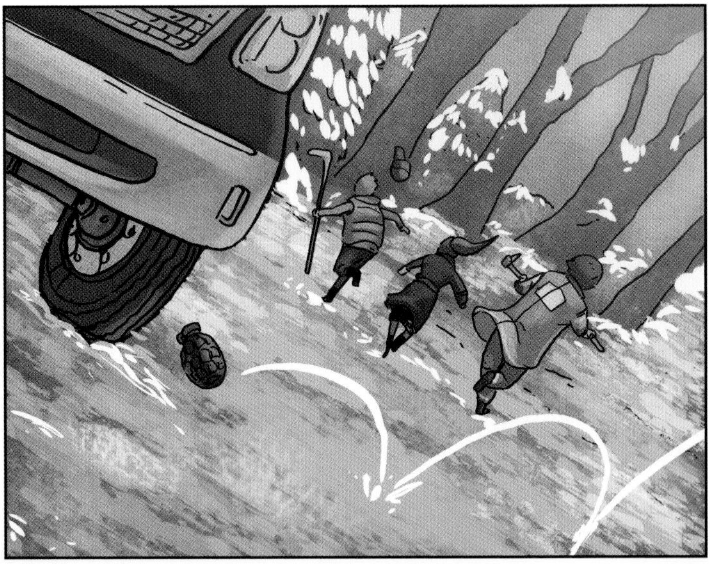
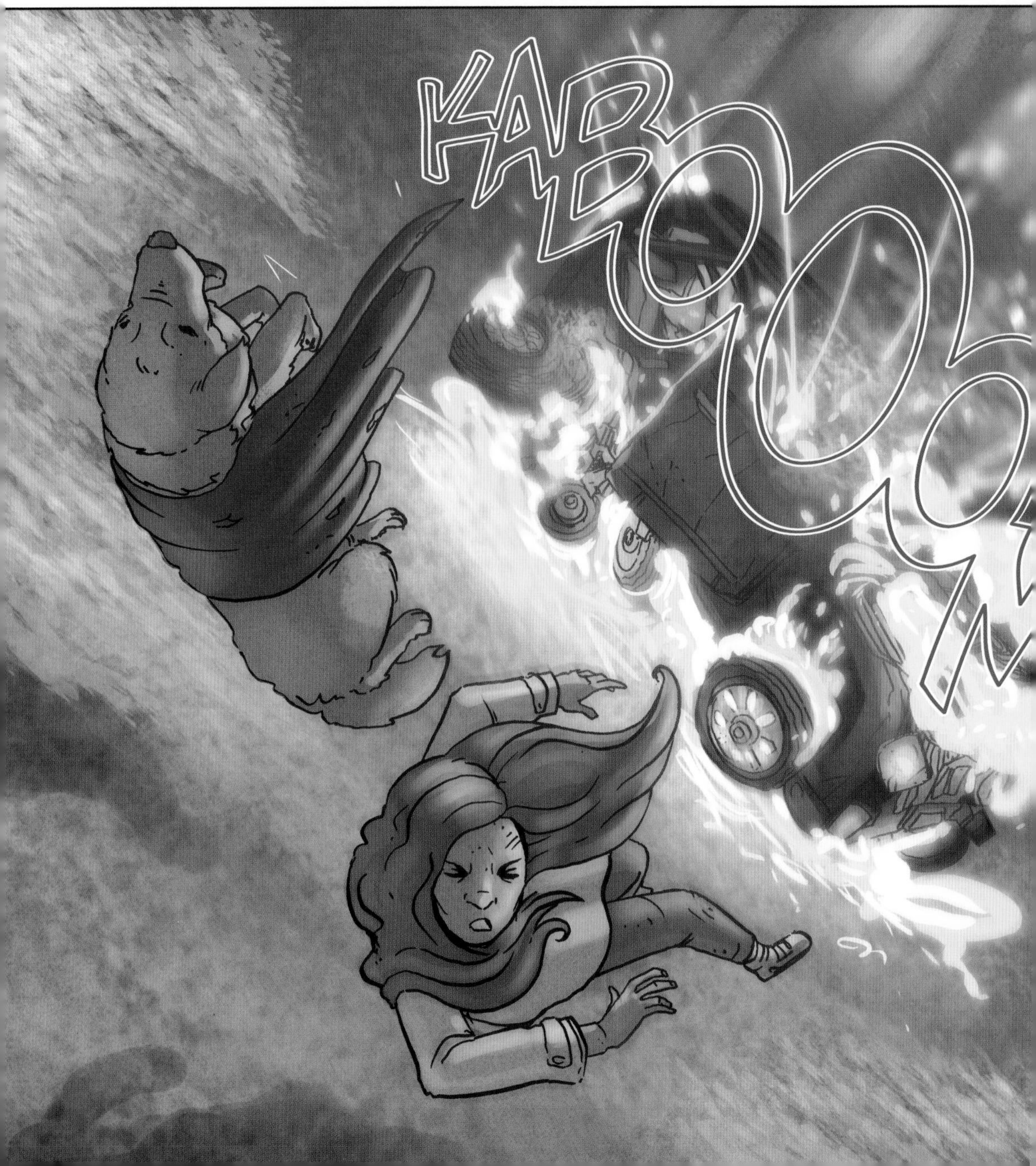
KABOOOOM

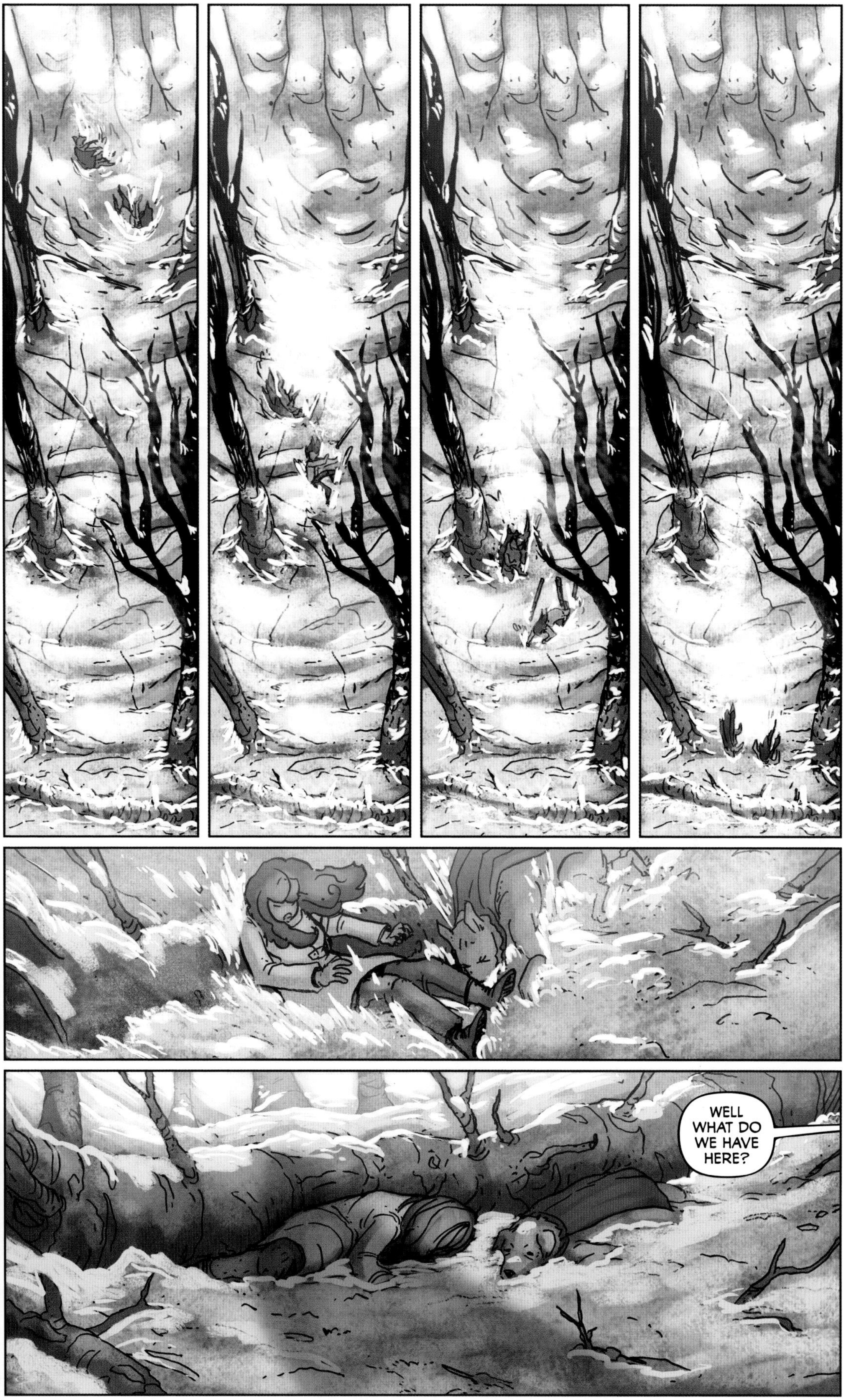
WELL WHAT DO WE HAVE HERE?

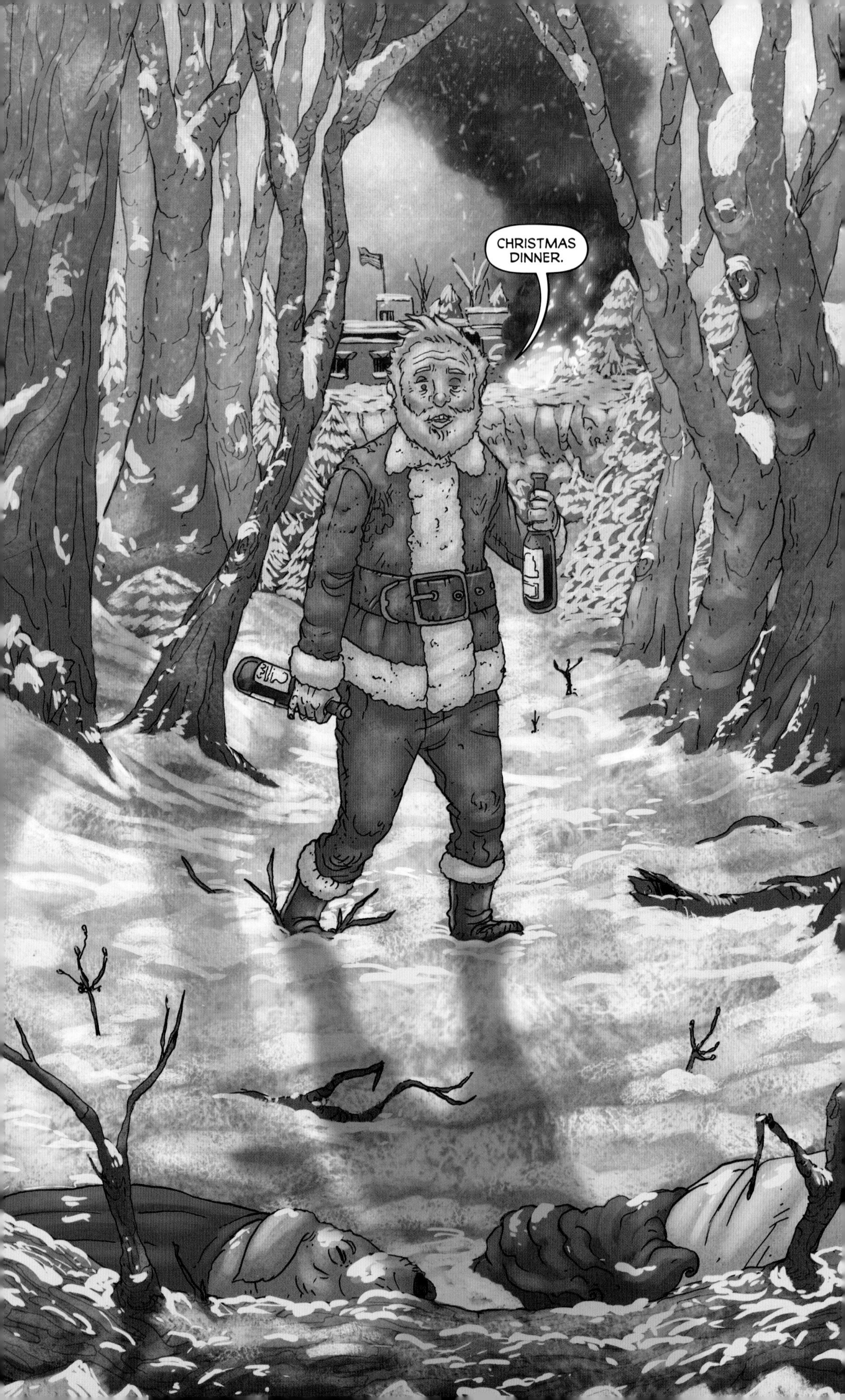
CHRISTMAS DINNER.

CHAPTER TWO

WHAT DO YOU MEAN HE CAN'T DRIVE A CAR?

PRODUCER

TRAI

SPARKY

I'M NOT SURE HOW ELSE TO SAY IT.

HE'S A *DOG*. HE CAN'T DRIVE A CAR.

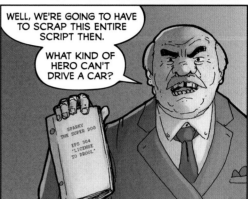

WELL, WE'RE GOING TO HAVE TO SCRAP THIS ENTIRE SCRIPT THEN.

WHAT KIND OF HERO CAN'T DRIVE A CAR?

SPARKY THE SUPER DOG

EPS. 304 "LICENSE TO DROOL"

EXIT

HE'S A DOG, MAN.

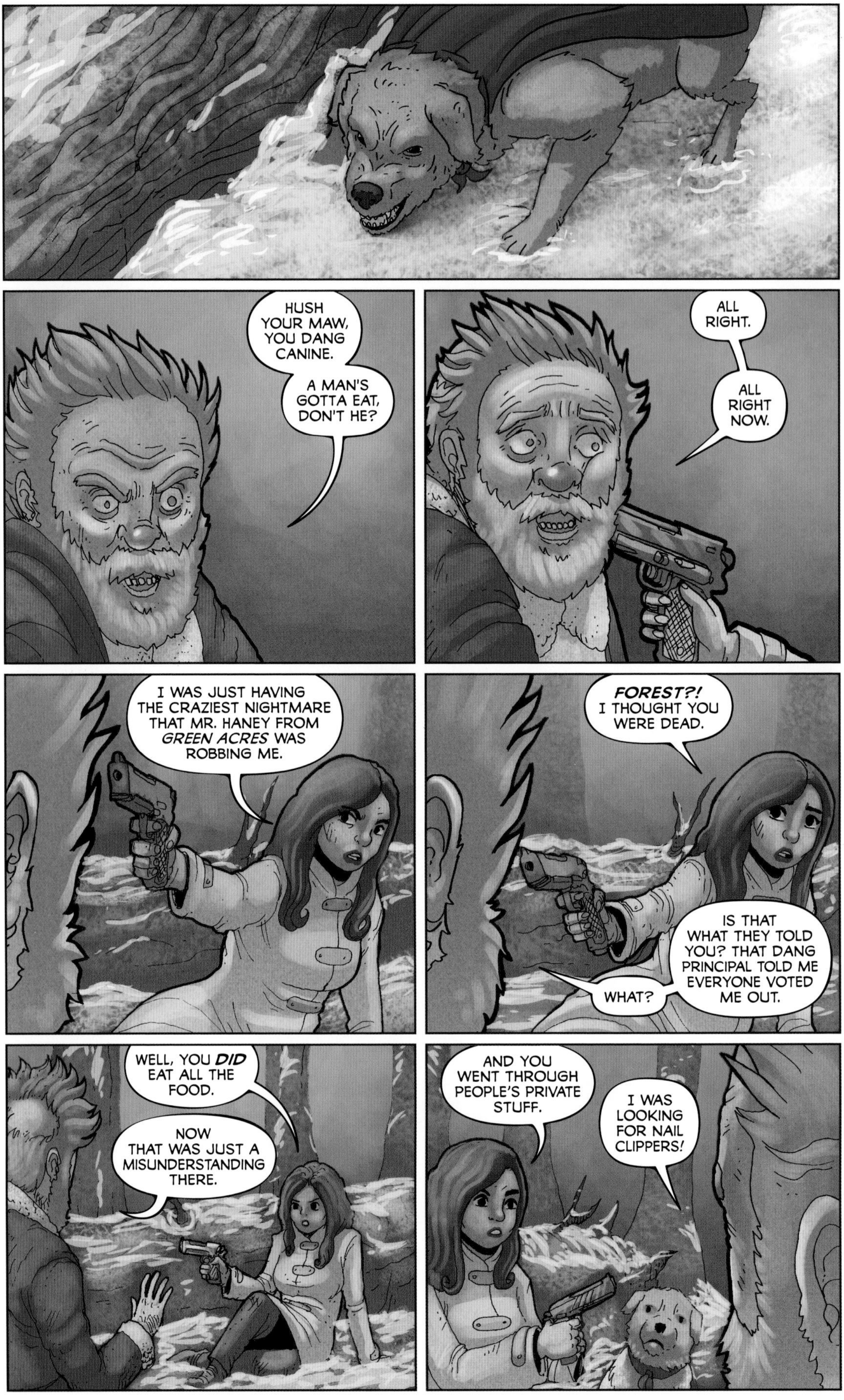
HUSH YOUR MAW, YOU DANG CANINE.
A MAN'S GOTTA EAT, DON'T HE?
ALL RIGHT.
ALL RIGHT NOW.
I WAS JUST HAVING THE CRAZIEST NIGHTMARE THAT MR. HANEY FROM *GREEN ACRES* WAS ROBBING ME.
FOREST?! I THOUGHT YOU WERE DEAD.
WHAT?
IS THAT WHAT THEY TOLD YOU? THAT DANG PRINCIPAL TOLD ME EVERYONE VOTED ME OUT.
WELL, YOU ***DID*** EAT ALL THE FOOD.
NOW THAT WAS JUST A MISUNDERSTANDING THERE.
AND YOU WENT THROUGH PEOPLE'S PRIVATE STUFF.
I WAS LOOKING FOR NAIL CLIPPERS!

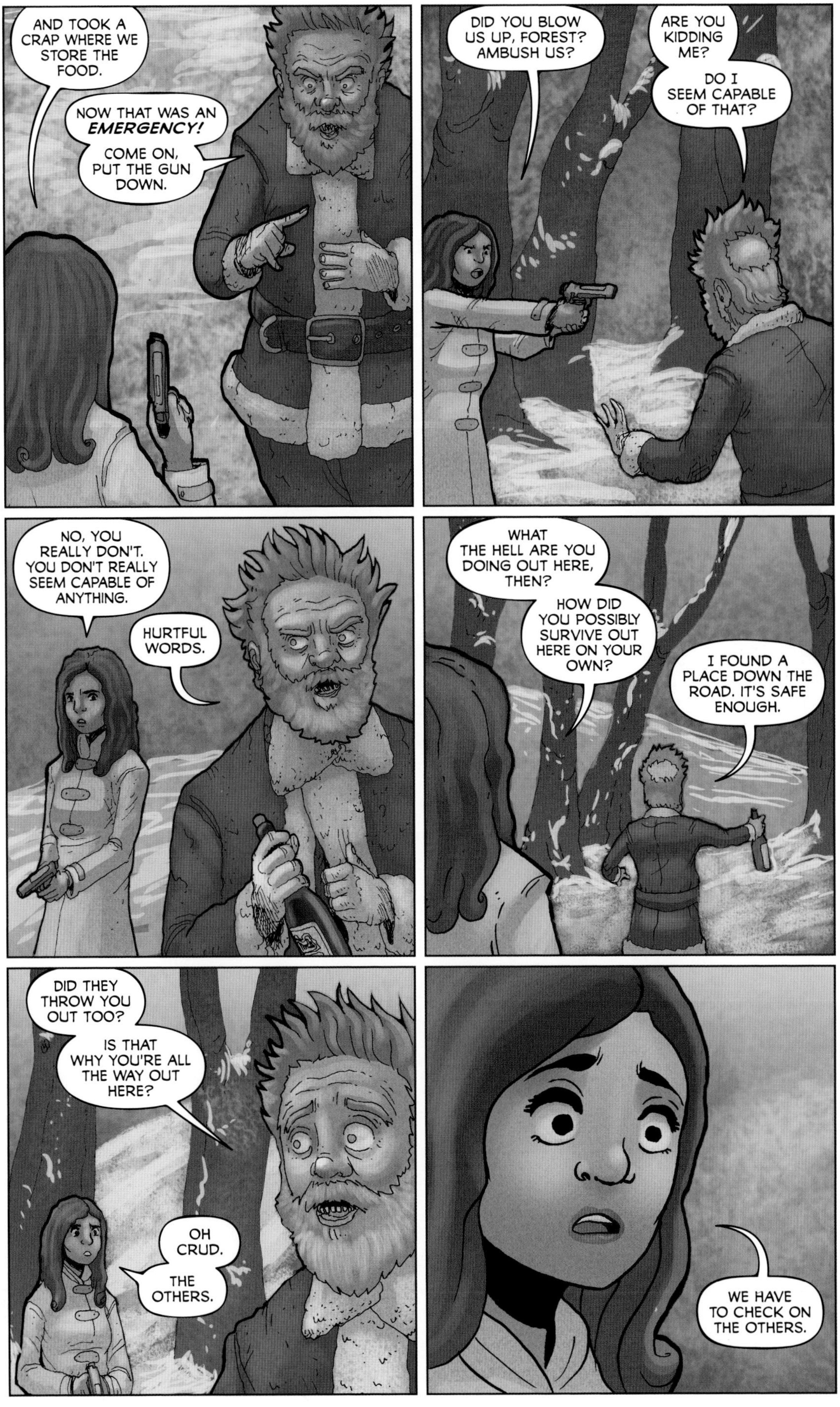
AND TOOK A CRAP WHERE WE STORE THE FOOD.
NOW THAT WAS AN ***EMERGENCY!***
COME ON, PUT THE GUN DOWN.
DID YOU BLOW US UP, FOREST? AMBUSH US?
ARE YOU KIDDING ME?
DO I SEEM CAPABLE OF THAT?
NO, YOU REALLY DON'T. YOU DON'T REALLY SEEM CAPABLE OF ANYTHING.
HURTFUL WORDS.
WHAT THE HELL ARE YOU DOING OUT HERE, THEN?
HOW DID YOU POSSIBLY SURVIVE OUT HERE ON YOUR OWN?
I FOUND A PLACE DOWN THE ROAD. IT'S SAFE ENOUGH.
DID THEY THROW YOU OUT TOO?
IS THAT WHY YOU'RE ALL THE WAY OUT HERE?
OH CRUD.
THE OTHERS.
WE HAVE TO CHECK ON THE OTHERS.

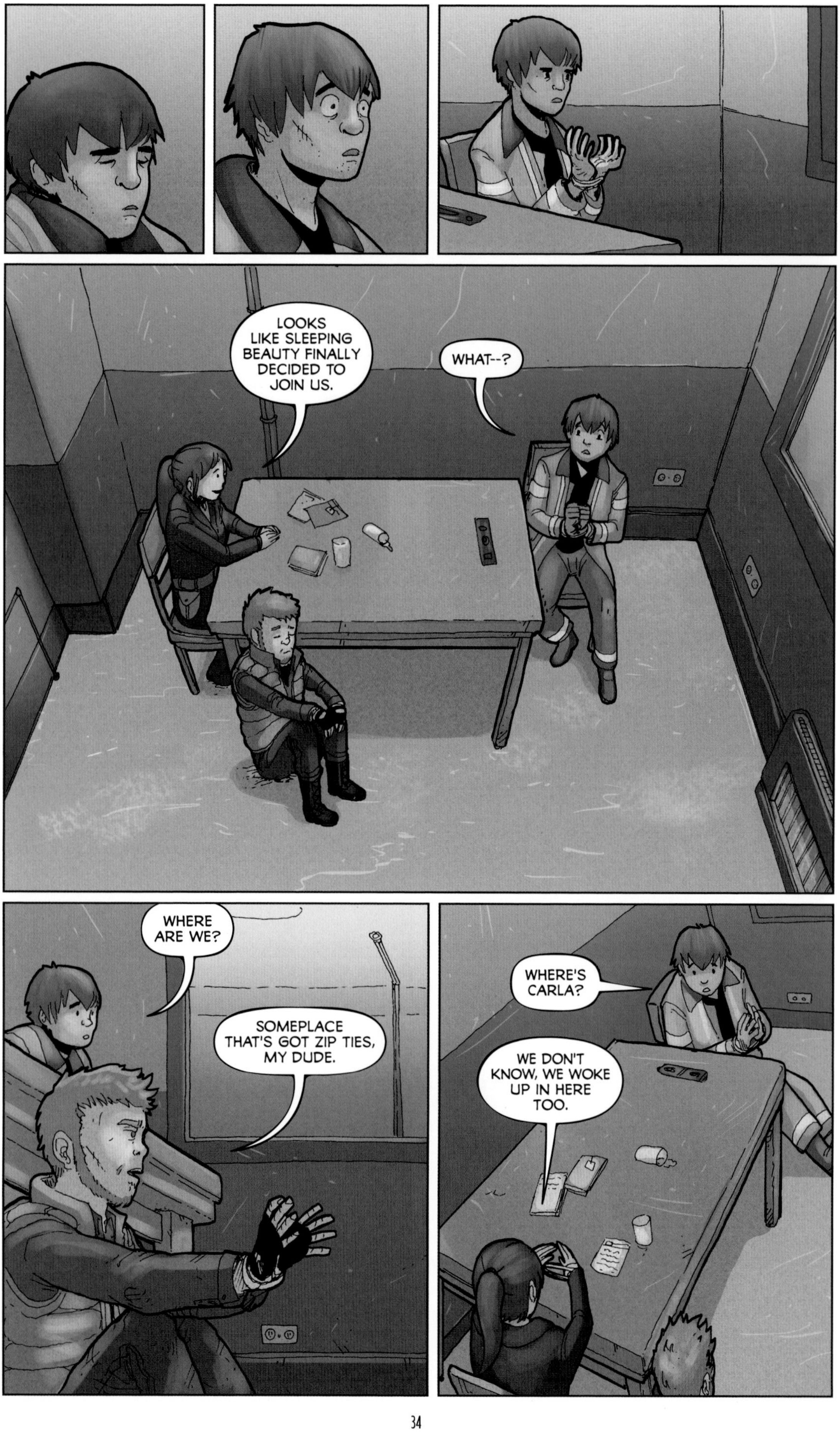
LOOKS LIKE SLEEPING BEAUTY FINALLY DECIDED TO JOIN US.
WHAT--?
WHERE ARE WE?
SOMEPLACE THAT'S GOT ZIP TIES, MY DUDE.
WHERE'S CARLA?
WE DON'T KNOW, WE WOKE UP IN HERE TOO.

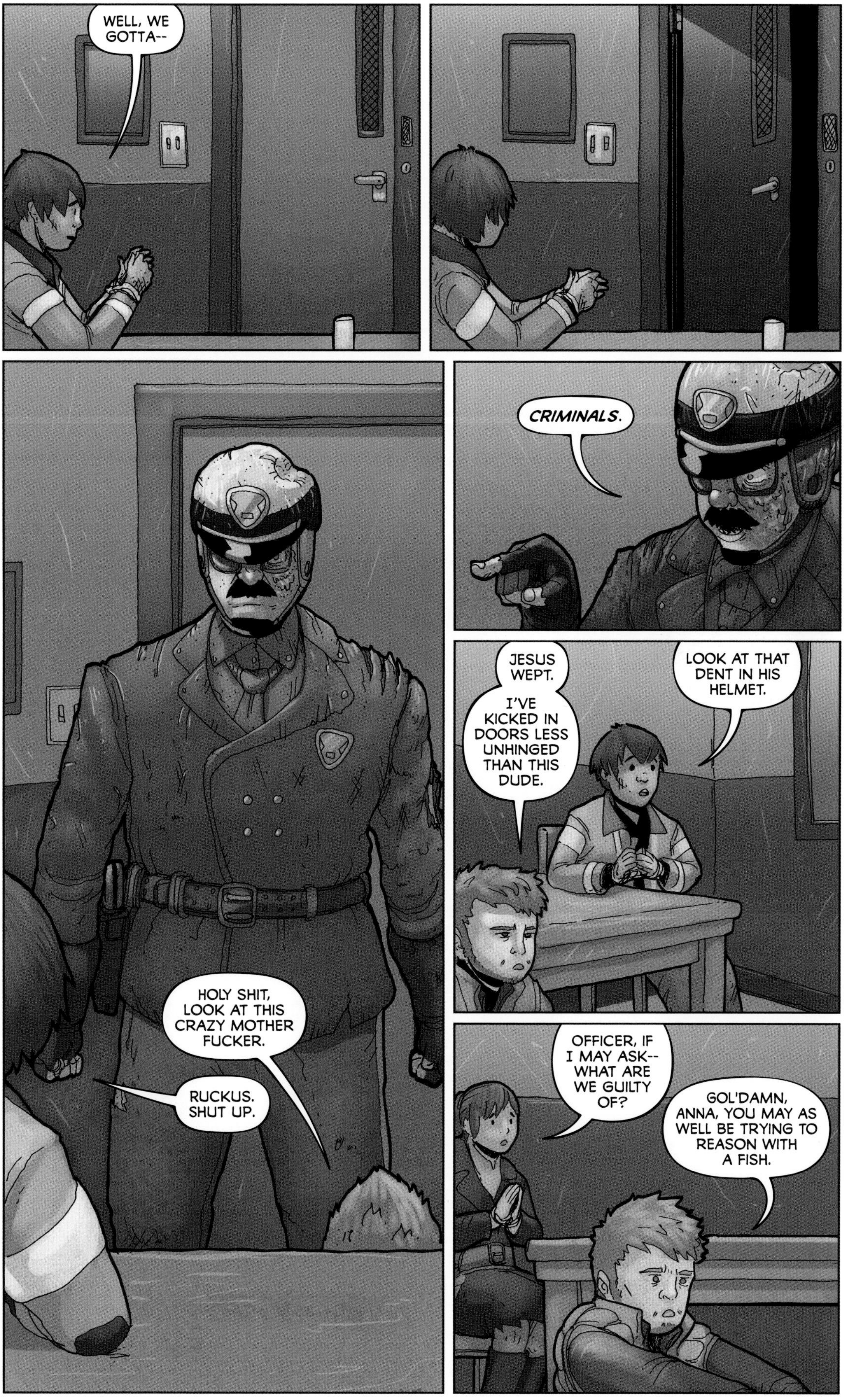
WELL, WE GOTTA--
CRIMINALS.
HOLY SHIT, LOOK AT THIS CRAZY MOTHER FUCKER.
RUCKUS. SHUT UP.
JESUS WEPT.
I'VE KICKED IN DOORS LESS UNHINGED THAN THIS DUDE.
LOOK AT THAT DENT IN HIS HELMET.
OFFICER, IF I MAY ASK-- WHAT ARE WE GUILTY OF?
GOL'DAMN, ANNA, YOU MAY AS WELL BE TRYING TO REASON WITH A FISH.

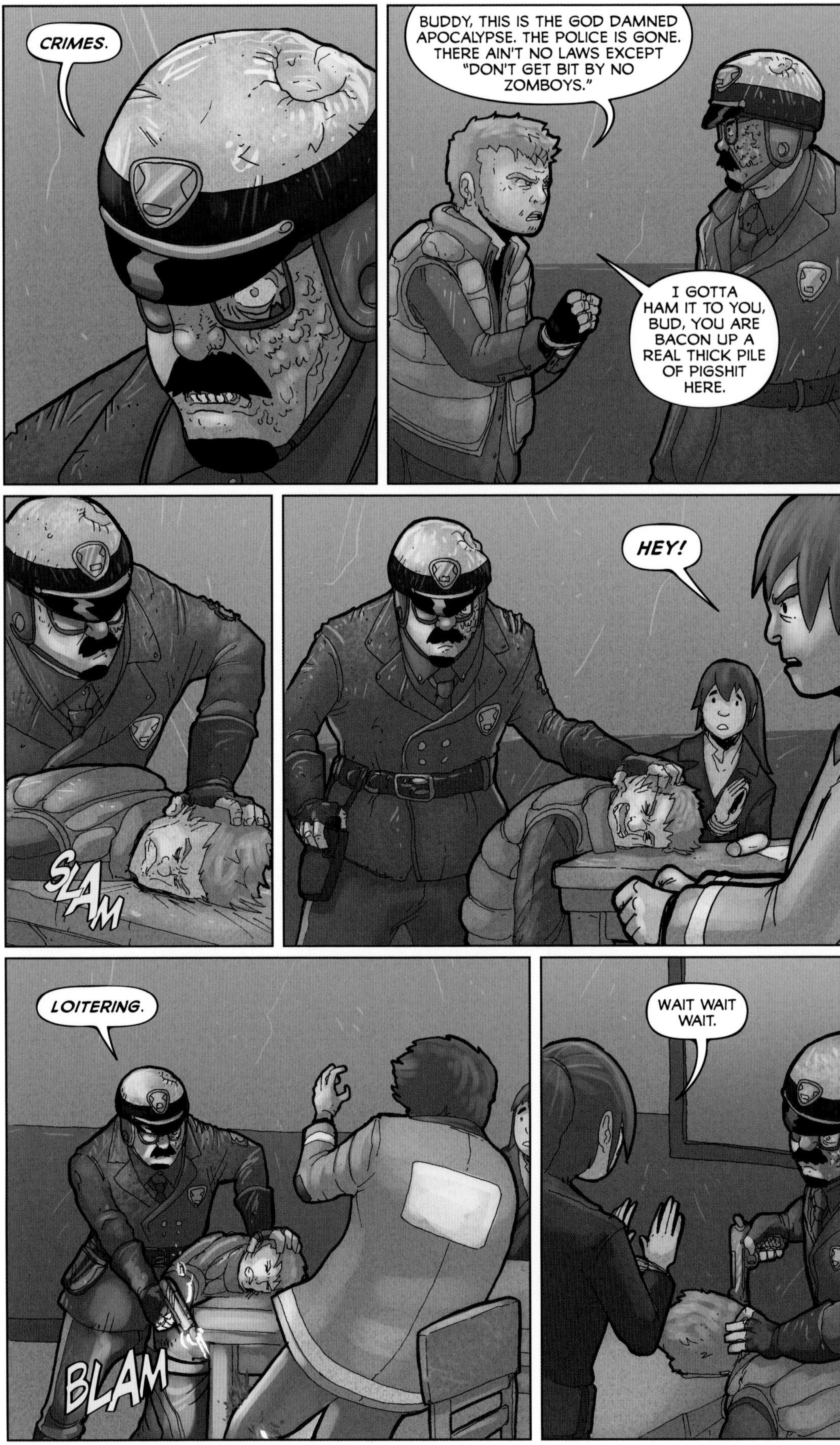
CRIMES.
BUDDY, THIS IS THE GOD DAMNED APOCALYPSE. THE POLICE IS GONE. THERE AIN'T NO LAWS EXCEPT "DON'T GET BIT BY NO ZOMBOYS."
I GOTTA HAM IT TO YOU, BUD, YOU ARE BACON UP A REAL THICK PILE OF PIGSHIT HERE.
SLAM
HEY!
LOITERING.
BLAM
WAIT WAIT WAIT.

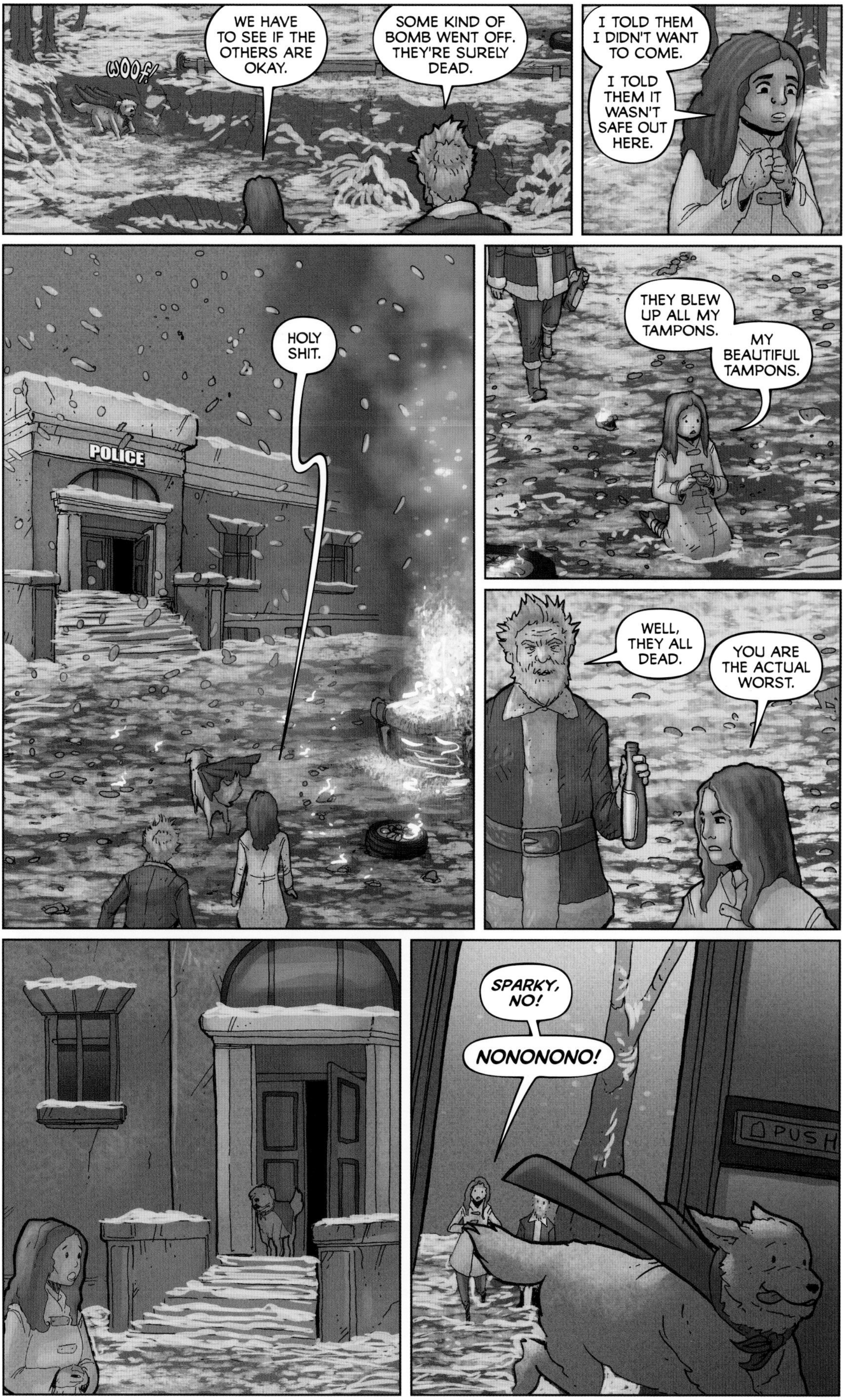
WOOF!
WE HAVE TO SEE IF THE OTHERS ARE OKAY.
SOME KIND OF BOMB WENT OFF. THEY'RE SURELY DEAD.
I TOLD THEM I DIDN'T WANT TO COME.
I TOLD THEM IT WASN'T SAFE OUT HERE.
POLICE
HOLY SHIT.
THEY BLEW UP ALL MY TAMPONS.
MY BEAUTIFUL TAMPONS.
WELL, THEY ALL DEAD.
YOU ARE THE ACTUAL WORST.
SPARKY, NO!
NONONONO!

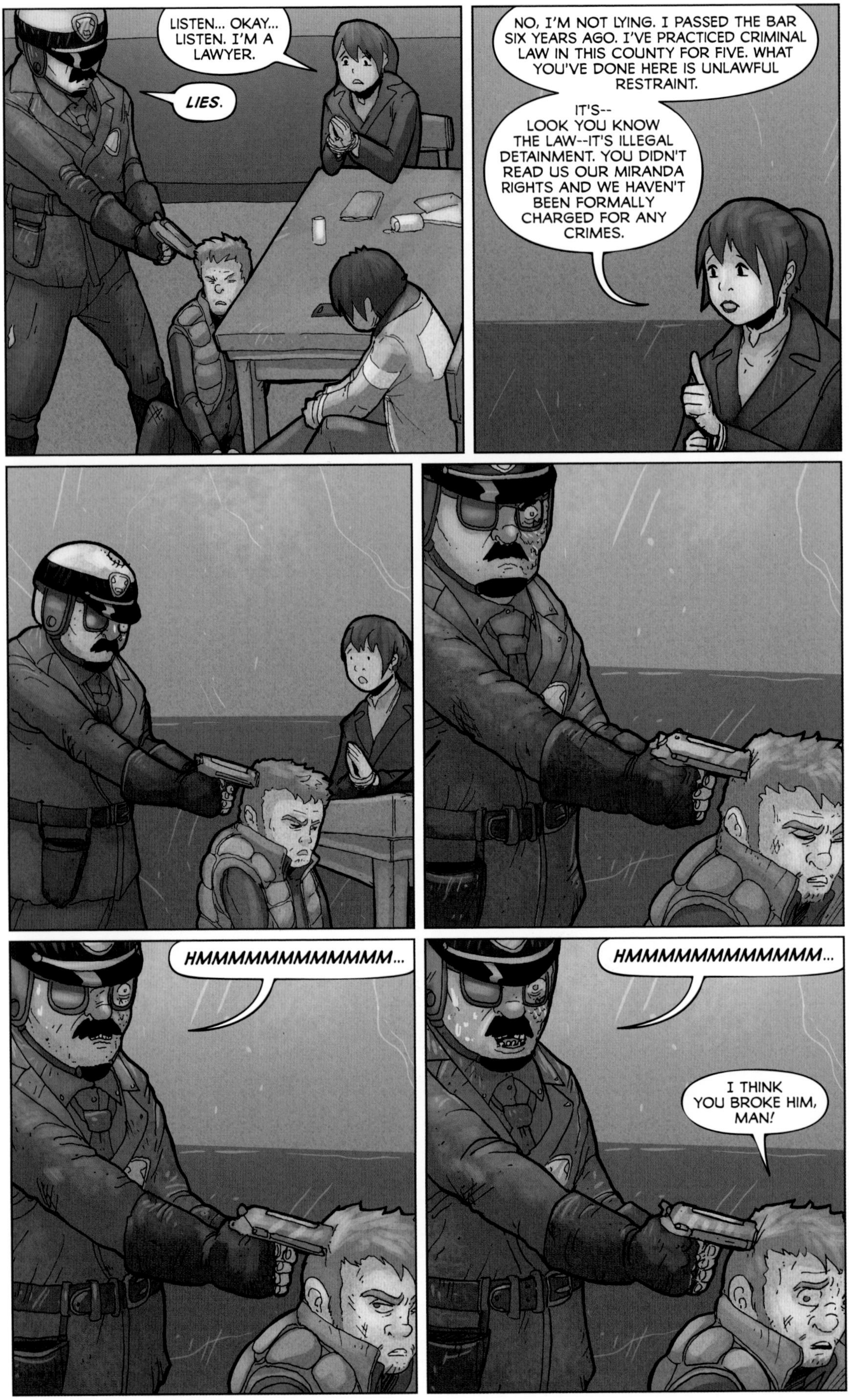
LISTEN... OKAY... LISTEN. I'M A LAWYER.
LIES.
NO, I'M NOT LYING. I PASSED THE BAR SIX YEARS AGO. I'VE PRACTICED CRIMINAL LAW IN THIS COUNTY FOR FIVE. WHAT YOU'VE DONE HERE IS UNLAWFUL RESTRAINT.
IT'S-- LOOK YOU KNOW THE LAW--IT'S ILLEGAL DETAINMENT. YOU DIDN'T READ US OUR MIRANDA RIGHTS AND WE HAVEN'T BEEN FORMALLY CHARGED FOR ANY CRIMES.
HMMMMMMMMMMMMM...
HMMMMMMMMMMMMM...
I THINK YOU BROKE HIM, MAN!

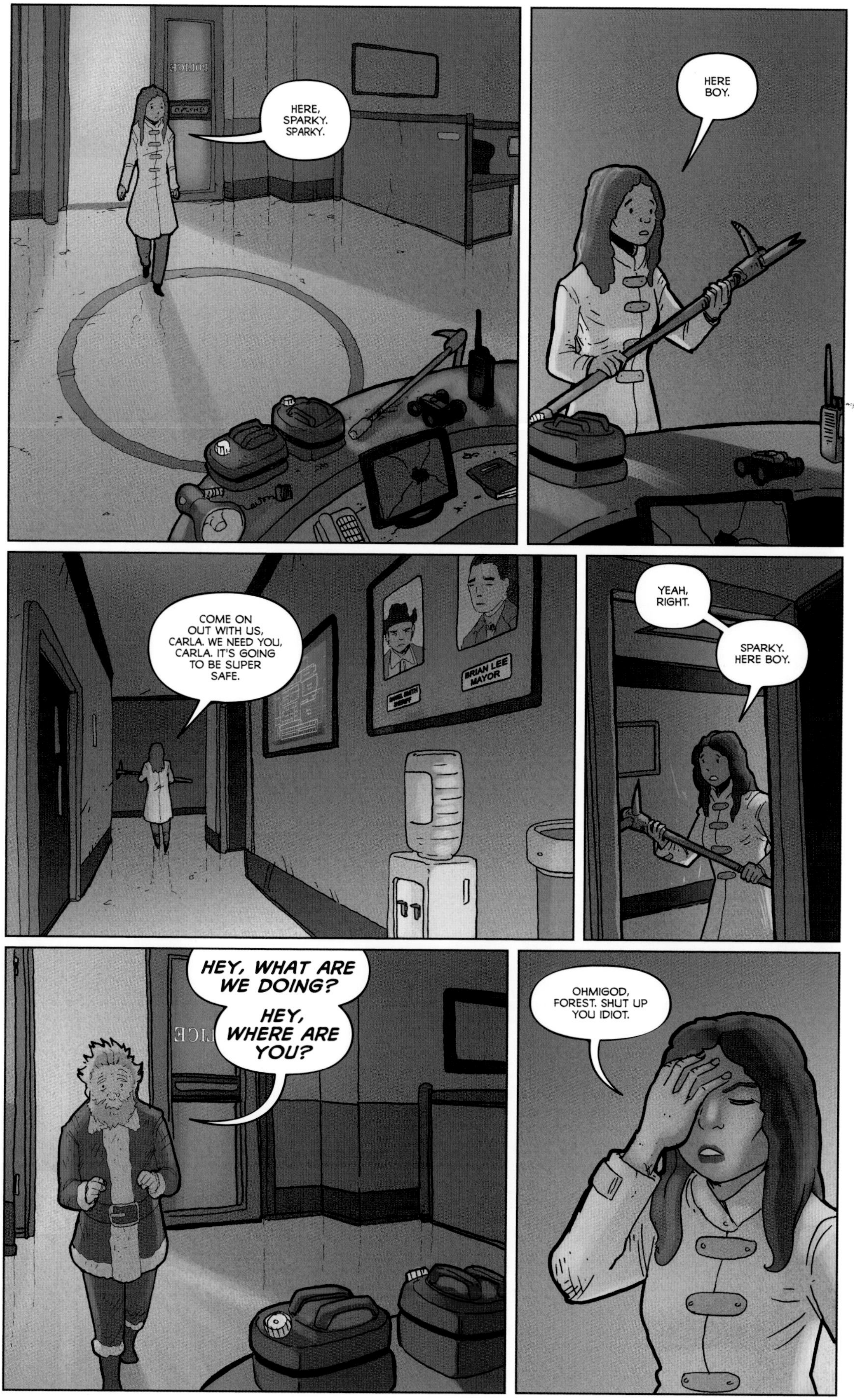
HERE, SPARKY. SPARKY.
HERE BOY.
COME ON OUT WITH US, CARLA. WE NEED YOU, CARLA. IT'S GOING TO BE SUPER SAFE.
BRIAN LEE MAYOR
YEAH, RIGHT.
SPARKY. HERE BOY.
HEY, WHAT ARE WE DOING?
HEY, WHERE ARE YOU?
OHMIGOD, FOREST. SHUT UP YOU IDIOT.

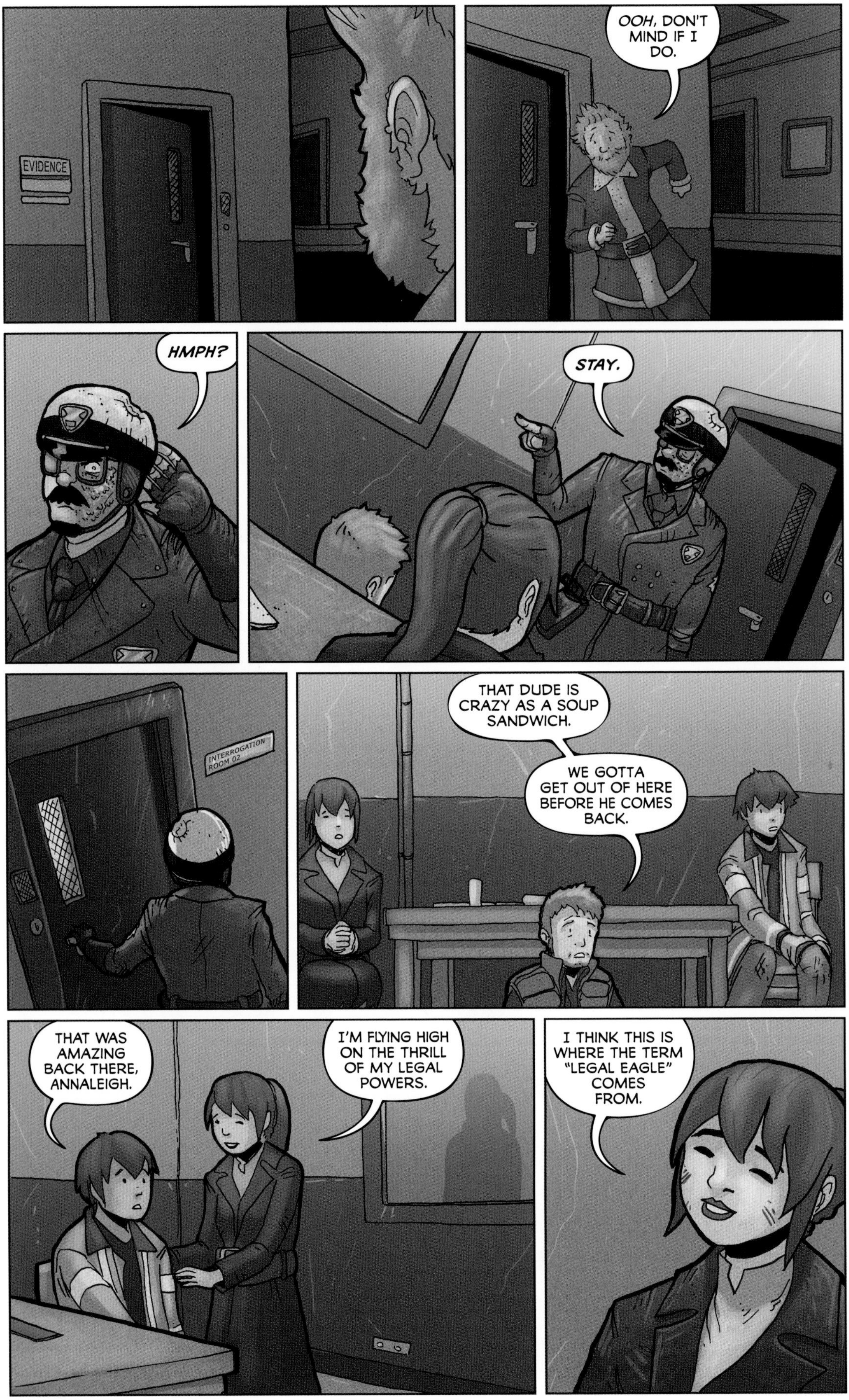
EVIDENCE
OOH, DON'T MIND IF I DO.
HMPH?
STAY.
INTERROGATION ROOM 02
THAT DUDE IS CRAZY AS A SOUP SANDWICH.
WE GOTTA GET OUT OF HERE BEFORE HE COMES BACK.
THAT WAS AMAZING BACK THERE, ANNALEIGH.
I'M FLYING HIGH ON THE THRILL OF MY LEGAL POWERS.
I THINK THIS IS WHERE THE TERM "LEGAL EAGLE" COMES FROM.

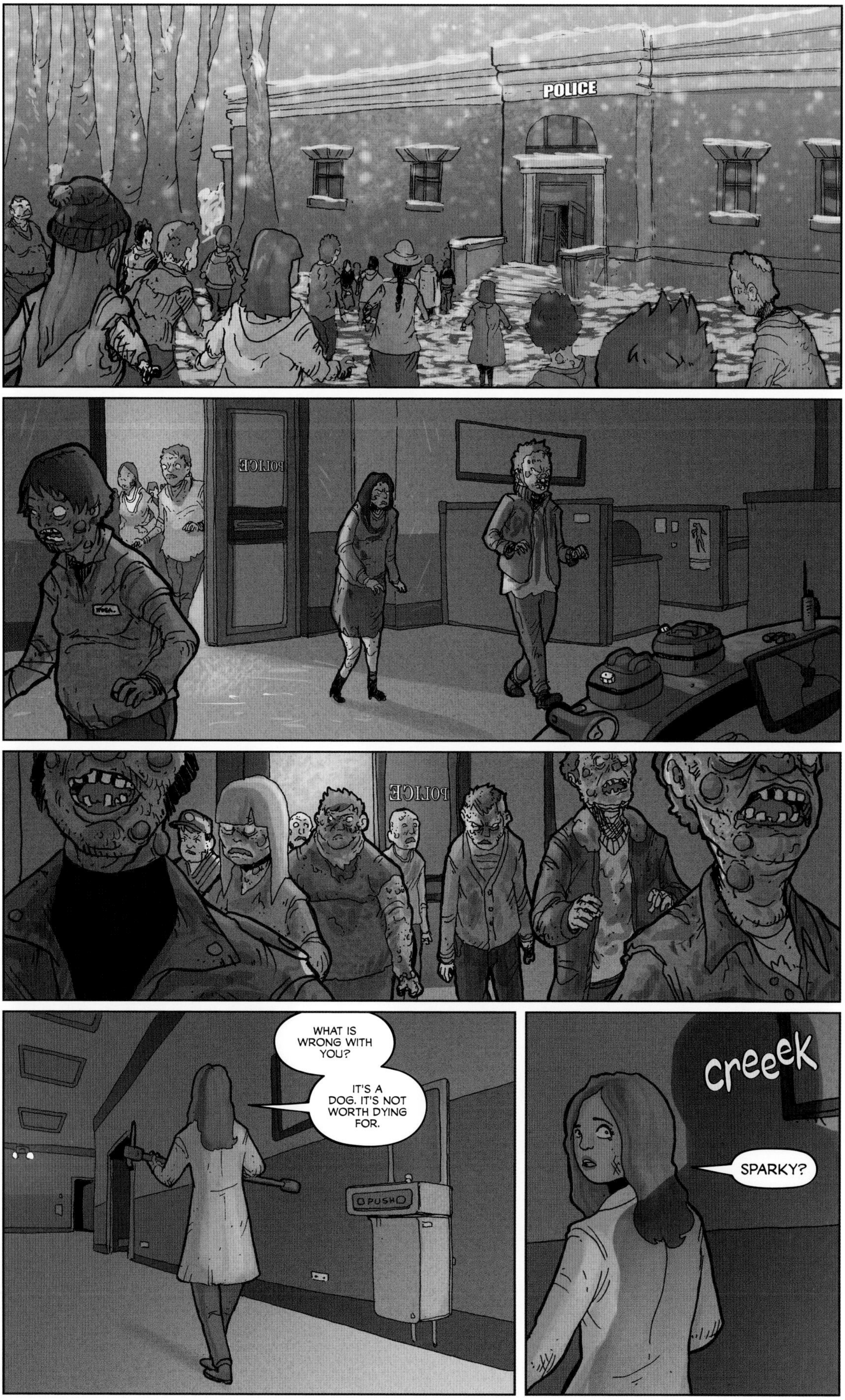
POLICE
WHAT IS WRONG WITH YOU?
IT'S A DOG. IT'S NOT WORTH DYING FOR.
PUSH
creeek
SPARKY?

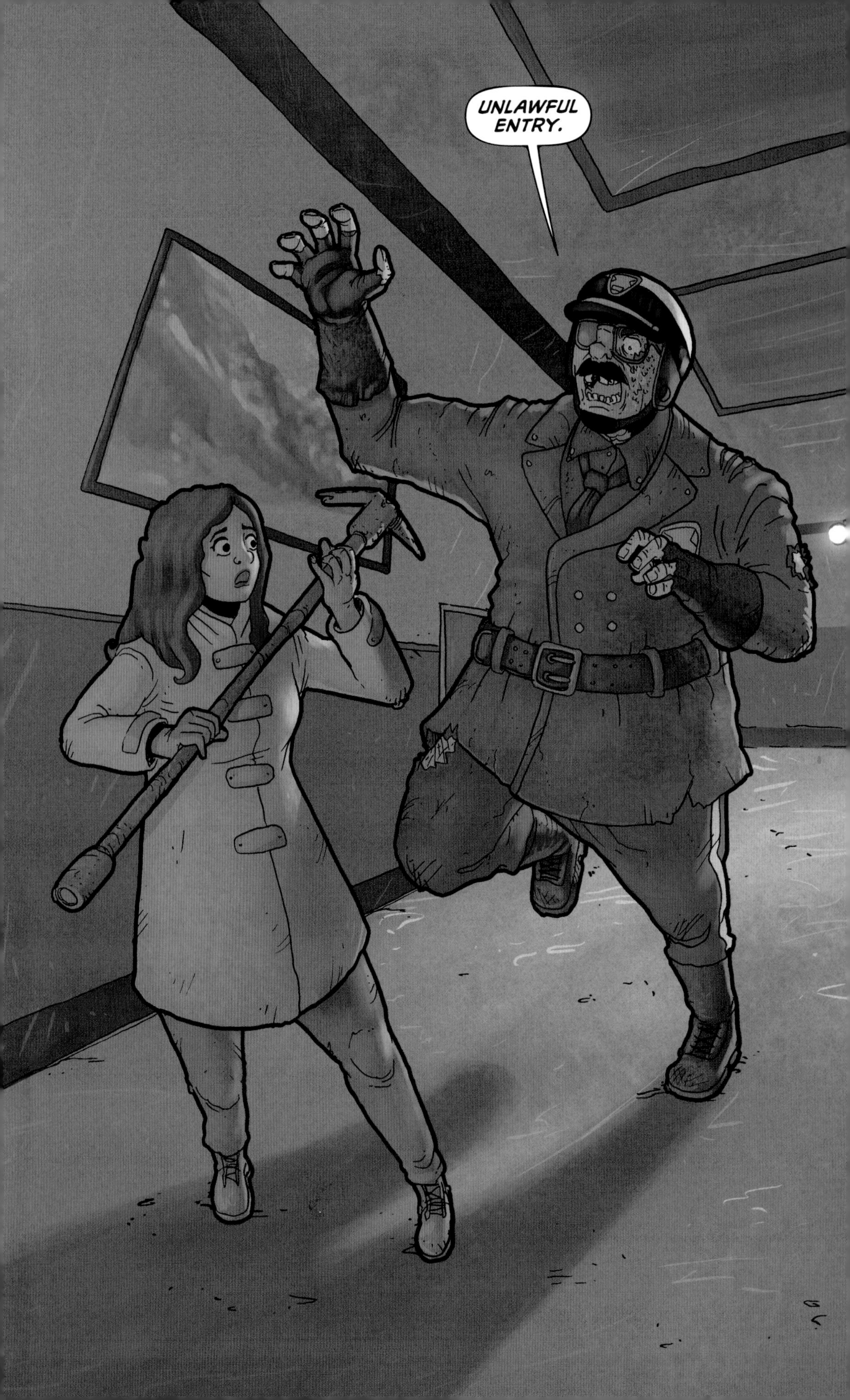
UNLAWFUL ENTRY.

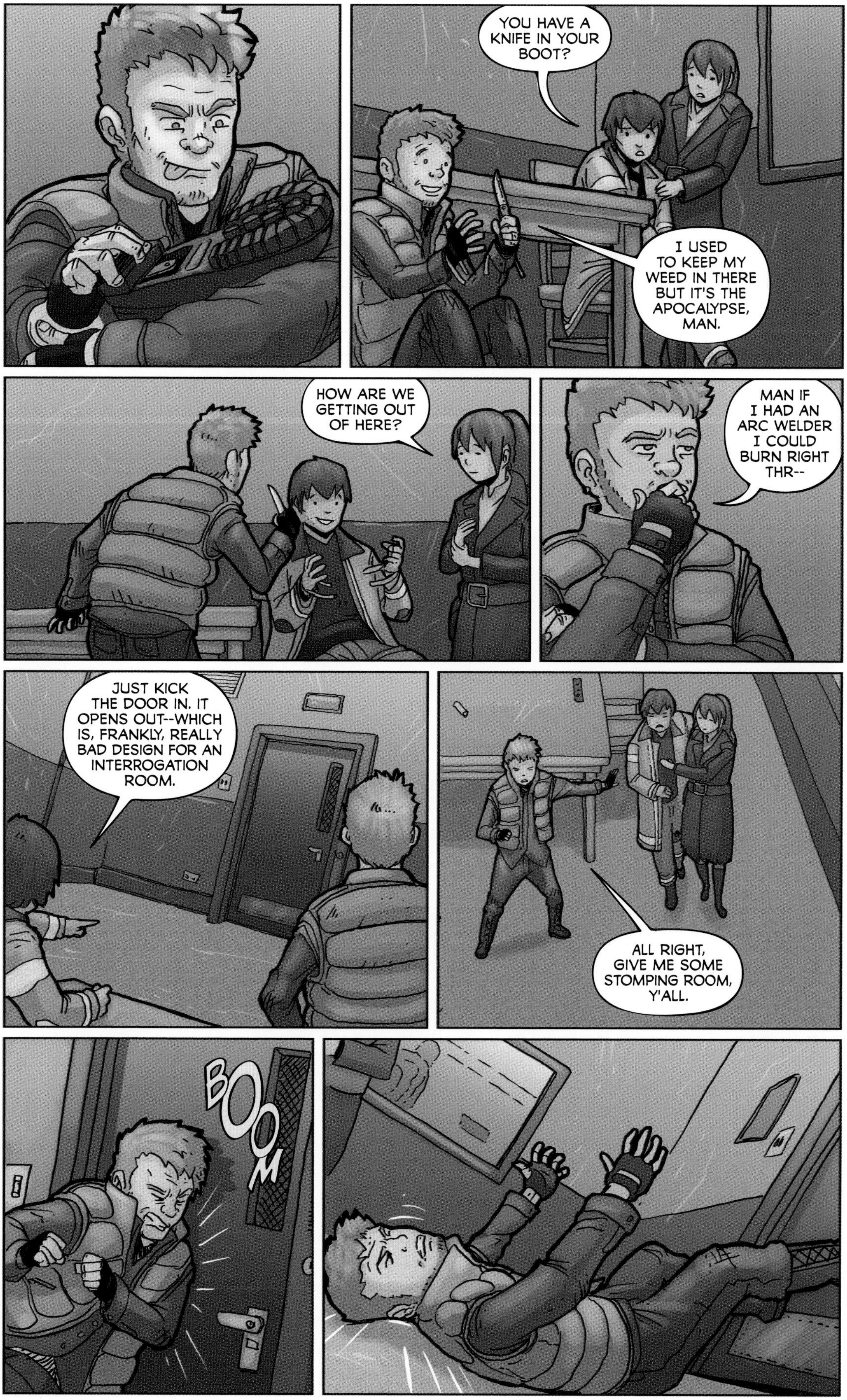
YOU HAVE A KNIFE IN YOUR BOOT?
I USED TO KEEP MY WEED IN THERE BUT IT'S THE APOCALYPSE, MAN.
HOW ARE WE GETTING OUT OF HERE?
MAN IF I HAD AN ARC WELDER I COULD BURN RIGHT THR--
JUST KICK THE DOOR IN. IT OPENS OUT--WHICH IS, FRANKLY, REALLY BAD DESIGN FOR AN INTERROGATION ROOM.
...
ALL RIGHT, GIVE ME SOME STOMPING ROOM, Y'ALL.
BOOM

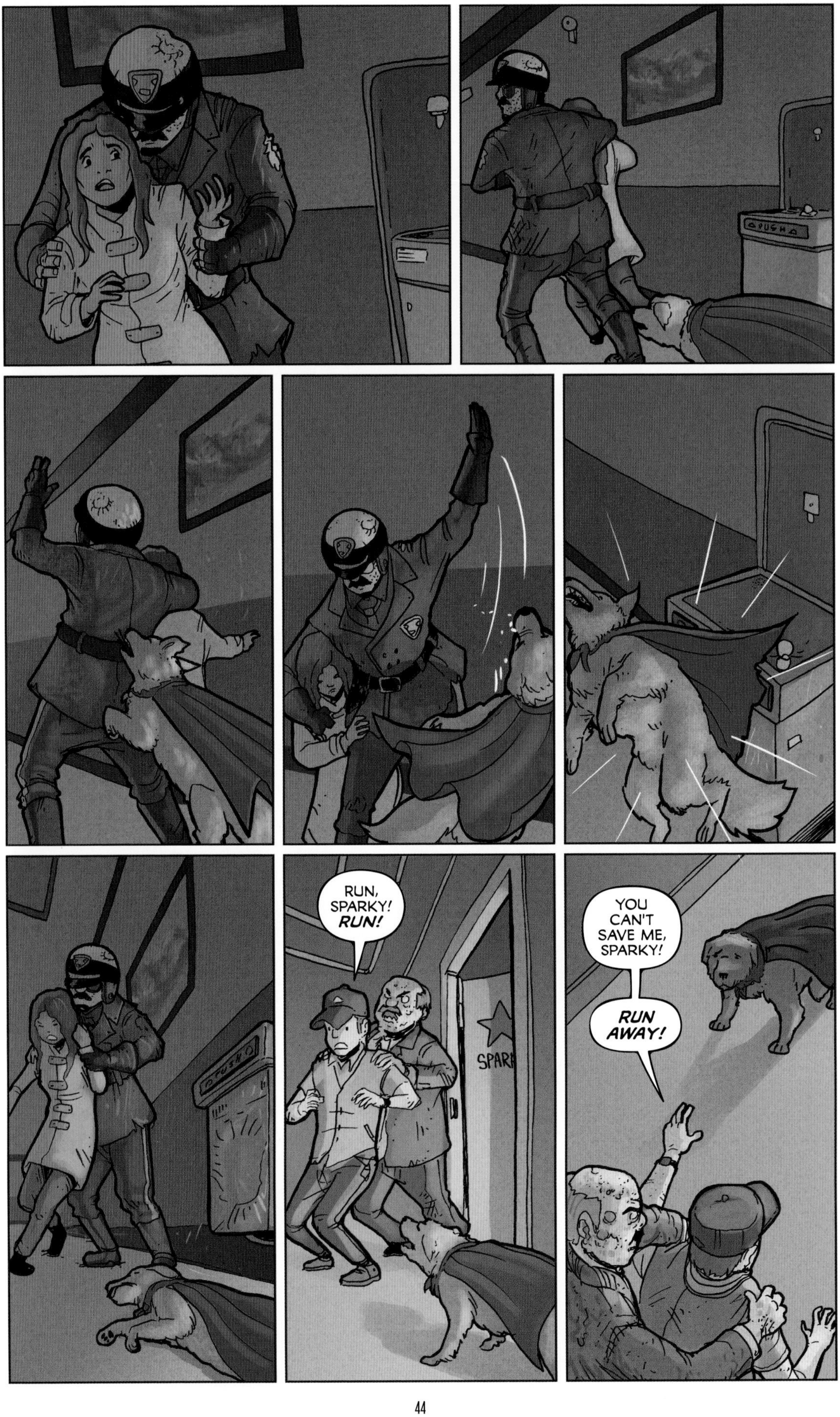
PUSH
PUSH
SPARK
RUN, SPARKY! RUN!
YOU CAN'T SAVE ME, SPARKY!
RUN AWAY!

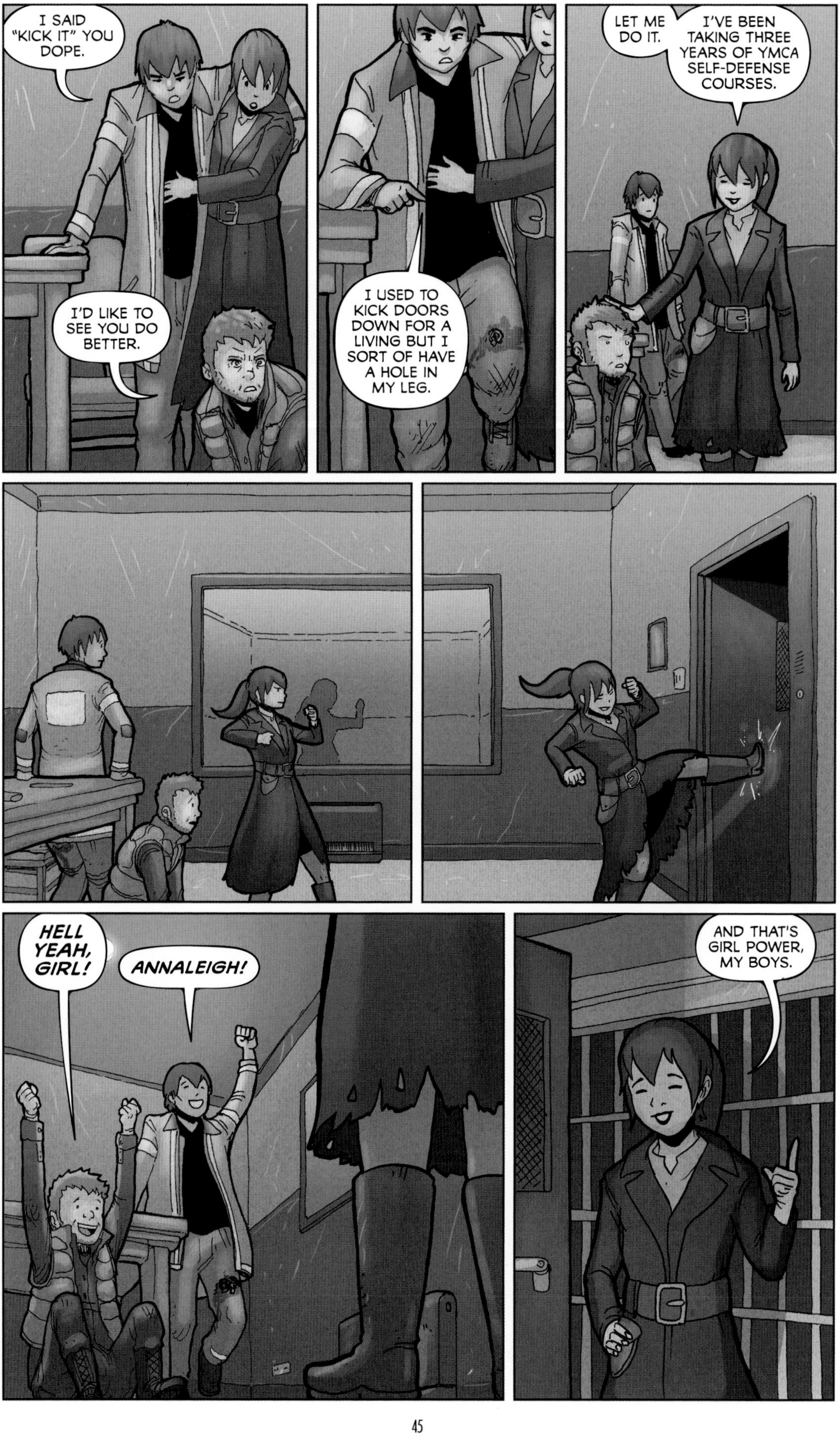
I SAID "KICK IT" YOU DOPE.
I'D LIKE TO SEE YOU DO BETTER.
I USED TO KICK DOORS DOWN FOR A LIVING BUT I SORT OF HAVE A HOLE IN MY LEG.
LET ME DO IT.
I'VE BEEN TAKING THREE YEARS OF YMCA SELF-DEFENSE COURSES.
HELL YEAH, GIRL!
ANNALEIGH!
AND THAT'S GIRL POWER, MY BOYS.

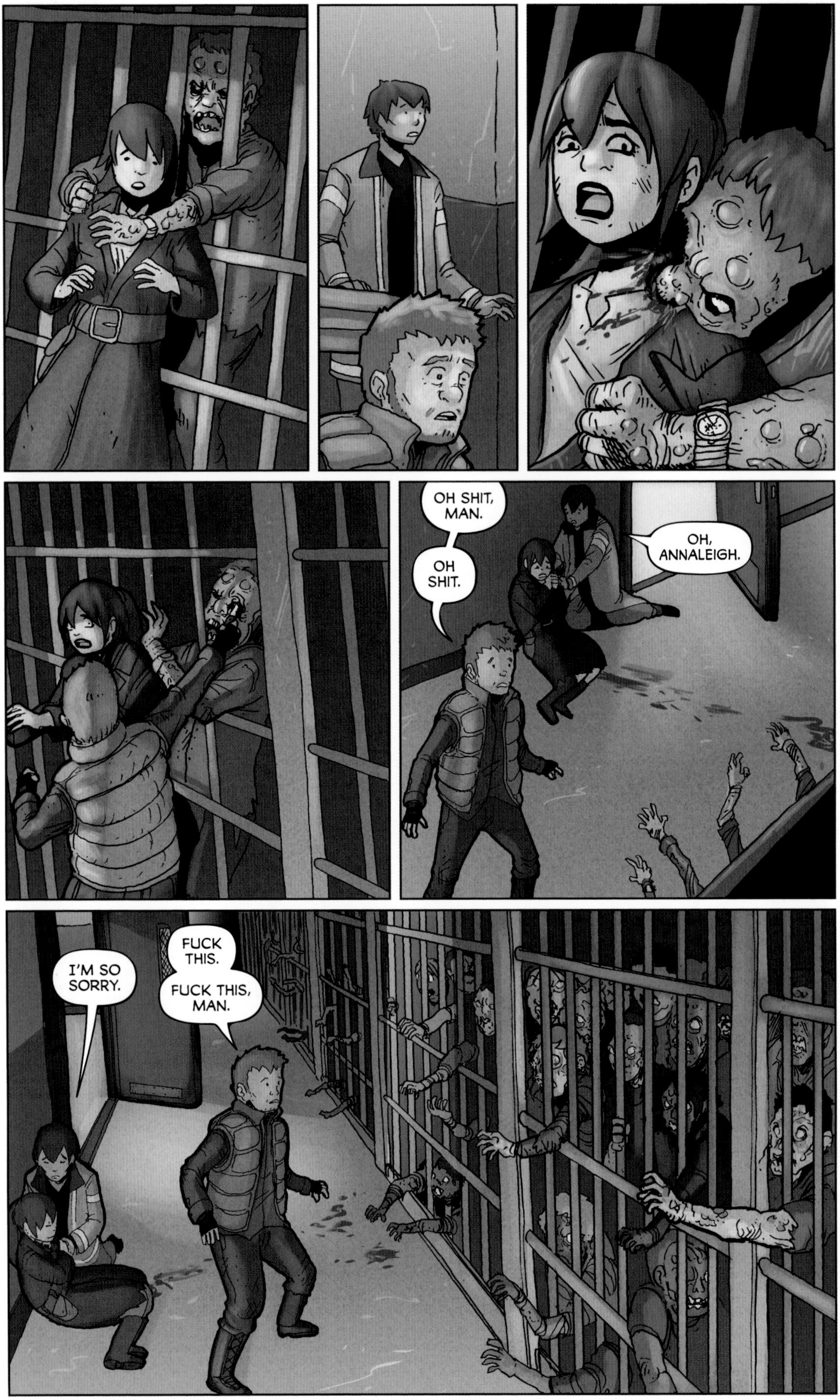
OH SHIT, MAN.
OH SHIT.
OH, ANNALEIGH.
I'M SO SORRY.
FUCK THIS.
FUCK THIS, MAN.

PUSH

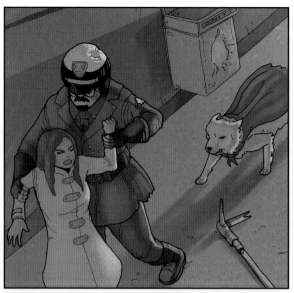

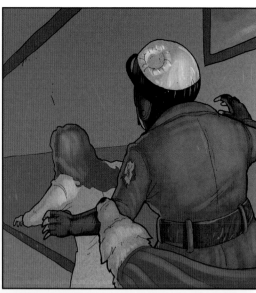

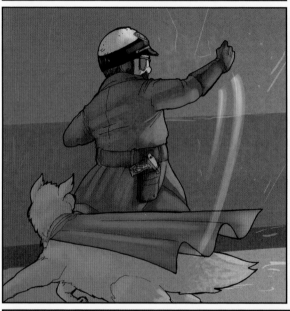

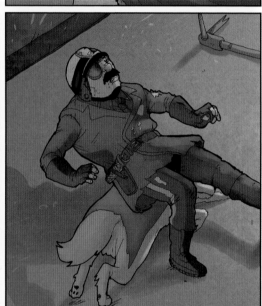

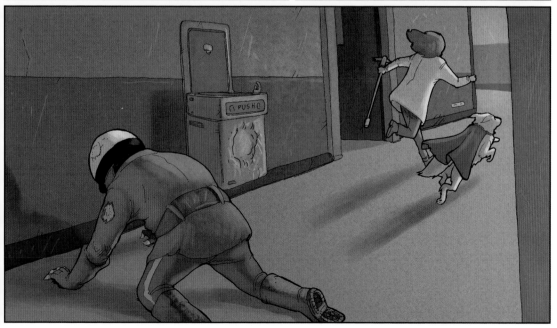

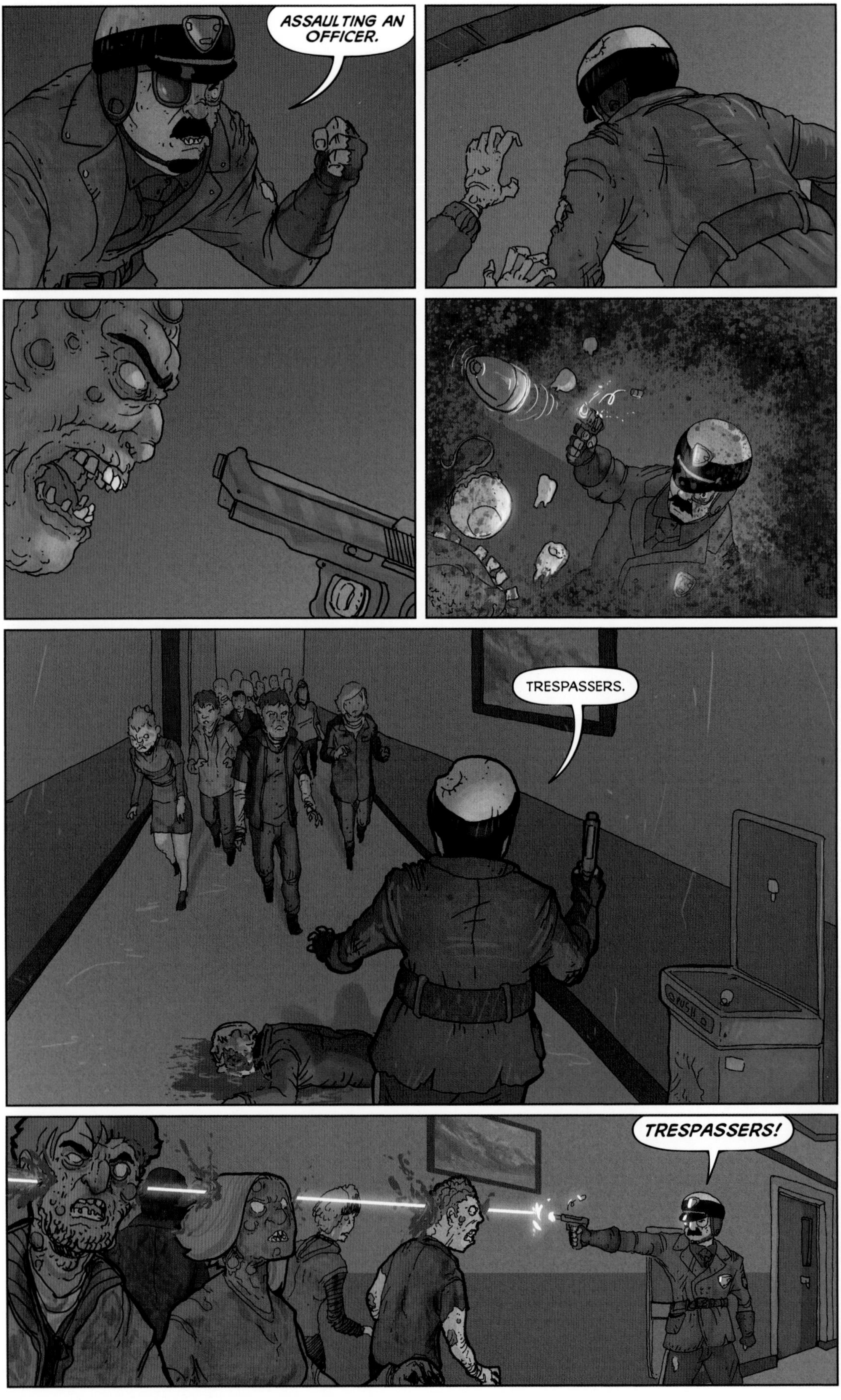
ASSAULTING AN OFFICER.
TRESPASSERS.
TRESPASSERS!
PUSH

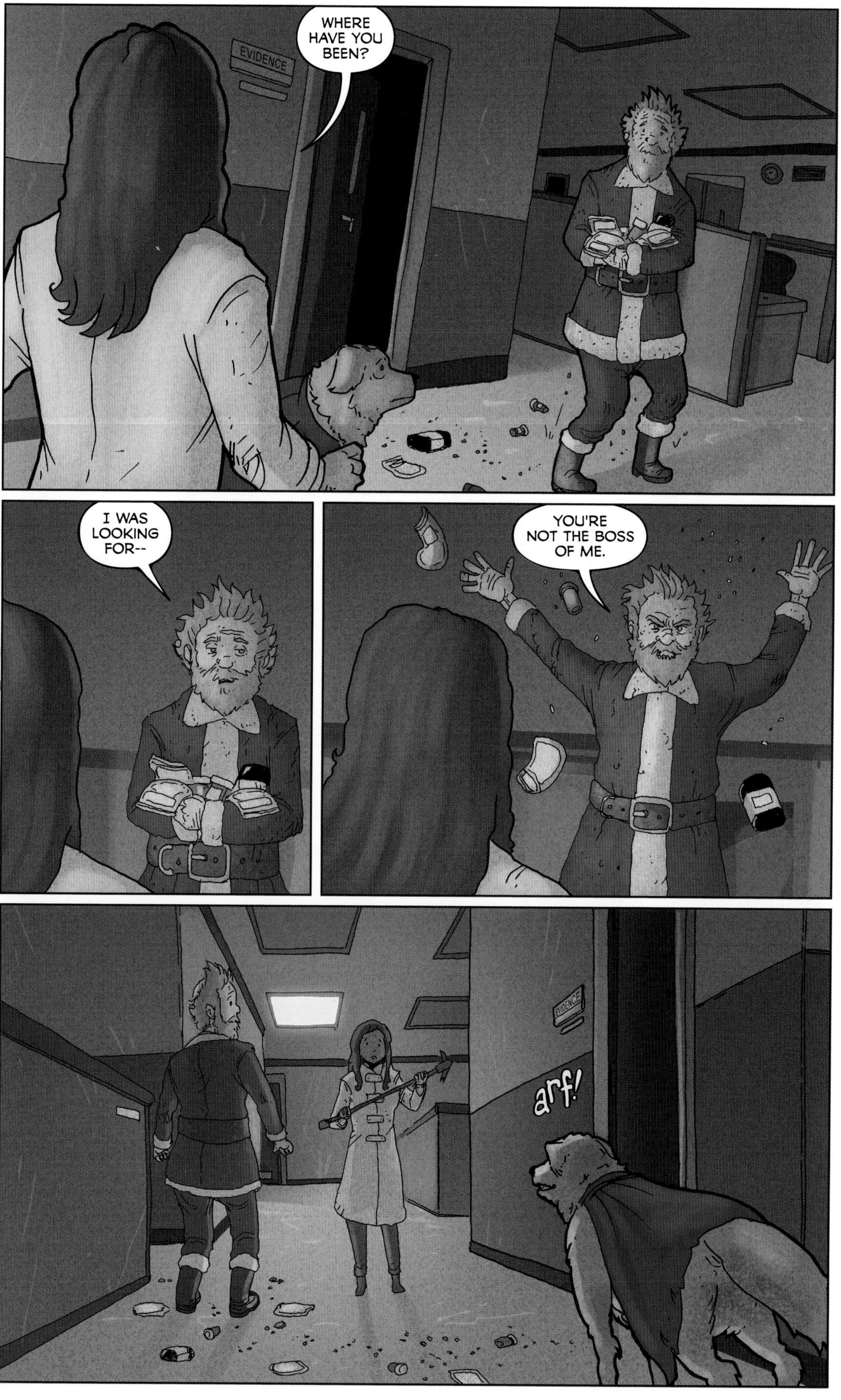
EVIDENCE
WHERE HAVE YOU BEEN?
I WAS LOOKING FOR--
YOU'RE NOT THE BOSS OF ME.
EVIDENCE
arf!

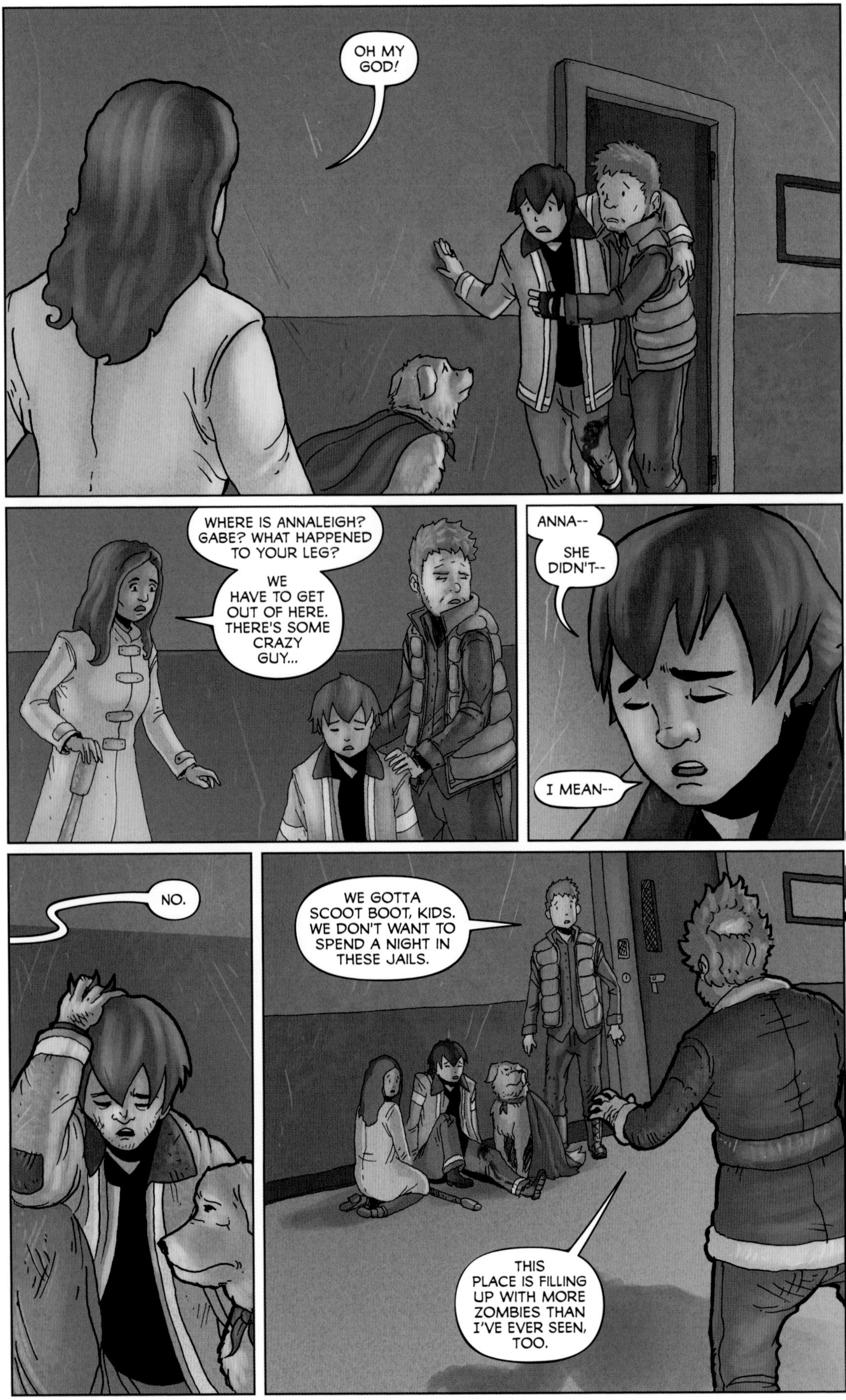
OH MY GOD!
WHERE IS ANNALEIGH? GABE? WHAT HAPPENED TO YOUR LEG?
WE HAVE TO GET OUT OF HERE. THERE'S SOME CRAZY GUY...
ANNA--
SHE DIDN'T--
I MEAN--
NO.
WE GOTTA SCOOT BOOT, KIDS. WE DON'T WANT TO SPEND A NIGHT IN THESE JAILS.
THIS PLACE IS FILLING UP WITH MORE ZOMBIES THAN I'VE EVER SEEN, TOO.

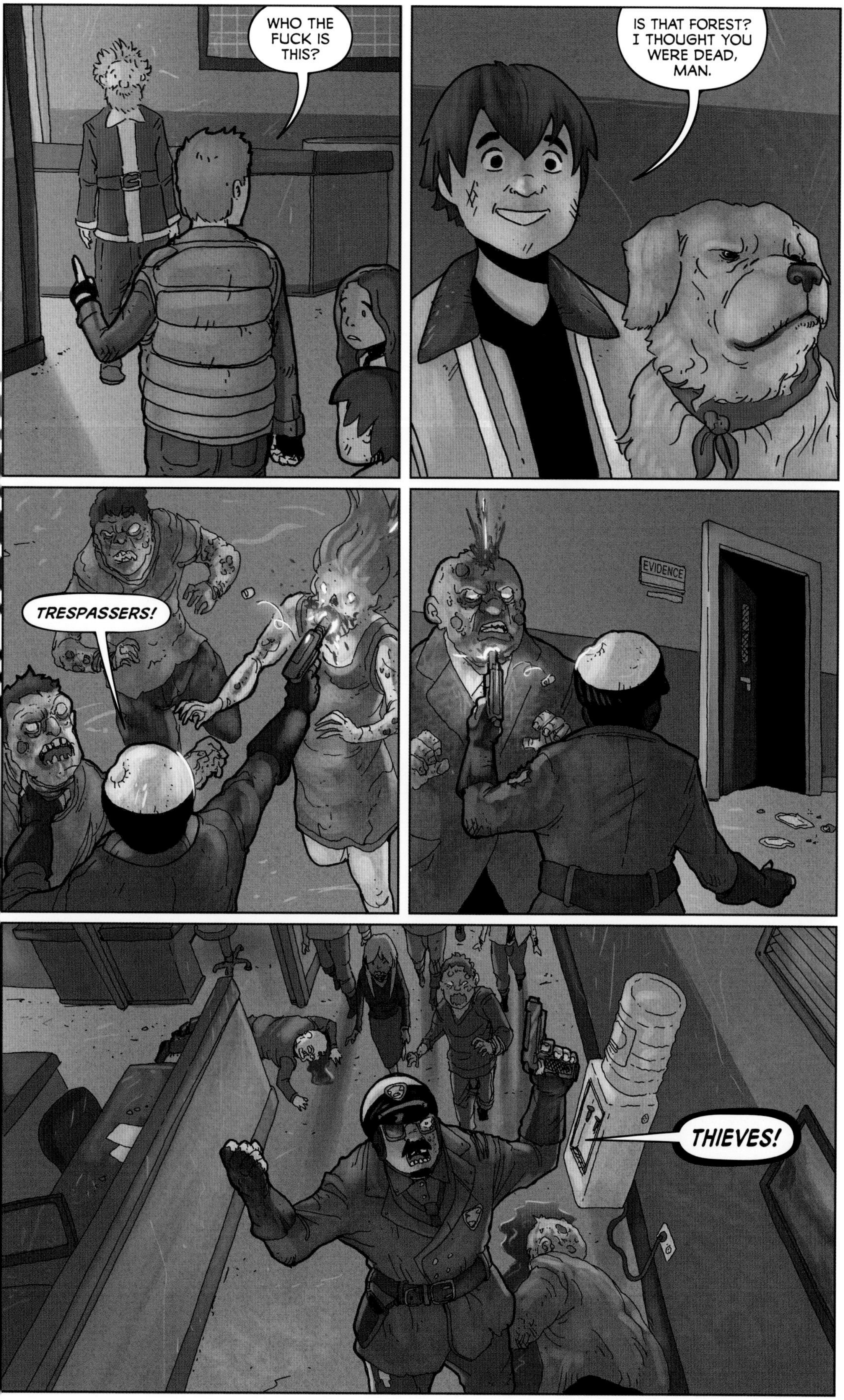
WHO THE FUCK IS THIS?
IS THAT FOREST? I THOUGHT YOU WERE DEAD, MAN.
TRESPASSERS!
EVIDENCE
THIEVES!

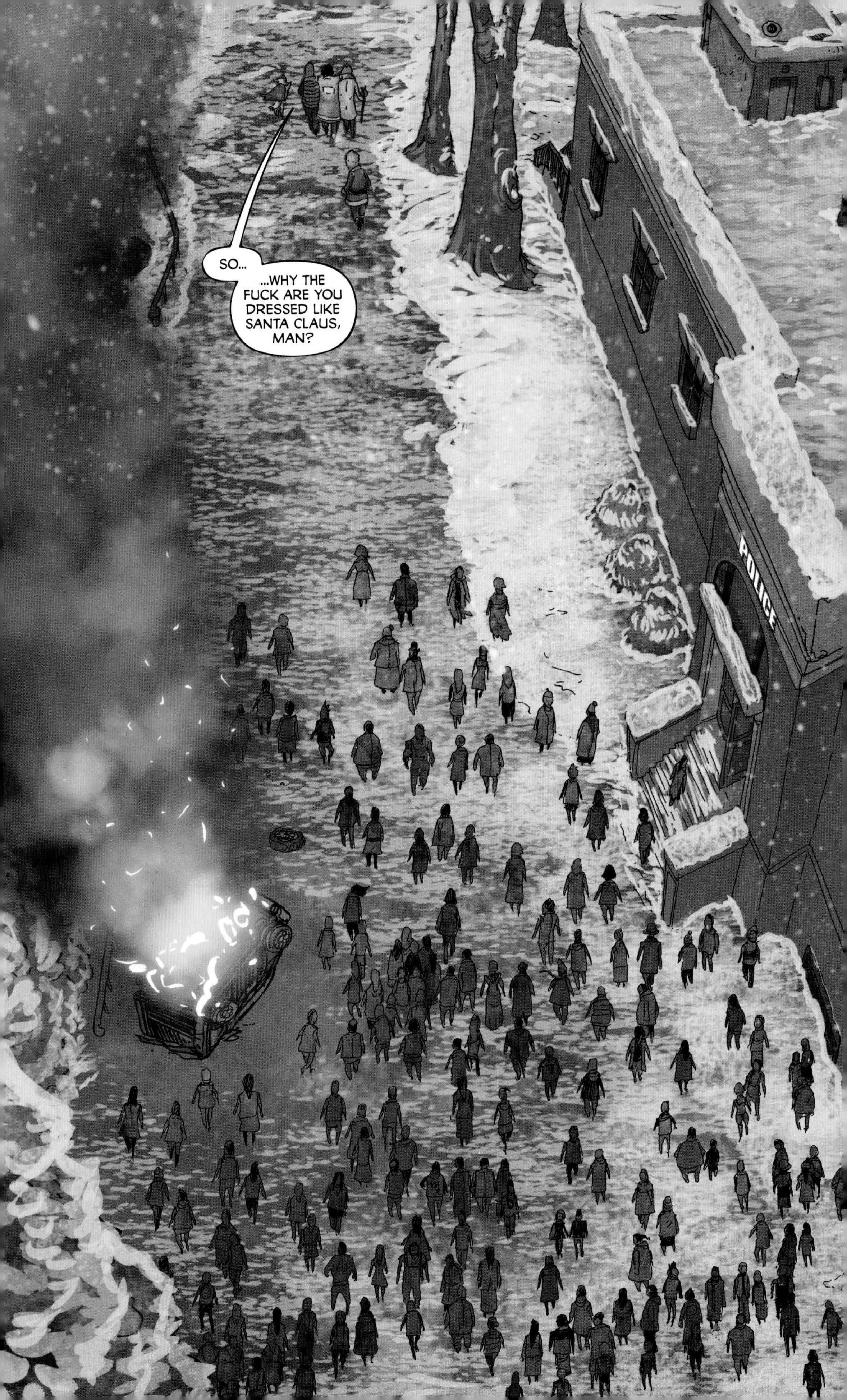
SO...
...WHY THE FUCK ARE YOU DRESSED LIKE SANTA CLAUS, MAN?
POLICE

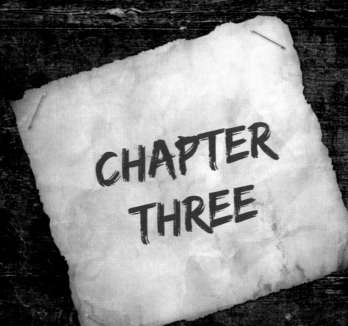

CHAPTER THREE

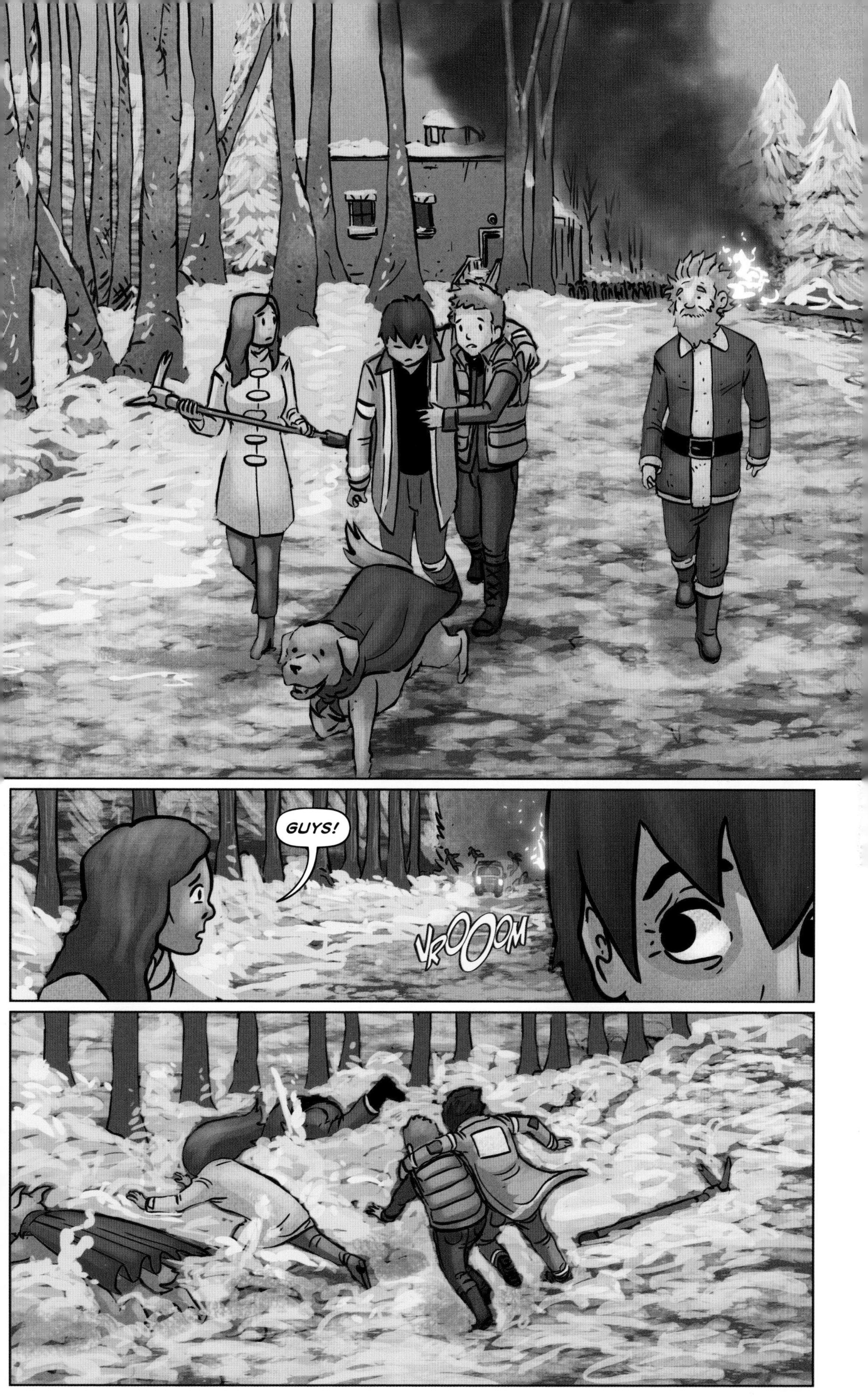
GUYS!
VROOOM

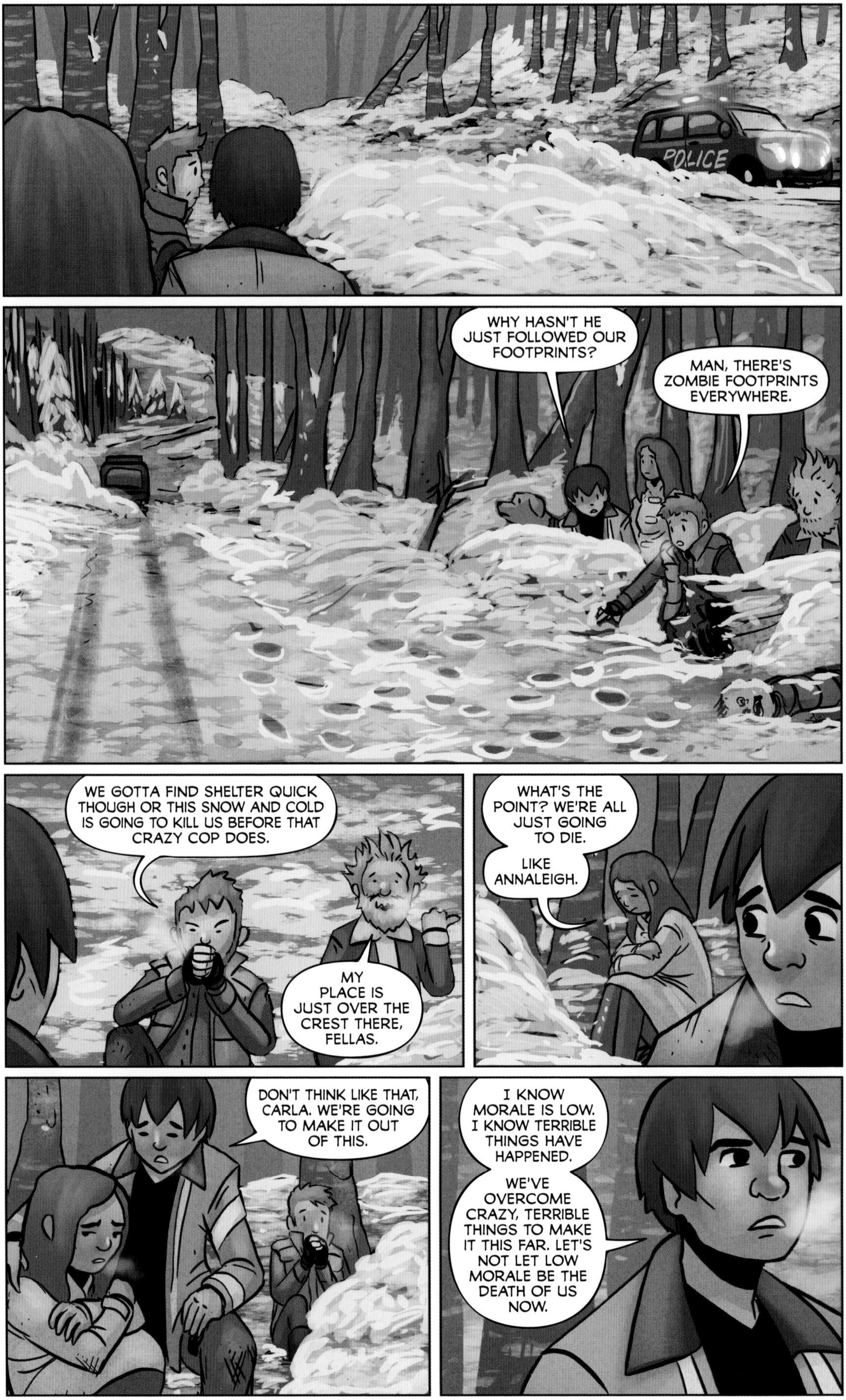
POLICE
WHY HASN'T HE JUST FOLLOWED OUR FOOTPRINTS?
MAN, THERE'S ZOMBIE FOOTPRINTS EVERYWHERE.
WE GOTTA FIND SHELTER QUICK THOUGH OR THIS SNOW AND COLD IS GOING TO KILL US BEFORE THAT CRAZY COP DOES.
MY PLACE IS JUST OVER THE CREST THERE, FELLAS.
WHAT'S THE POINT? WE'RE ALL JUST GOING TO DIE.
LIKE ANNALEIGH.
DON'T THINK LIKE THAT, CARLA. WE'RE GOING TO MAKE IT OUT OF THIS.
I KNOW MORALE IS LOW. I KNOW TERRIBLE THINGS HAVE HAPPENED.
WE'VE OVERCOME CRAZY, TERRIBLE THINGS TO MAKE IT THIS FAR. LET'S NOT LET LOW MORALE BE THE DEATH OF US NOW.

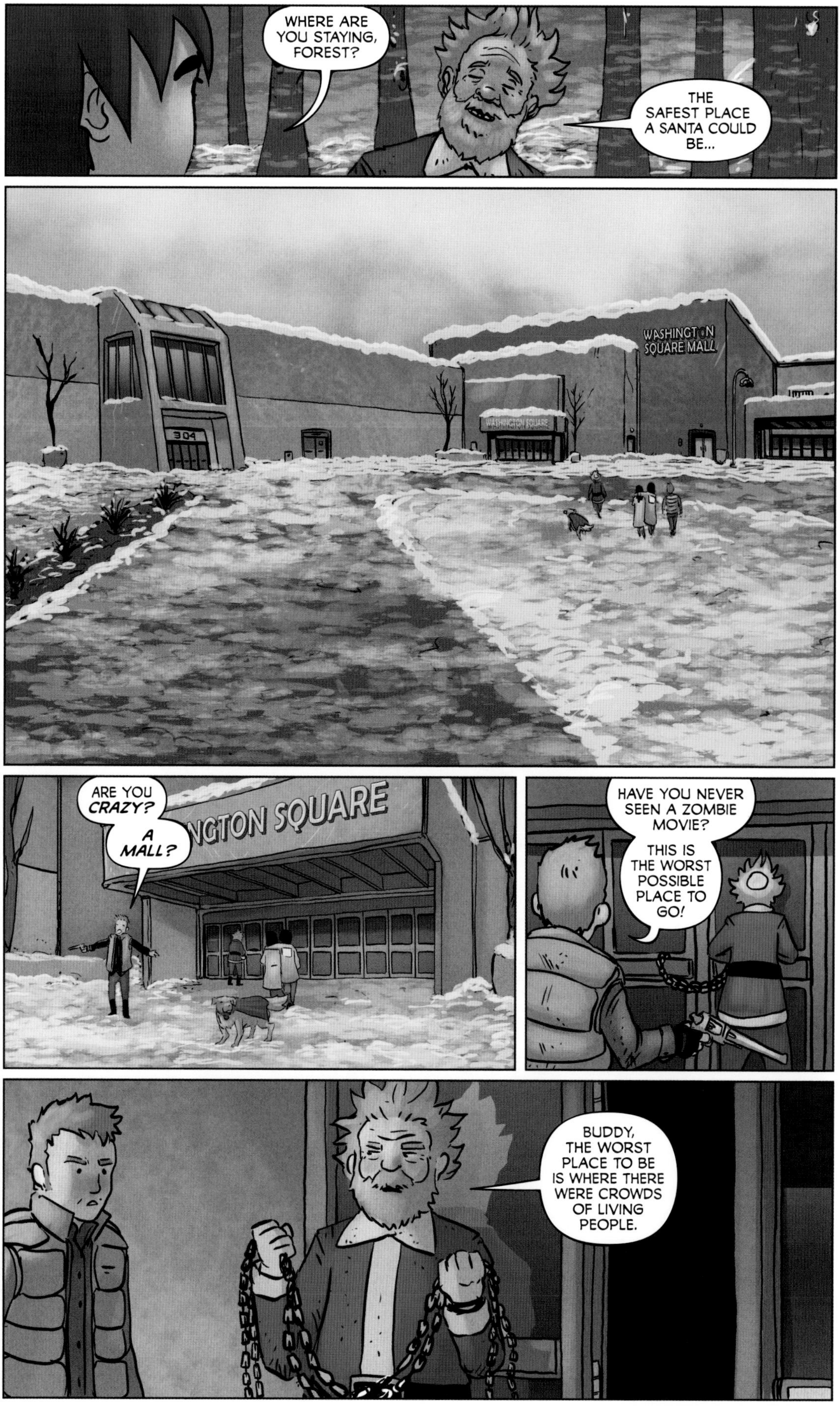
WHERE ARE YOU STAYING, FOREST?
THE SAFEST PLACE A SANTA COULD BE...
WASHINGTON SQUARE MALL
304
WASHINGTON SQUARE
NGTON SQUARE
ARE YOU CRAZY?
A MALL?
HAVE YOU NEVER SEEN A ZOMBIE MOVIE?
THIS IS THE WORST POSSIBLE PLACE TO GO!
BUDDY, THE WORST PLACE TO BE IS WHERE THERE WERE CROWDS OF LIVING PEOPLE.

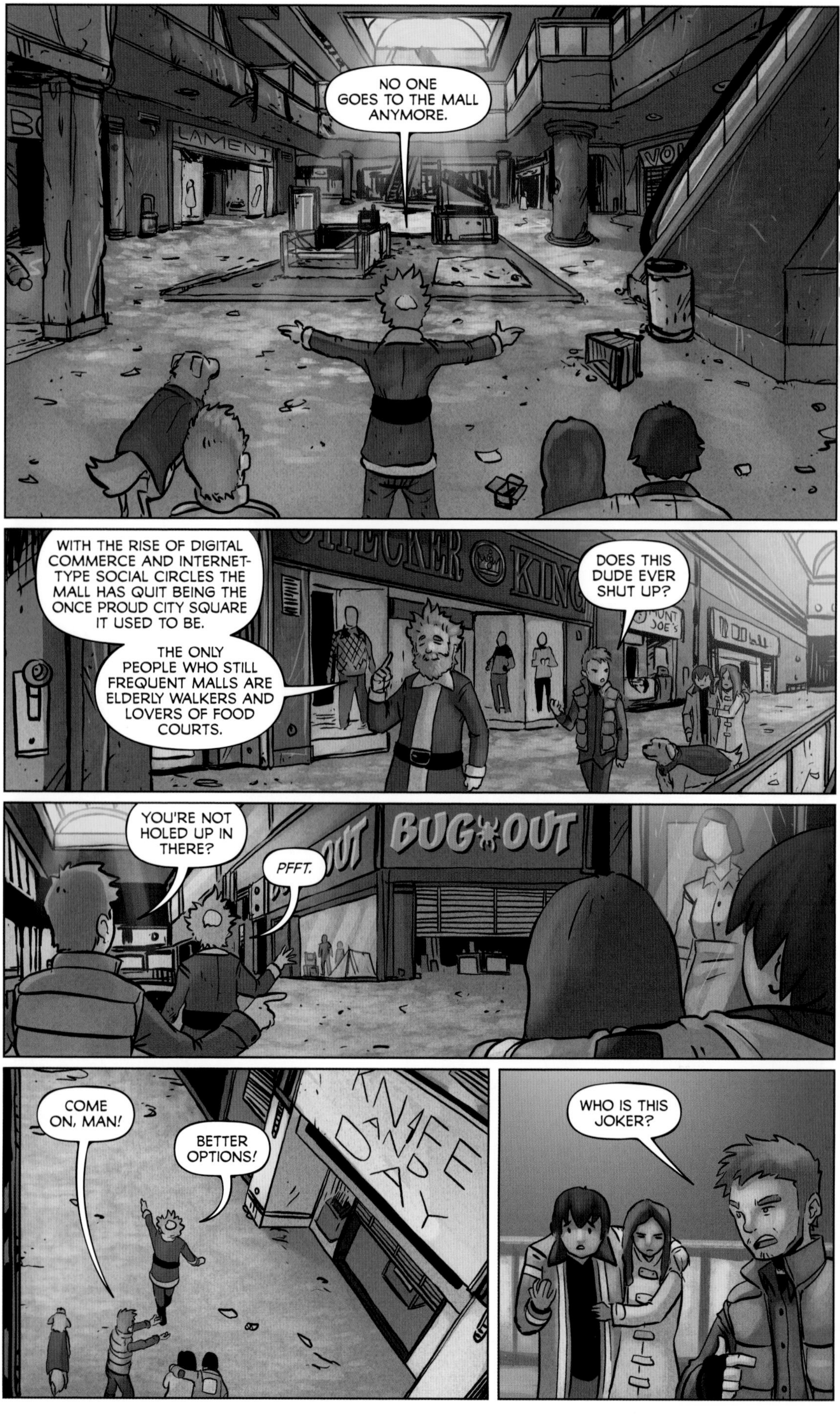
NO ONE GOES TO THE MALL ANYMORE.
LAMENT
WITH THE RISE OF DIGITAL COMMERCE AND INTERNET-TYPE SOCIAL CIRCLES THE MALL HAS QUIT BEING THE ONCE PROUD CITY SQUARE IT USED TO BE.
THE ONLY PEOPLE WHO STILL FREQUENT MALLS ARE ELDERLY WALKERS AND LOVERS OF FOOD COURTS.
DOES THIS DUDE EVER SHUT UP?
KING
YOU'RE NOT HOLED UP IN THERE?
PFFT.
BUG OUT
COME ON, MAN!
BETTER OPTIONS!
KNIFE DANDY
WHO IS THIS JOKER?

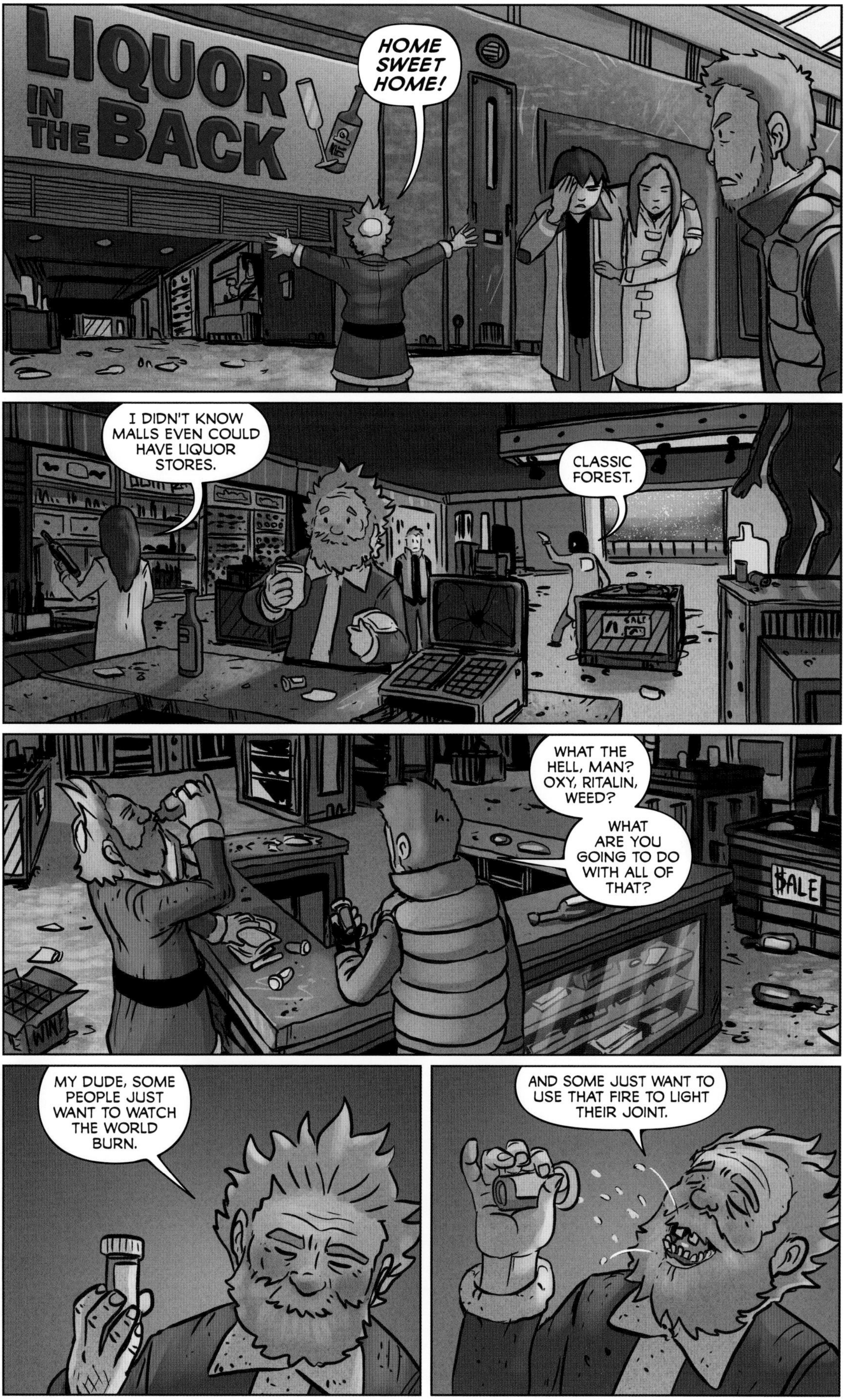
LIQUOR IN THE BACK
HOME SWEET HOME!
I DIDN'T KNOW MALLS EVEN COULD HAVE LIQUOR STORES.
CLASSIC FOREST.
WHAT THE HELL, MAN? OXY, RITALIN, WEED?
WHAT ARE YOU GOING TO DO WITH ALL OF THAT?
$ALE
MY DUDE, SOME PEOPLE JUST WANT TO WATCH THE WORLD BURN.
AND SOME JUST WANT TO USE THAT FIRE TO LIGHT THEIR JOINT.

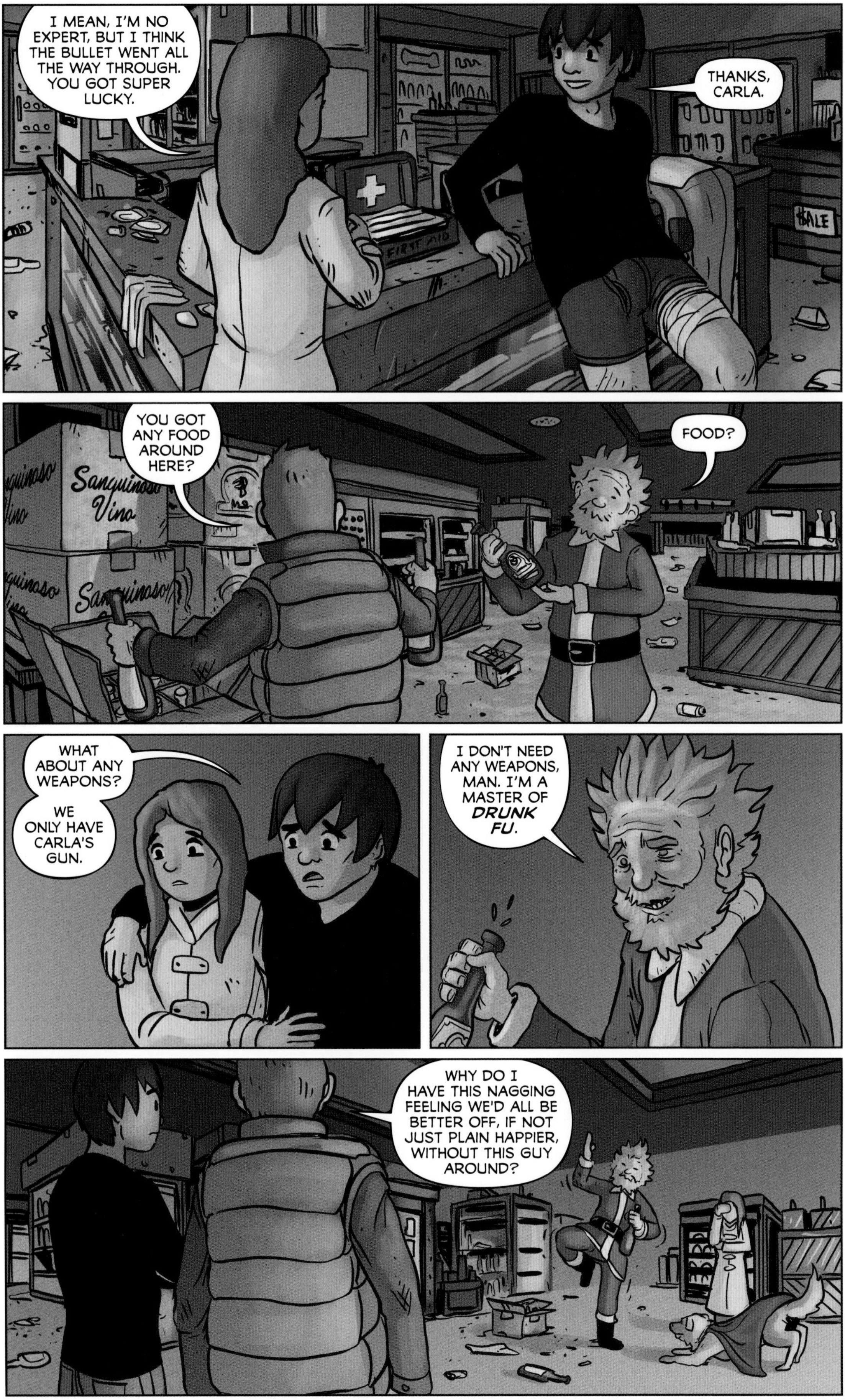
I MEAN, I'M NO EXPERT, BUT I THINK THE BULLET WENT ALL THE WAY THROUGH. YOU GOT SUPER LUCKY.
THANKS, CARLA.
FIRST AID
SALE
YOU GOT ANY FOOD AROUND HERE?
FOOD?
Sanguinoso Vino
WHAT ABOUT ANY WEAPONS?
WE ONLY HAVE CARLA'S GUN.
I DON'T NEED ANY WEAPONS, MAN. I'M A MASTER OF *DRUNK FU*.
WHY DO I HAVE THIS NAGGING FEELING WE'D ALL BE BETTER OFF, IF NOT JUST PLAIN HAPPIER, WITHOUT THIS GUY AROUND?

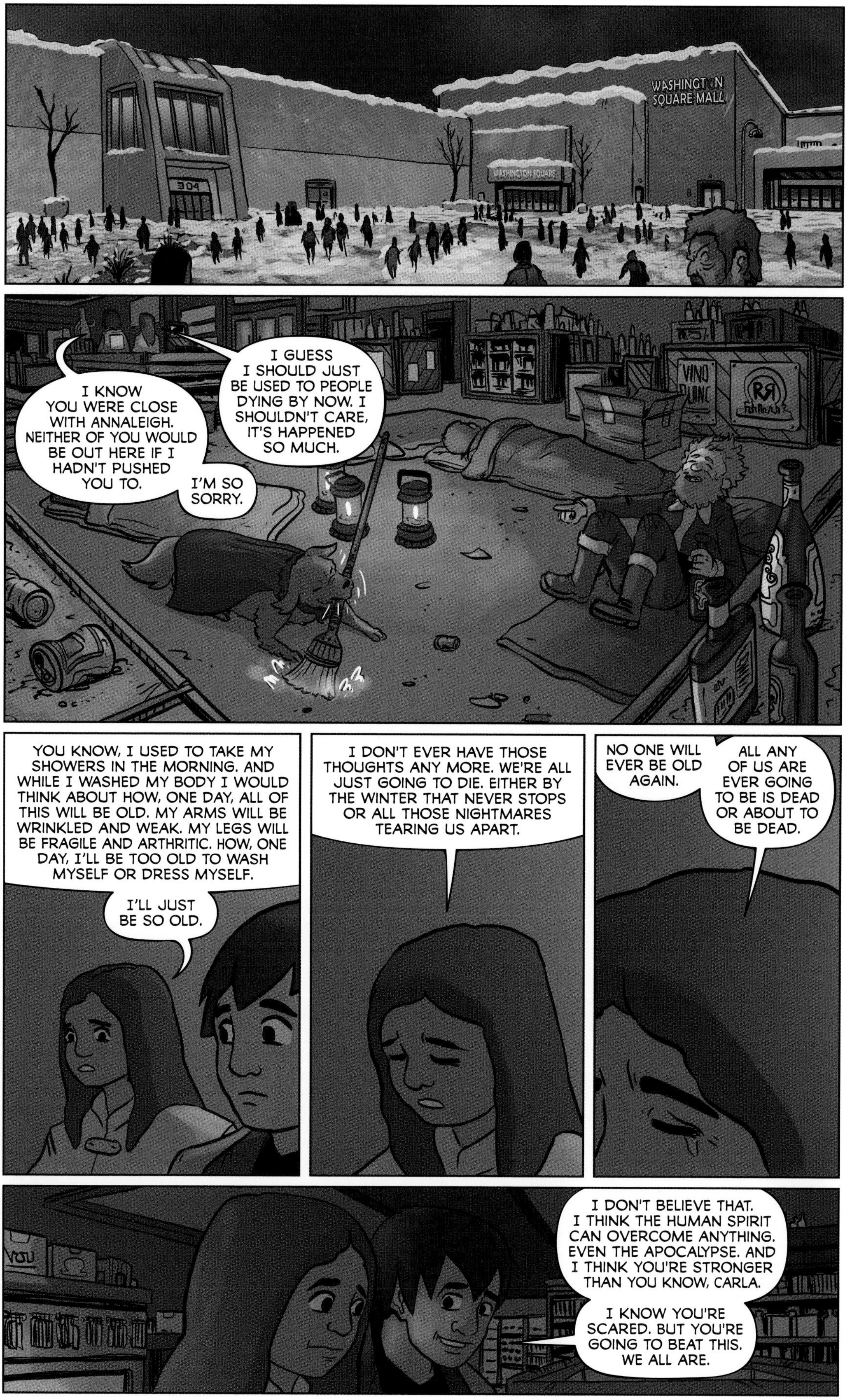
WASHINGTON SQUARE MALL
WASHINGTON SQUARE
I KNOW YOU WERE CLOSE WITH ANNALEIGH. NEITHER OF YOU WOULD BE OUT HERE IF I HADN'T PUSHED YOU TO.
I'M SO SORRY.
I GUESS I SHOULD JUST BE USED TO PEOPLE DYING BY NOW. I SHOULDN'T CARE, IT'S HAPPENED SO MUCH.
VINO BLANC
YOU KNOW, I USED TO TAKE MY SHOWERS IN THE MORNING. AND WHILE I WASHED MY BODY I WOULD THINK ABOUT HOW, ONE DAY, ALL OF THIS WILL BE OLD. MY ARMS WILL BE WRINKLED AND WEAK. MY LEGS WILL BE FRAGILE AND ARTHRITIC. HOW, ONE DAY, I'LL BE TOO OLD TO WASH MYSELF OR DRESS MYSELF.
I'LL JUST BE SO OLD.
I DON'T EVER HAVE THOSE THOUGHTS ANY MORE. WE'RE ALL JUST GOING TO DIE. EITHER BY THE WINTER THAT NEVER STOPS OR ALL THOSE NIGHTMARES TEARING US APART.
NO ONE WILL EVER BE OLD AGAIN.
ALL ANY OF US ARE EVER GOING TO BE IS DEAD OR ABOUT TO BE DEAD.
I DON'T BELIEVE THAT. I THINK THE HUMAN SPIRIT CAN OVERCOME ANYTHING. EVEN THE APOCALYPSE. AND I THINK YOU'RE STRONGER THAN YOU KNOW, CARLA.
I KNOW YOU'RE SCARED. BUT YOU'RE GOING TO BEAT THIS. WE ALL ARE.

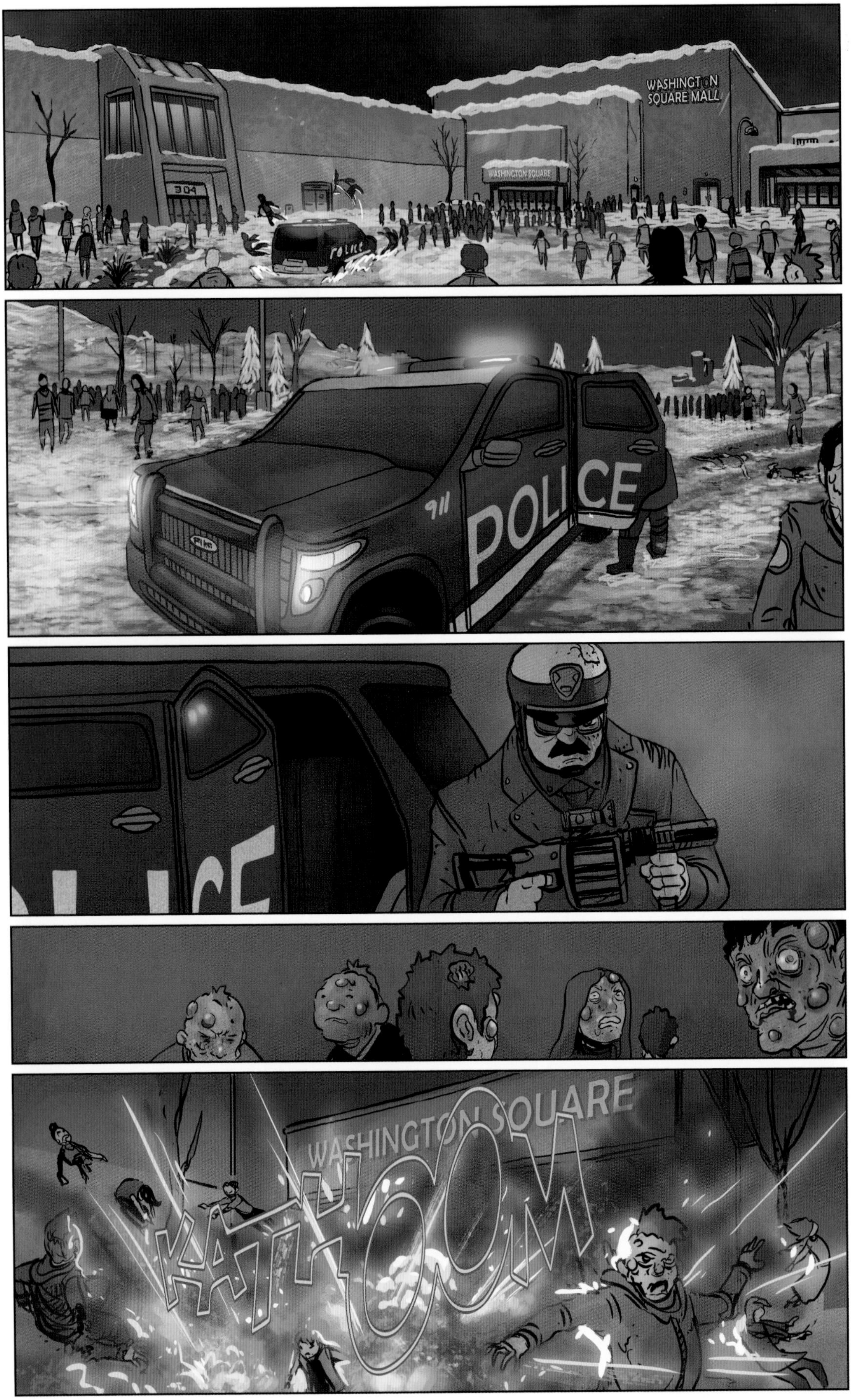
WASHINGTON SQUARE MALL
WASHINGTON SQUARE
304
POLICE
POLICE
911
POLICE
LICE
WASHINGTON SQUARE
KATHOOM

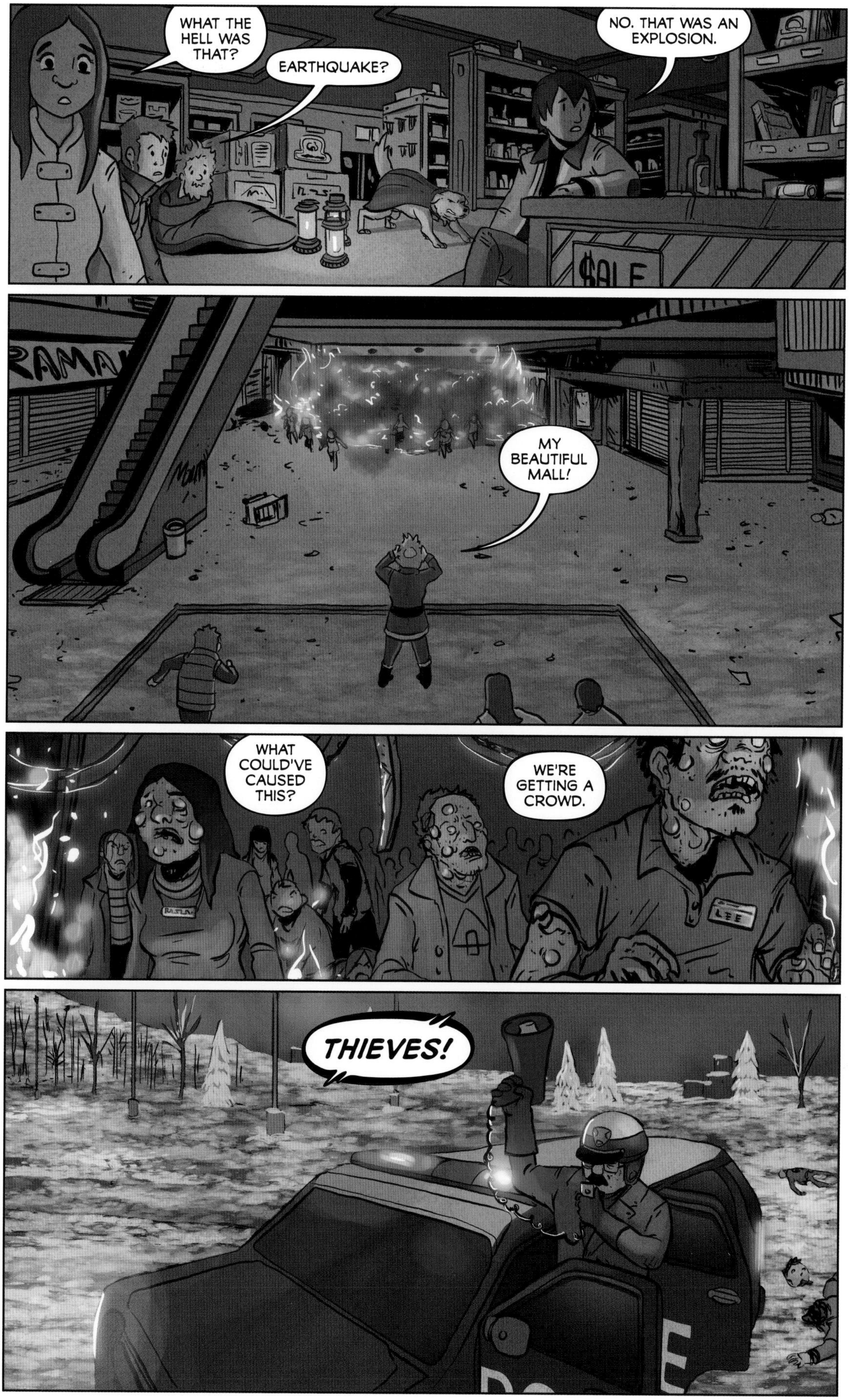
WHAT THE HELL WAS THAT?
EARTHQUAKE?
NO. THAT WAS AN EXPLOSION.
$ALE
MY BEAUTIFUL MALL!
WHAT COULD'VE CAUSED THIS?
WE'RE GETTING A CROWD.
LEE
THIEVES!

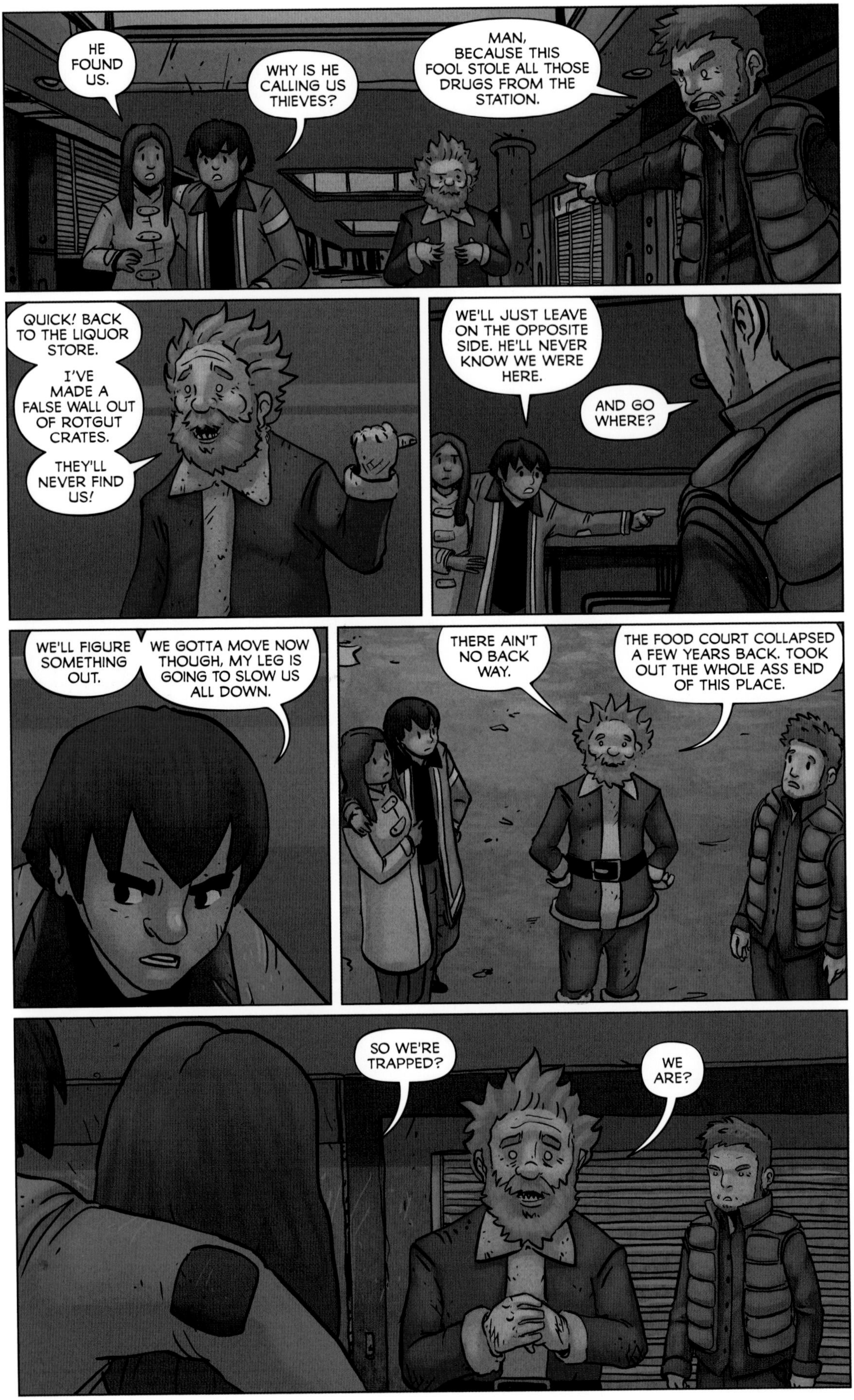
HE FOUND US.
WHY IS HE CALLING US THIEVES?
MAN, BECAUSE THIS FOOL STOLE ALL THOSE DRUGS FROM THE STATION.
QUICK! BACK TO THE LIQUOR STORE.
I'VE MADE A FALSE WALL OUT OF ROTGUT CRATES.
THEY'LL NEVER FIND US!
WE'LL JUST LEAVE ON THE OPPOSITE SIDE. HE'LL NEVER KNOW WE WERE HERE.
AND GO WHERE?
WE'LL FIGURE SOMETHING OUT.
WE GOTTA MOVE NOW THOUGH, MY LEG IS GOING TO SLOW US ALL DOWN.
THERE AIN'T NO BACK WAY.
THE FOOD COURT COLLAPSED A FEW YEARS BACK. TOOK OUT THE WHOLE ASS END OF THIS PLACE.
SO WE'RE TRAPPED?
WE ARE?

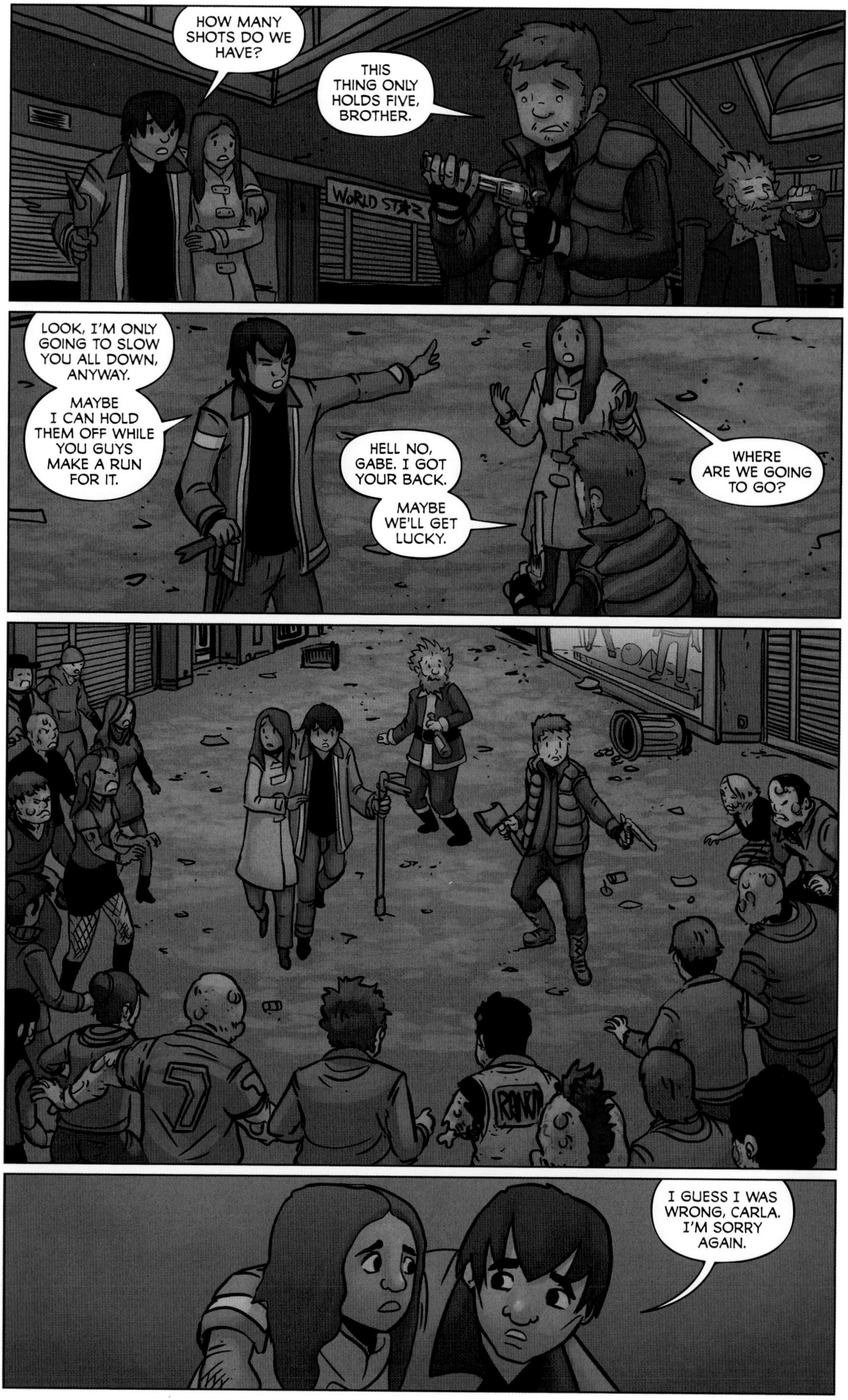
HOW MANY SHOTS DO WE HAVE?
THIS THING ONLY HOLDS FIVE, BROTHER.
WORLD STAR
LOOK, I'M ONLY GOING TO SLOW YOU ALL DOWN, ANYWAY.
MAYBE I CAN HOLD THEM OFF WHILE YOU GUYS MAKE A RUN FOR IT.
HELL NO, GABE. I GOT YOUR BACK.
MAYBE WE'LL GET LUCKY.
WHERE ARE WE GOING TO GO?
I GUESS I WAS WRONG, CARLA. I'M SORRY AGAIN.

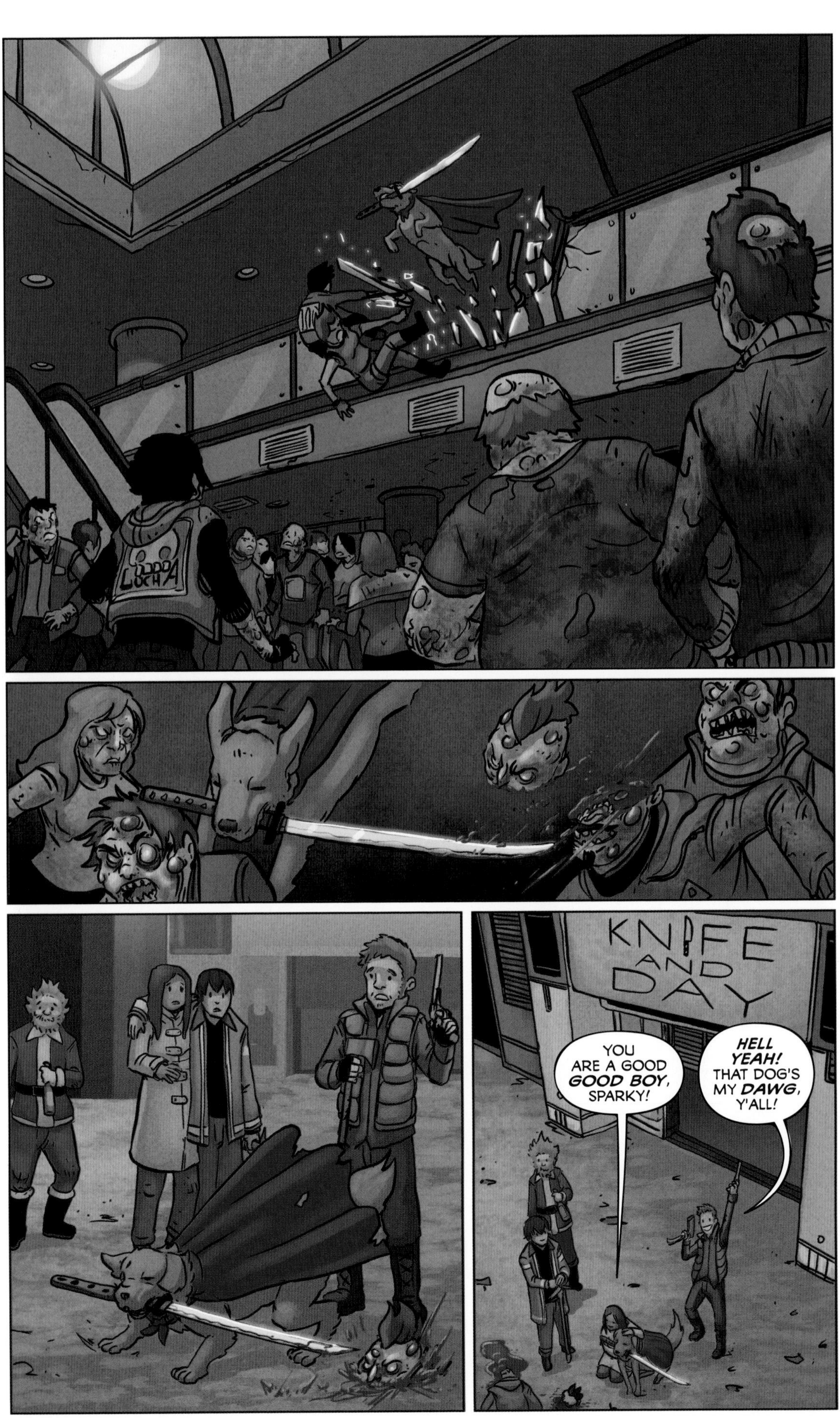

KNIFE AND DAY
YOU ARE A GOOD *GOOD BOY*, SPARKY!
HELL YEAH! THAT DOG'S MY ***DAWG***, Y'ALL!

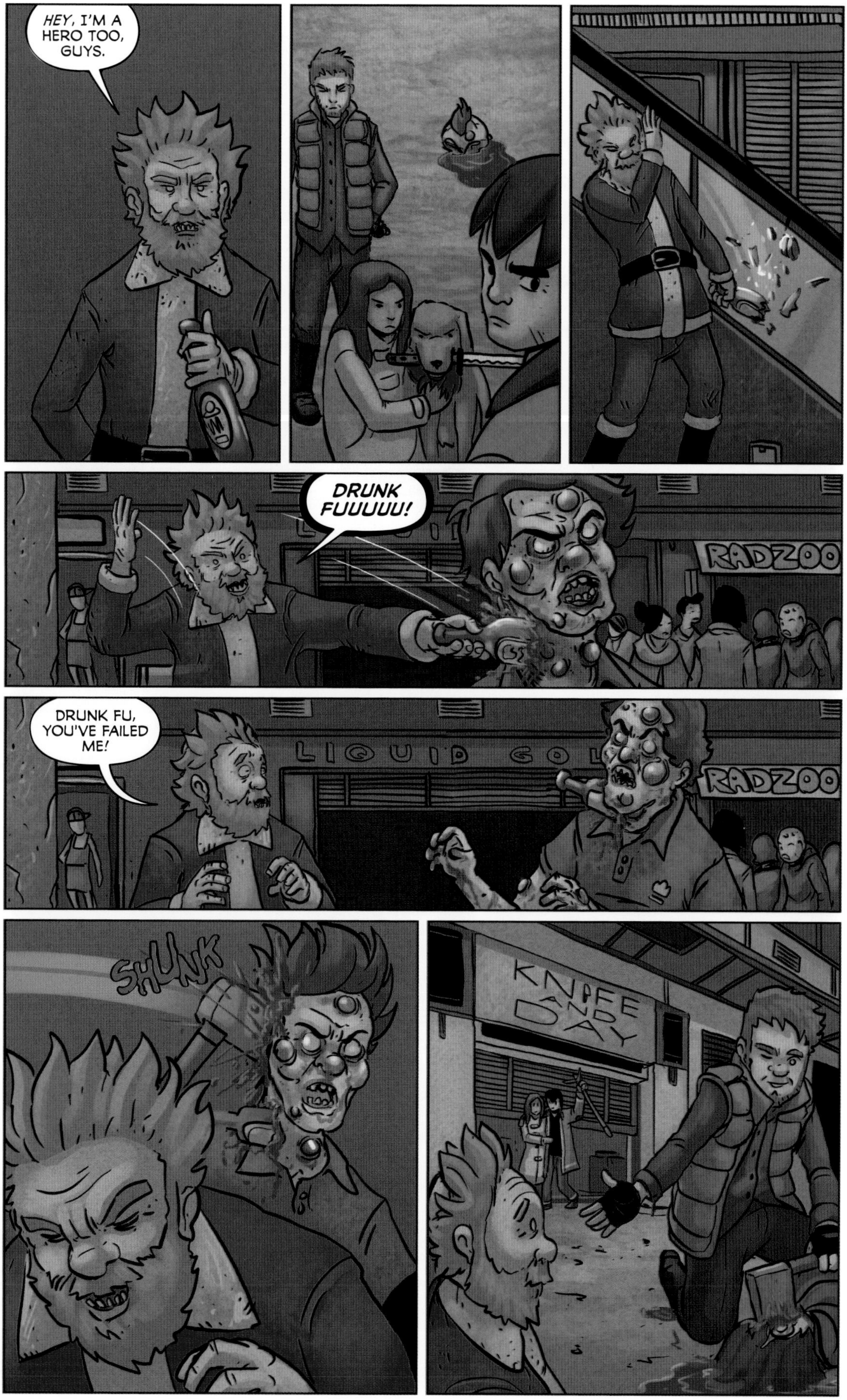
HEY, I'M A HERO TOO, GUYS.
DRUNK FUUUUU!
RADZOO
DRUNK FU, YOU'VE FAILED ME!
LIQUID GOL
RADZOO
SHUNK
KNIFE AND DAY

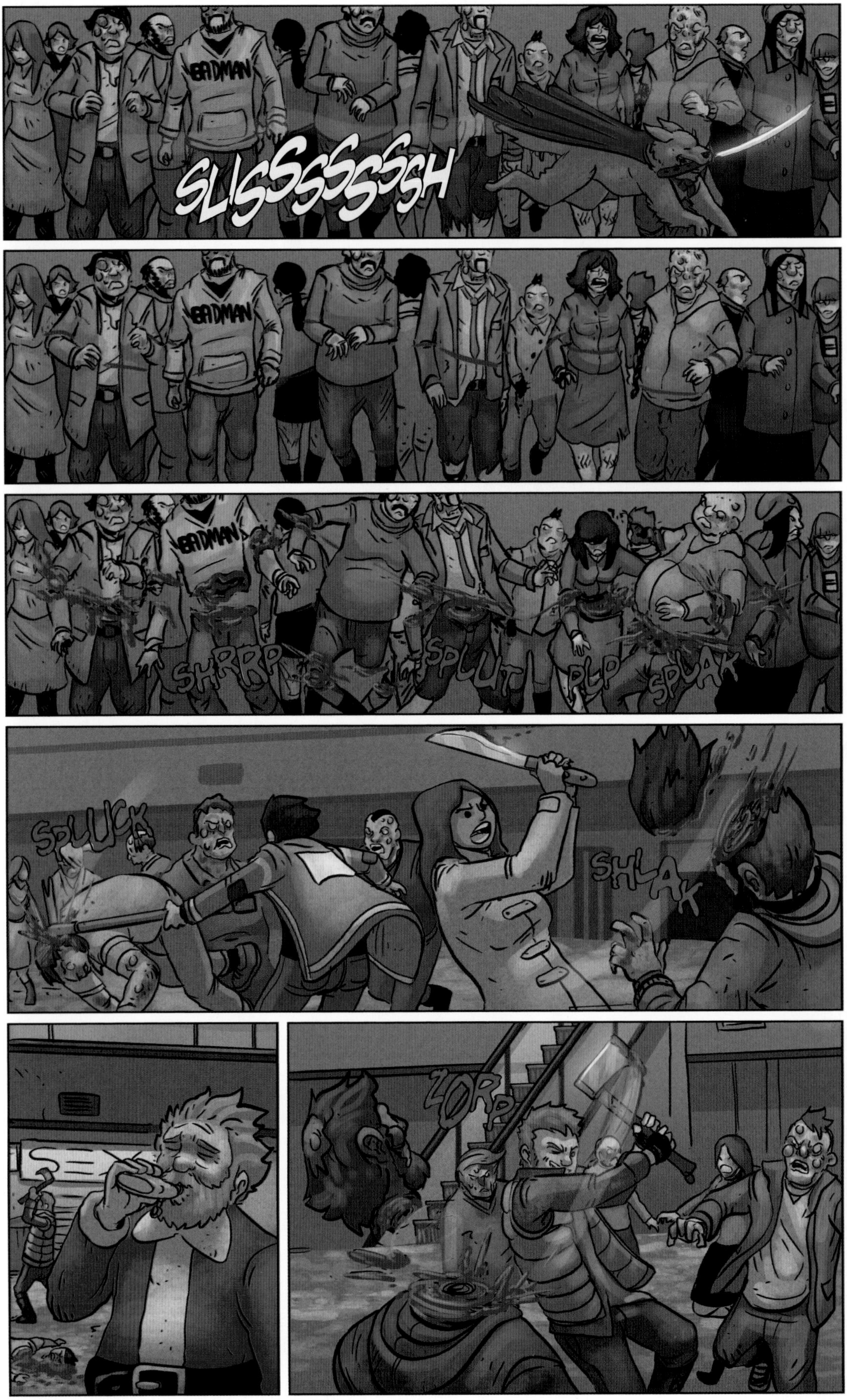
SLISSSSSSSH
BADMAN
SHRRP
SPLUT
PLP
SPLAK
SPLUCK
SHLAK
ZORP

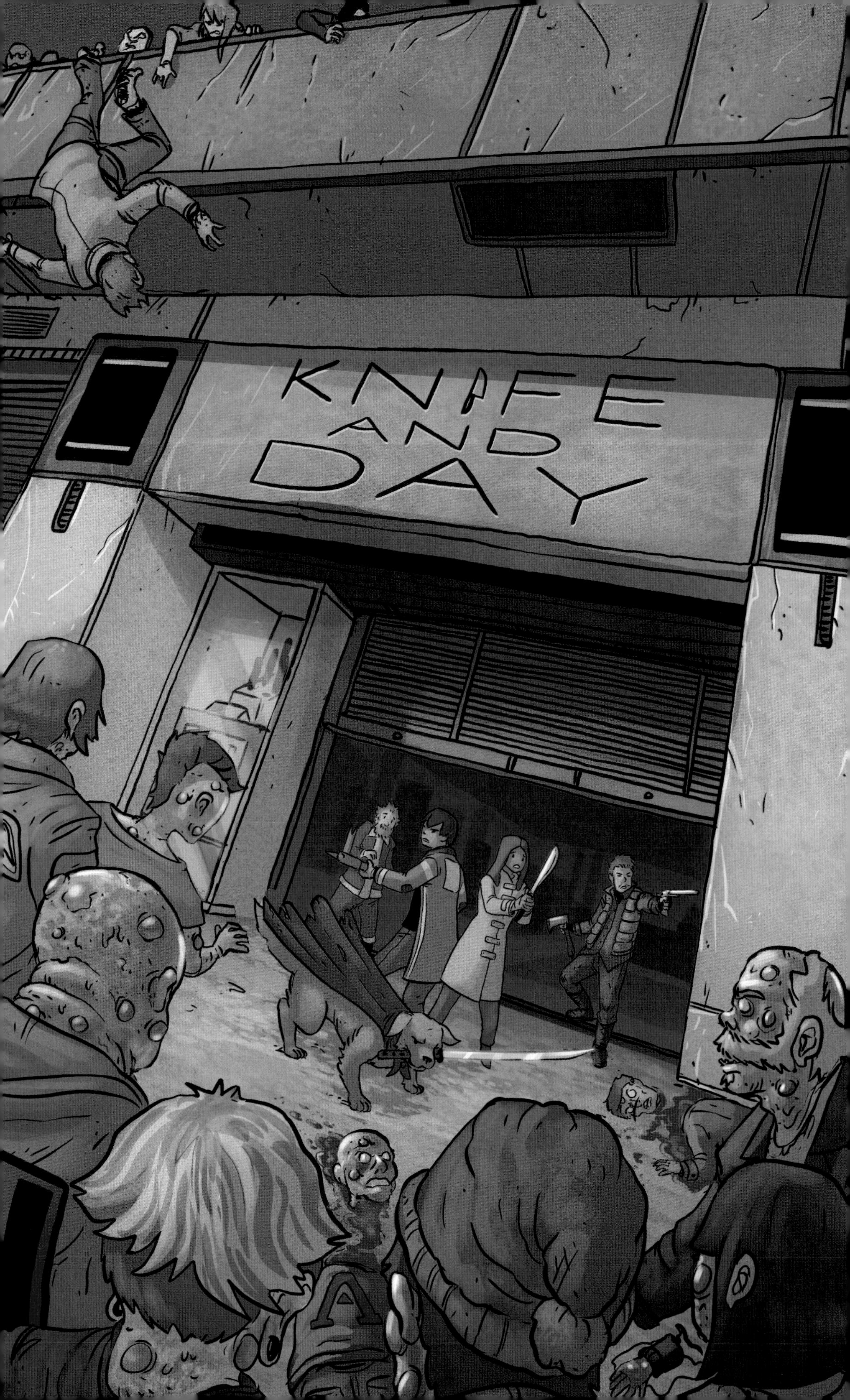
KNIFE
AND
DAY

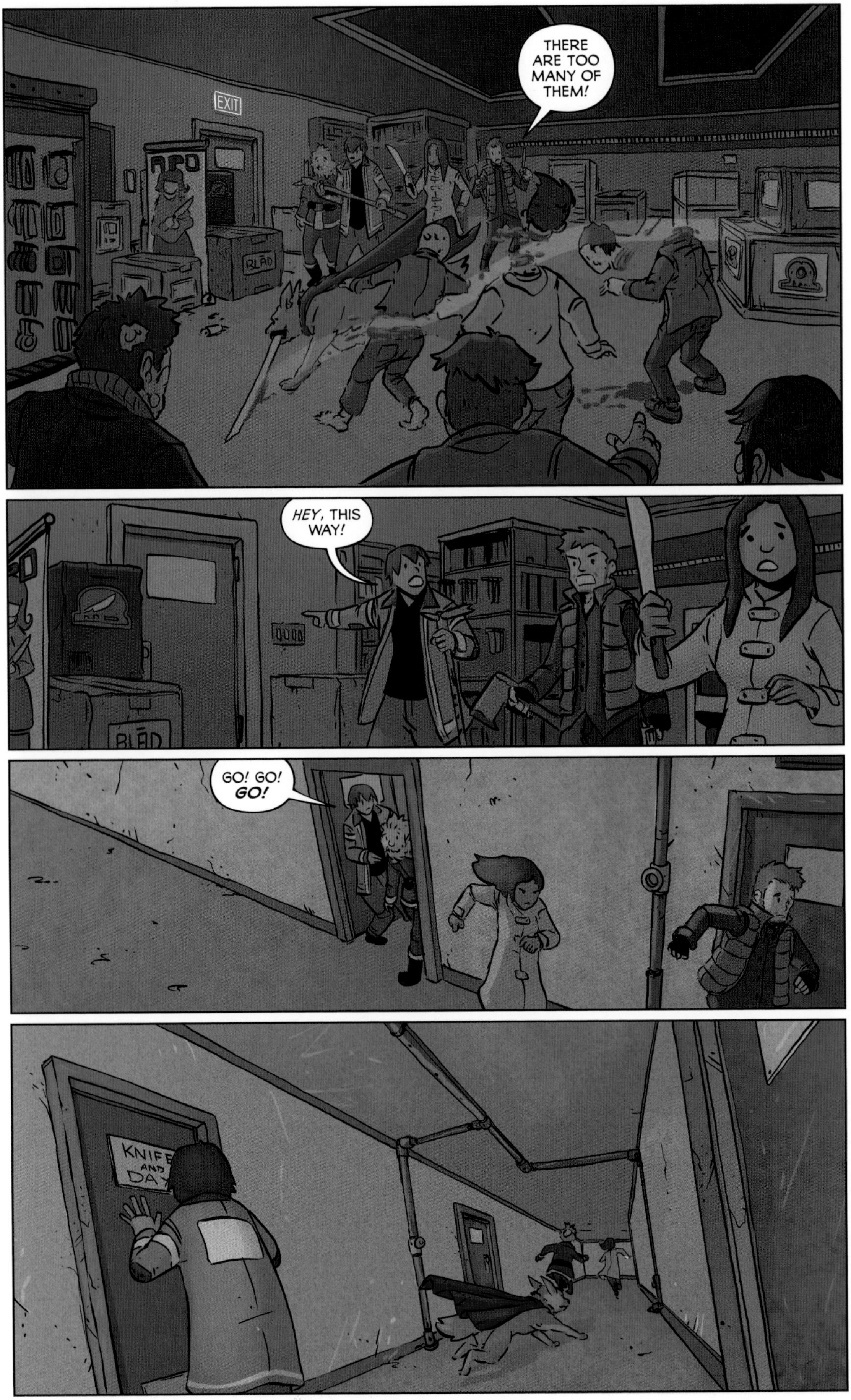
EXIT
BLĀD
THERE ARE TOO MANY OF THEM!
HEY, THIS WAY!
GO! GO! ***GO!***

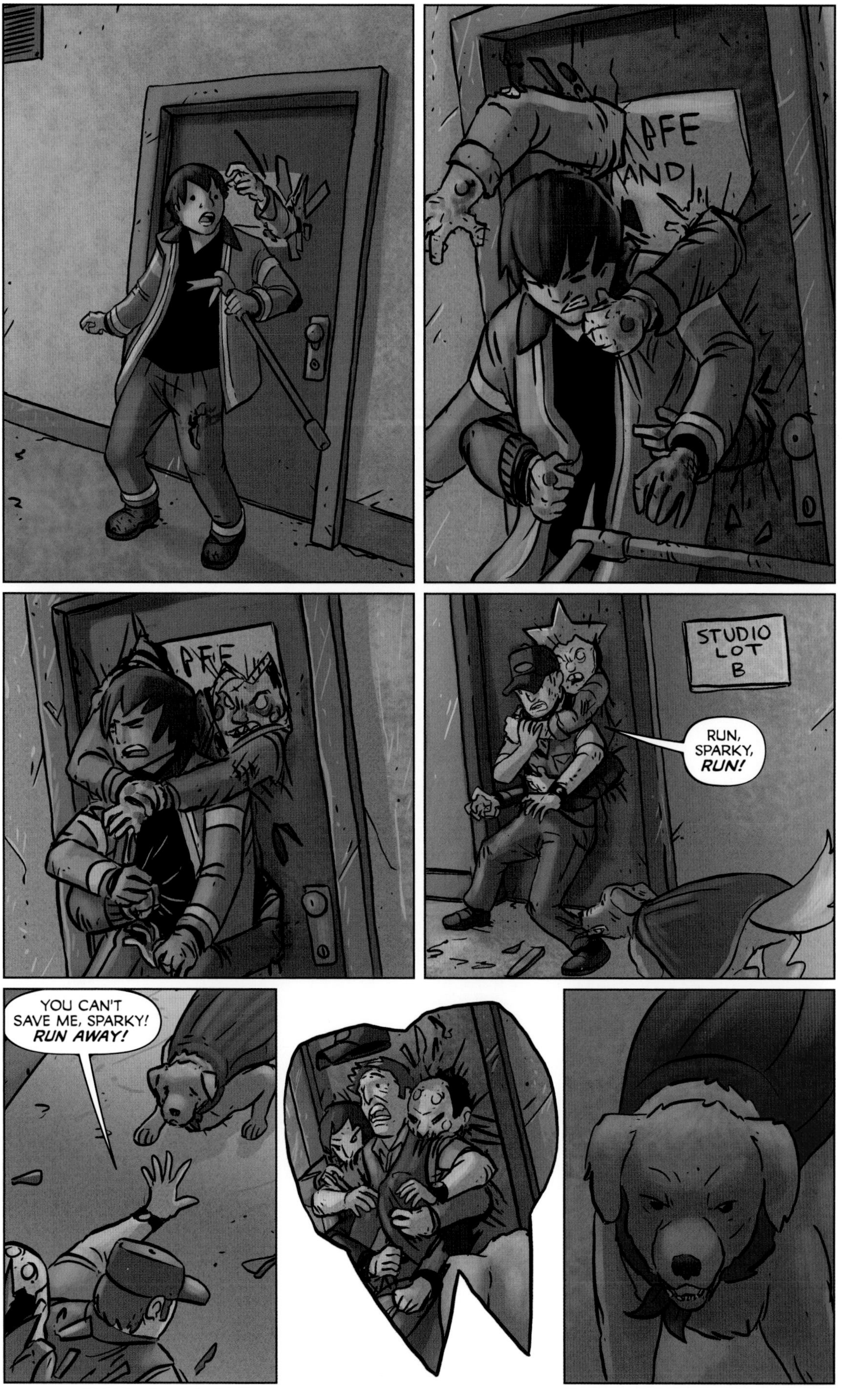
STUDIO LOT B
RUN, SPARKY, RUN!
YOU CAN'T SAVE ME, SPARKY! RUN AWAY!

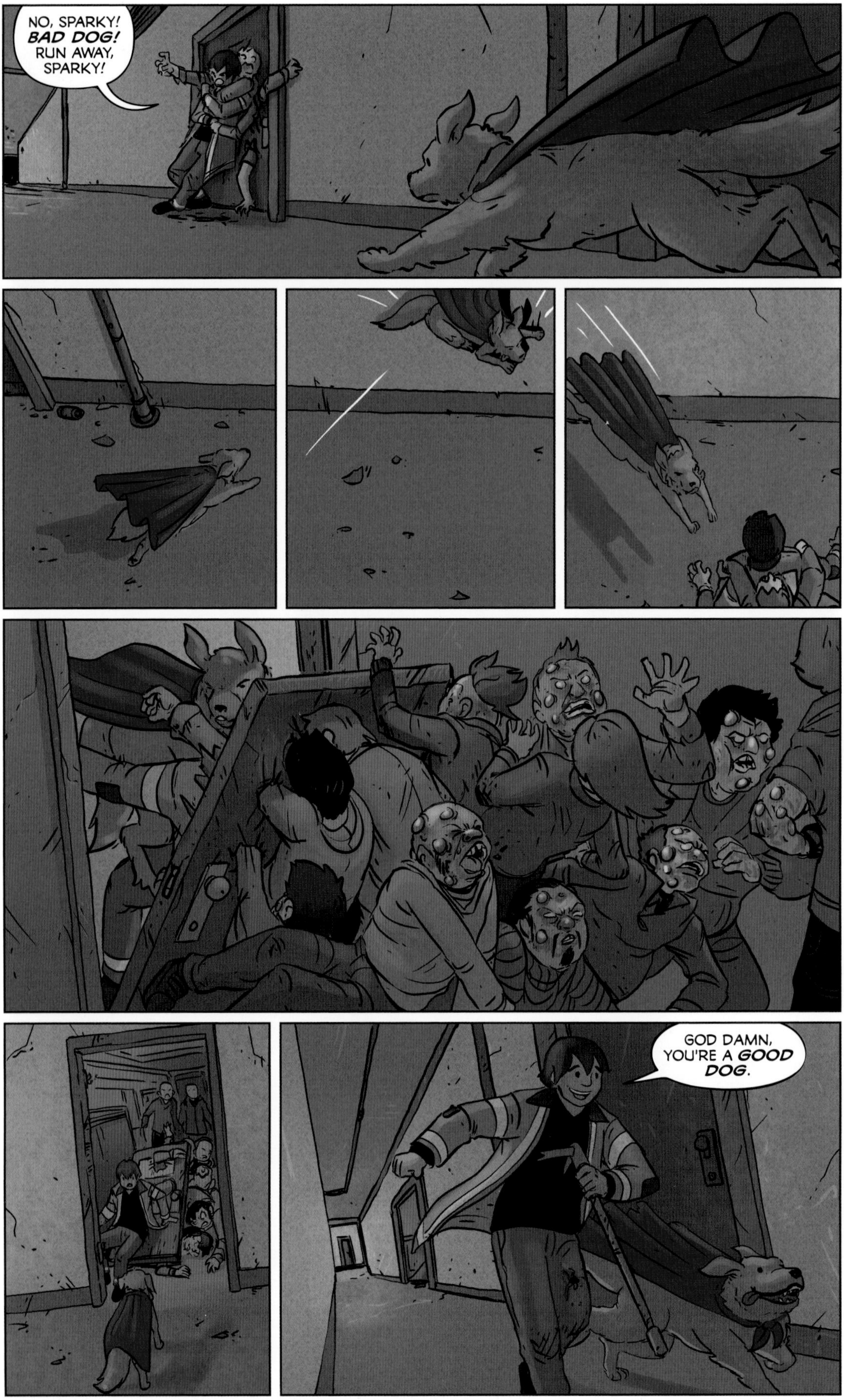
NO, SPARKY! BAD DOG! RUN AWAY, SPARKY!
GOD DAMN, YOU'RE A GOOD DOG.

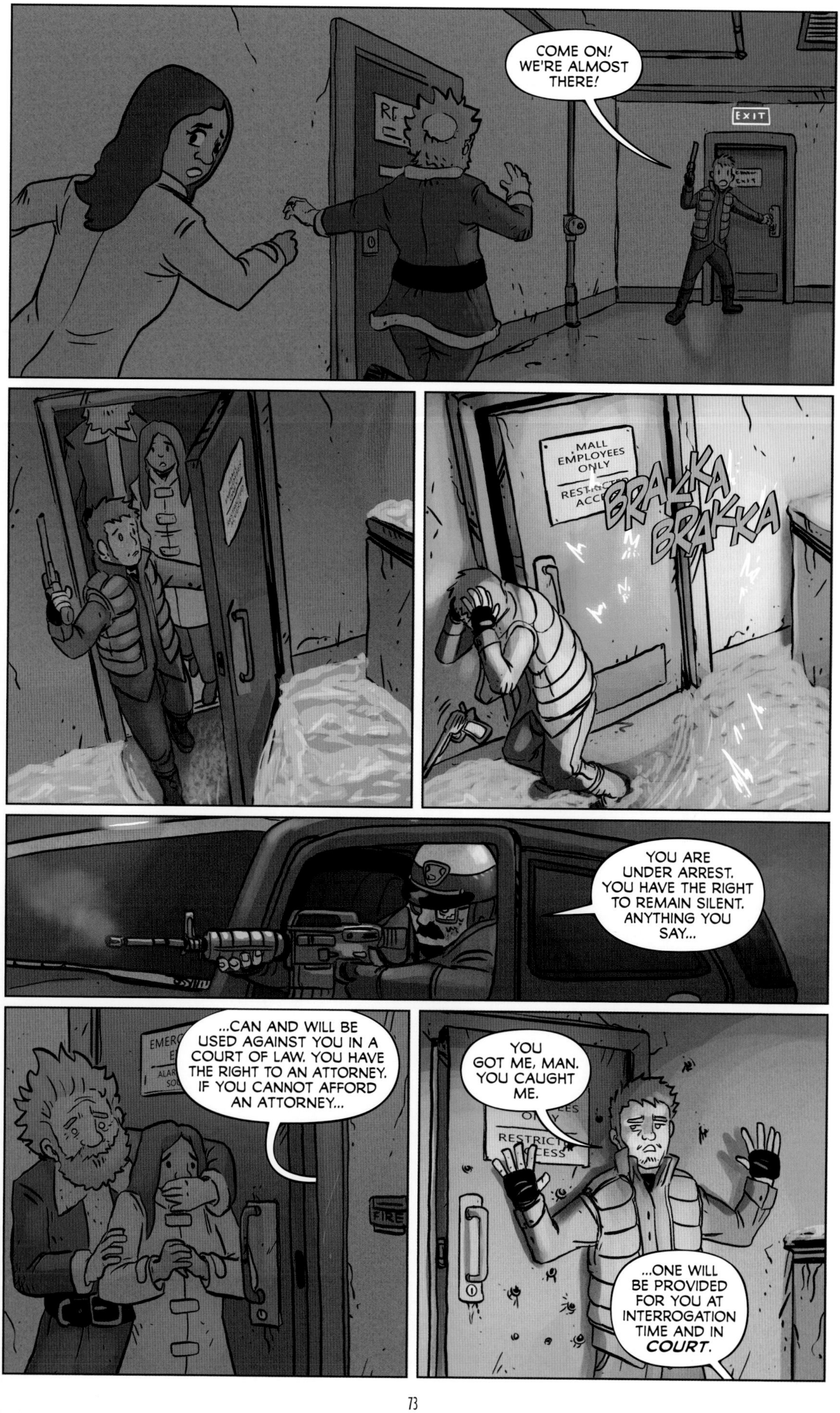
COME ON! WE'RE ALMOST THERE!
EXIT
MALL EMPLOYEES ONLY
BRAKKA BRAKKA
YOU ARE UNDER ARREST. YOU HAVE THE RIGHT TO REMAIN SILENT. ANYTHING YOU SAY...
...CAN AND WILL BE USED AGAINST YOU IN A COURT OF LAW. YOU HAVE THE RIGHT TO AN ATTORNEY. IF YOU CANNOT AFFORD AN ATTORNEY...
FIRE
YOU GOT ME, MAN. YOU CAUGHT ME.
...ONE WILL BE PROVIDED FOR YOU AT INTERROGATION TIME AND IN **COURT**.

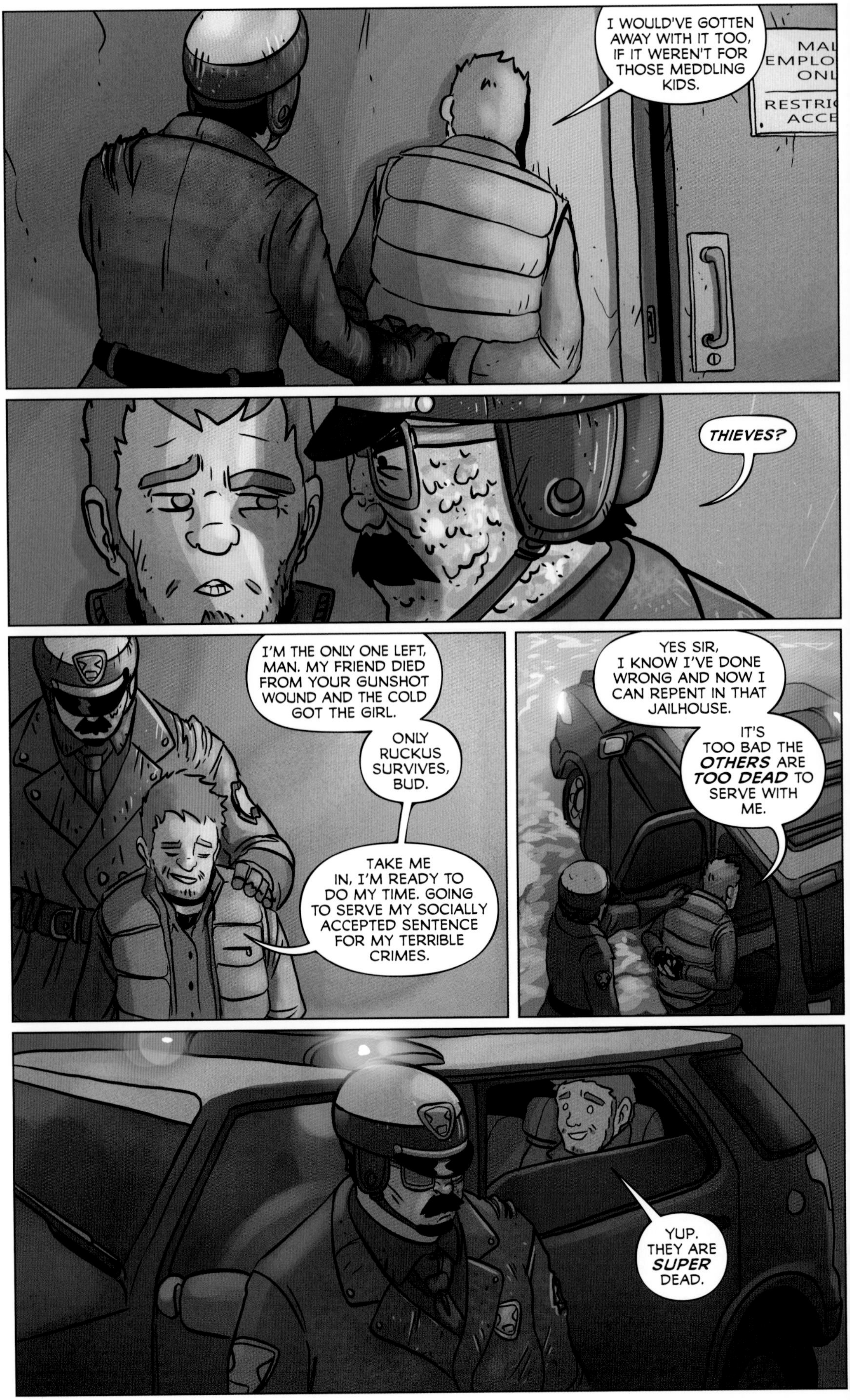
I WOULD'VE GOTTEN AWAY WITH IT TOO, IF IT WEREN'T FOR THOSE MEDDLING KIDS.
THIEVES?
I'M THE ONLY ONE LEFT, MAN. MY FRIEND DIED FROM YOUR GUNSHOT WOUND AND THE COLD GOT THE GIRL.
ONLY RUCKUS SURVIVES, BUD.
TAKE ME IN, I'M READY TO DO MY TIME. GOING TO SERVE MY SOCIALLY ACCEPTED SENTENCE FOR MY TERRIBLE CRIMES.
YES SIR, I KNOW I'VE DONE WRONG AND NOW I CAN REPENT IN THAT JAILHOUSE.
IT'S TOO BAD THE ***OTHERS*** ARE ***TOO DEAD*** TO SERVE WITH ME.
YUP. THEY ARE ***SUPER*** DEAD.

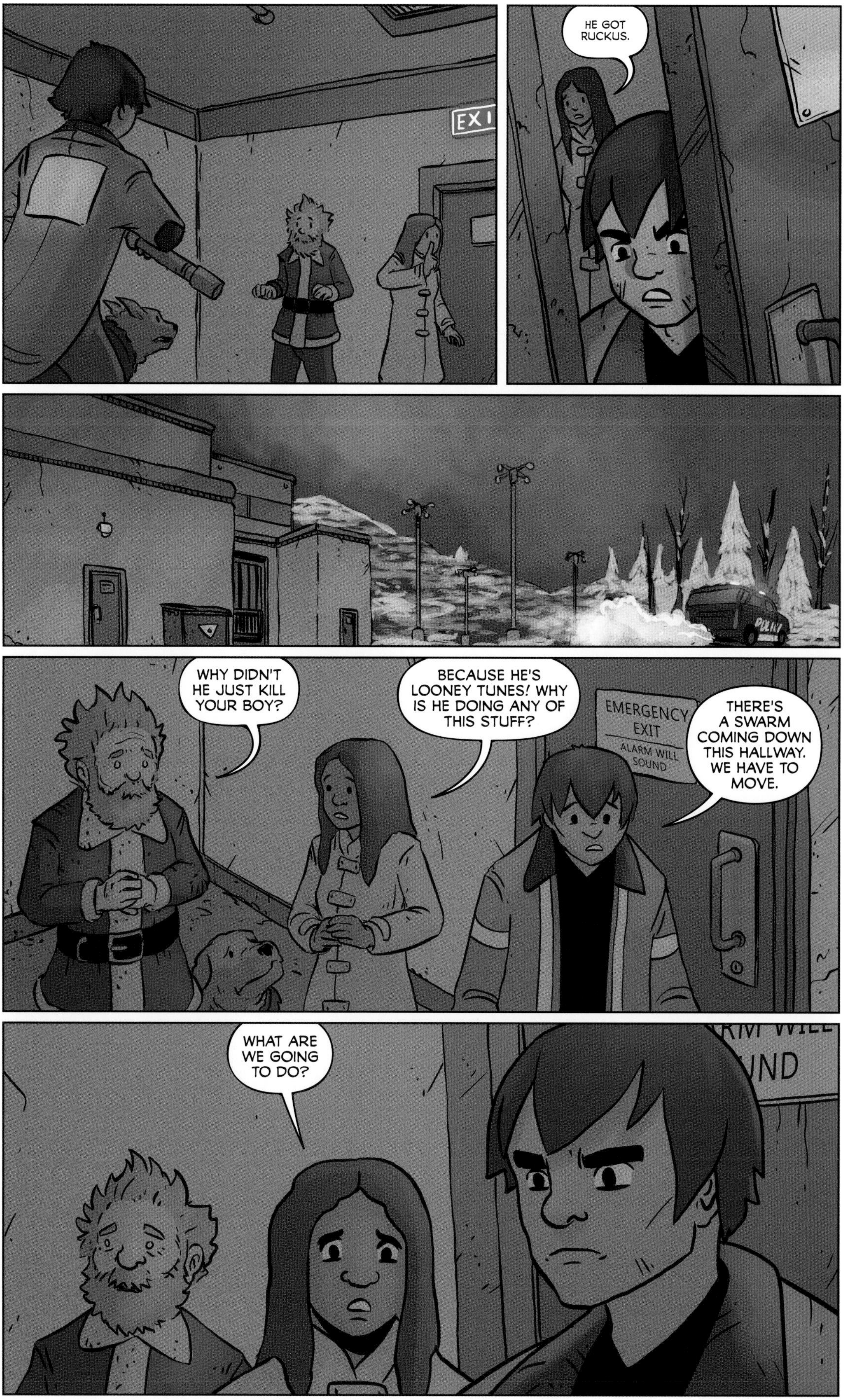
EXI
HE GOT RUCKUS.
WHY DIDN'T HE JUST KILL YOUR BOY?
BECAUSE HE'S LOONEY TUNES! WHY IS HE DOING ANY OF THIS STUFF?
EMERGENCY EXIT
ALARM WILL SOUND
THERE'S A SWARM COMING DOWN THIS HALLWAY. WE HAVE TO MOVE.
WHAT ARE WE GOING TO DO?

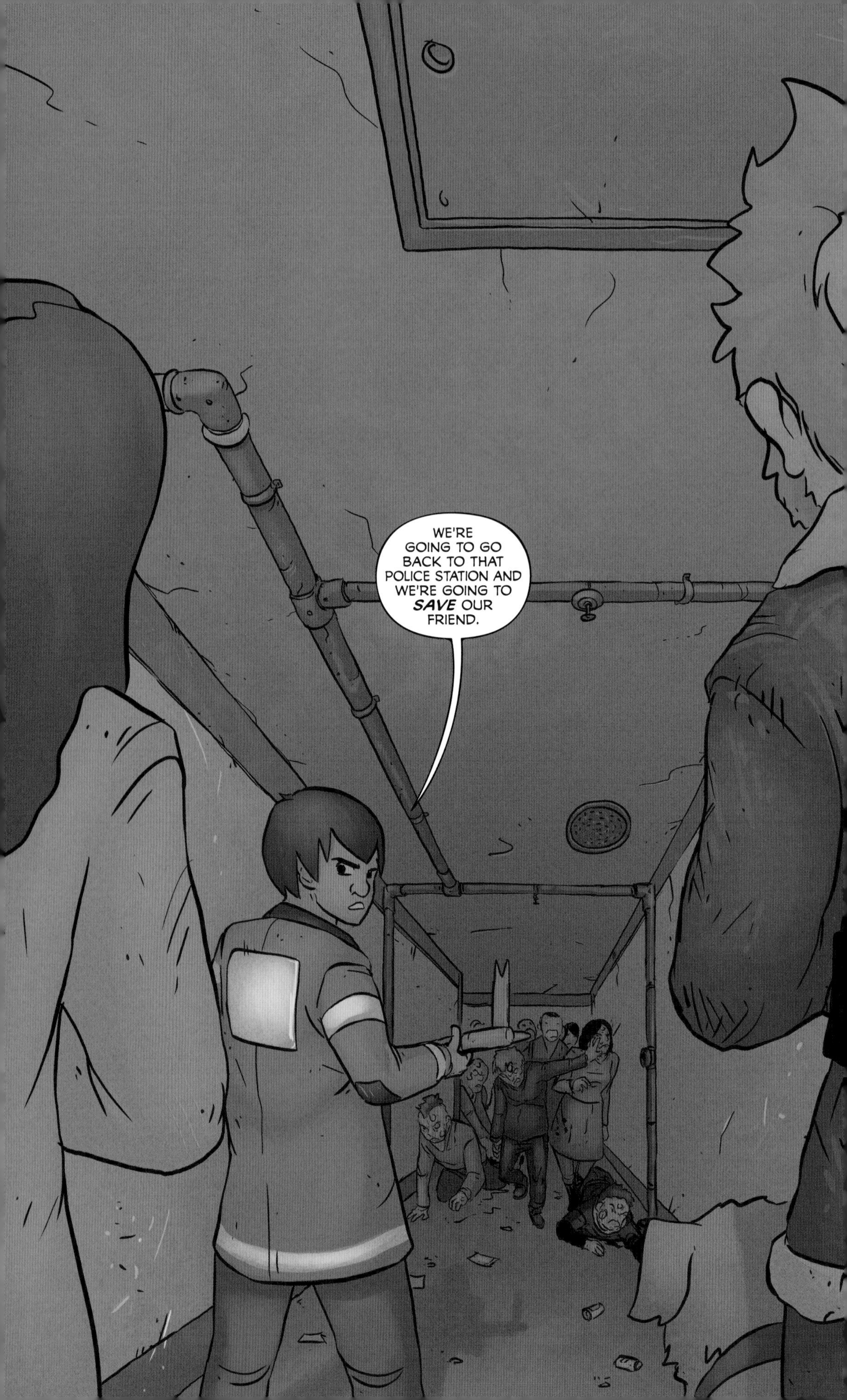
WE'RE GOING TO GO BACK TO THAT POLICE STATION AND WE'RE GOING TO *SAVE* OUR FRIEND.

CHAPTER FOUR

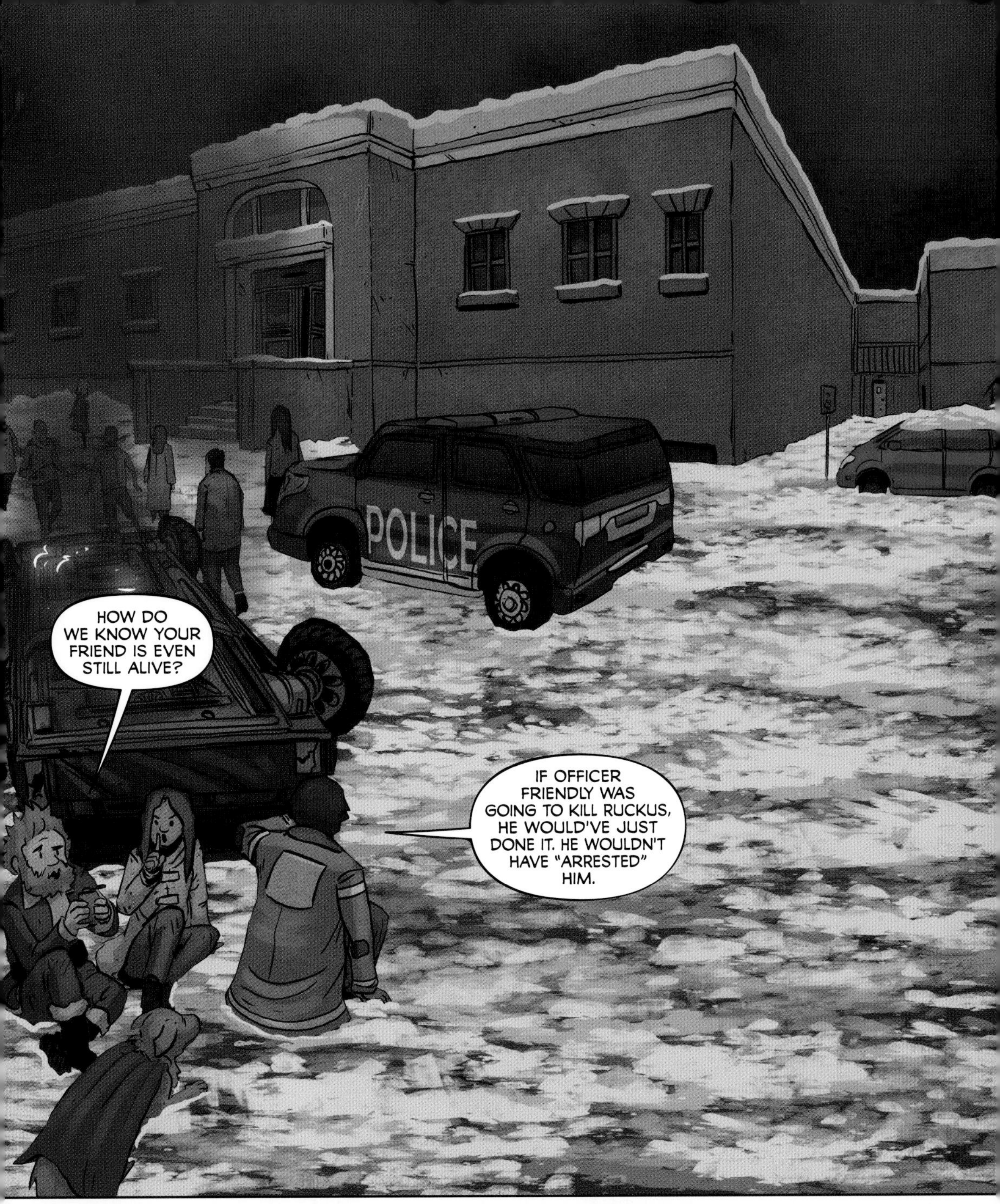
HOW DO WE KNOW YOUR FRIEND IS EVEN STILL ALIVE?
IF OFFICER FRIENDLY WAS GOING TO KILL RUCKUS, HE WOULD'VE JUST DONE IT. HE WOULDN'T HAVE "ARRESTED" HIM.

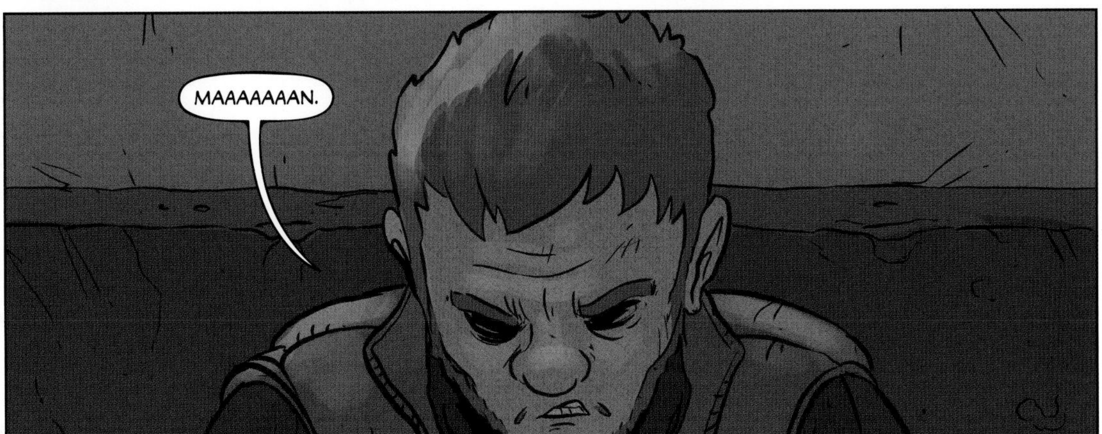
MAAAAAAAN.

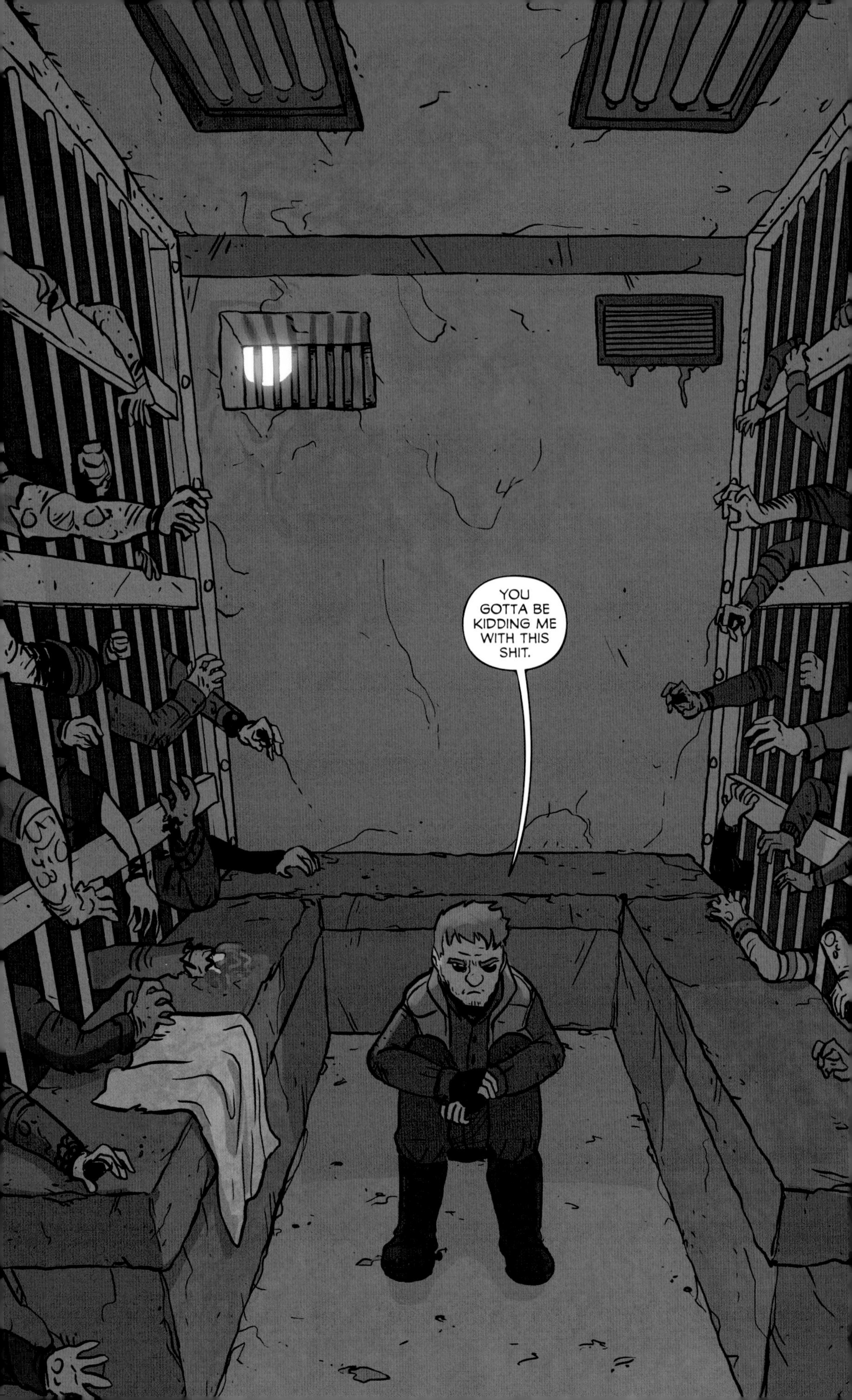
YOU GOTTA BE KIDDING ME WITH THIS SHIT.

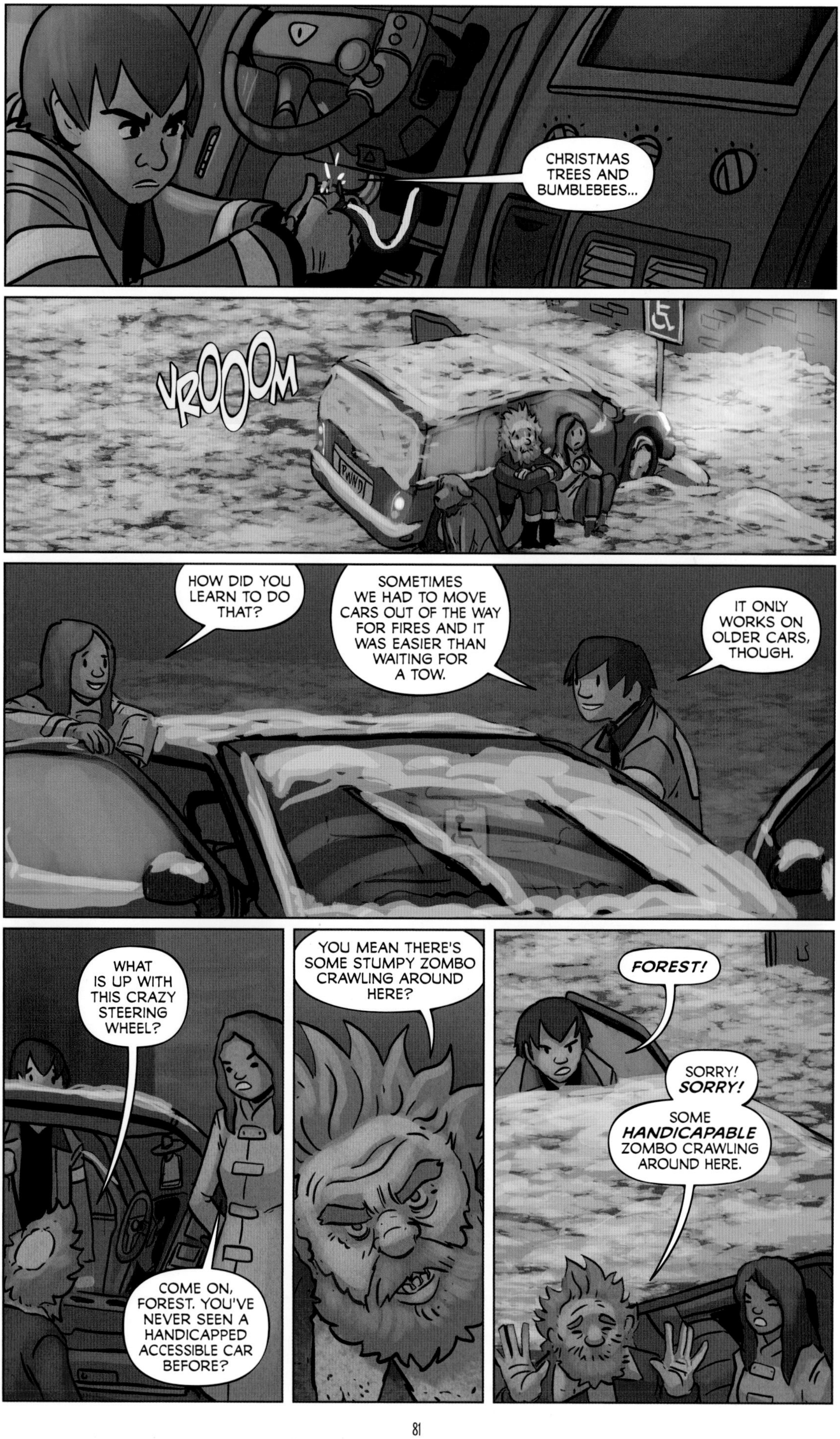
CHRISTMAS TREES AND BUMBLEBEES...
VROOOM
PWND
HOW DID YOU LEARN TO DO THAT?
SOMETIMES WE HAD TO MOVE CARS OUT OF THE WAY FOR FIRES AND IT WAS EASIER THAN WAITING FOR A TOW.
IT ONLY WORKS ON OLDER CARS, THOUGH.
WHAT IS UP WITH THIS CRAZY STEERING WHEEL?
COME ON, FOREST. YOU'VE NEVER SEEN A HANDICAPPED ACCESSIBLE CAR BEFORE?
YOU MEAN THERE'S SOME STUMPY ZOMBO CRAWLING AROUND HERE?
FOREST!
SORRY! SORRY!
SOME HANDICAPABLE ZOMBO CRAWLING AROUND HERE.

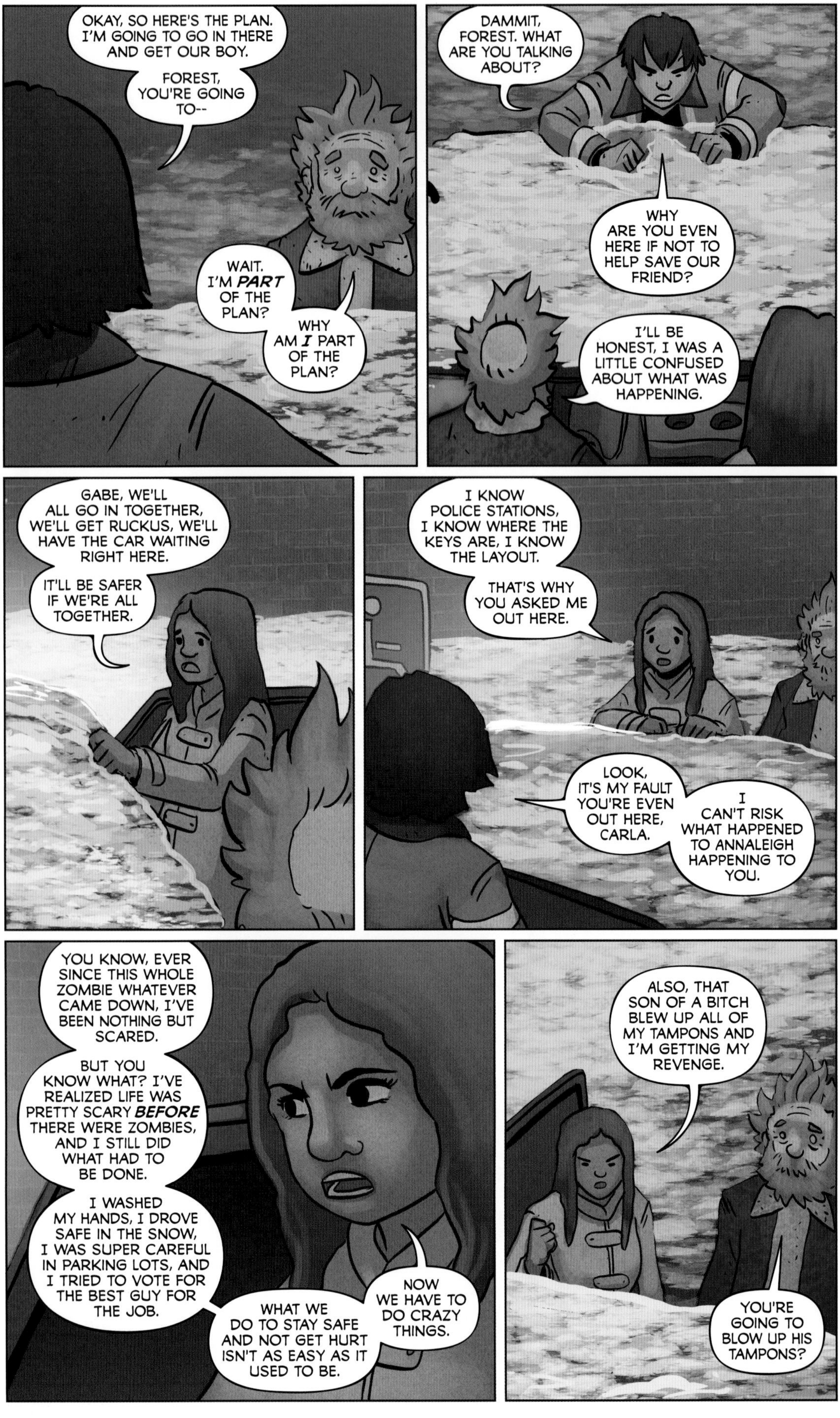
OKAY, SO HERE'S THE PLAN. I'M GOING TO GO IN THERE AND GET OUR BOY.
FOREST, YOU'RE GOING TO--
WAIT. I'M *PART* OF THE PLAN?
WHY AM *I* PART OF THE PLAN?
DAMMIT, FOREST. WHAT ARE YOU TALKING ABOUT?
WHY ARE YOU EVEN HERE IF NOT TO HELP SAVE OUR FRIEND?
I'LL BE HONEST, I WAS A LITTLE CONFUSED ABOUT WHAT WAS HAPPENING.
GABE, WE'LL ALL GO IN TOGETHER, WE'LL GET RUCKUS, WE'LL HAVE THE CAR WAITING RIGHT HERE.
IT'LL BE SAFER IF WE'RE ALL TOGETHER.
I KNOW POLICE STATIONS, I KNOW WHERE THE KEYS ARE, I KNOW THE LAYOUT.
THAT'S WHY YOU ASKED ME OUT HERE.
LOOK, IT'S MY FAULT YOU'RE EVEN OUT HERE, CARLA.
I CAN'T RISK WHAT HAPPENED TO ANNALEIGH HAPPENING TO YOU.
YOU KNOW, EVER SINCE THIS WHOLE ZOMBIE WHATEVER CAME DOWN, I'VE BEEN NOTHING BUT SCARED.
BUT YOU KNOW WHAT? I'VE REALIZED LIFE WAS PRETTY SCARY *BEFORE* THERE WERE ZOMBIES, AND I STILL DID WHAT HAD TO BE DONE.
I WASHED MY HANDS, I DROVE SAFE IN THE SNOW, I WAS SUPER CAREFUL IN PARKING LOTS, AND I TRIED TO VOTE FOR THE BEST GUY FOR THE JOB.
WHAT WE DO TO STAY SAFE AND NOT GET HURT ISN'T AS EASY AS IT USED TO BE.
NOW WE HAVE TO DO CRAZY THINGS.
ALSO, THAT SON OF A BITCH BLEW UP ALL OF MY TAMPONS AND I'M GETTING MY REVENGE.
YOU'RE GOING TO BLOW UP HIS TAMPONS?

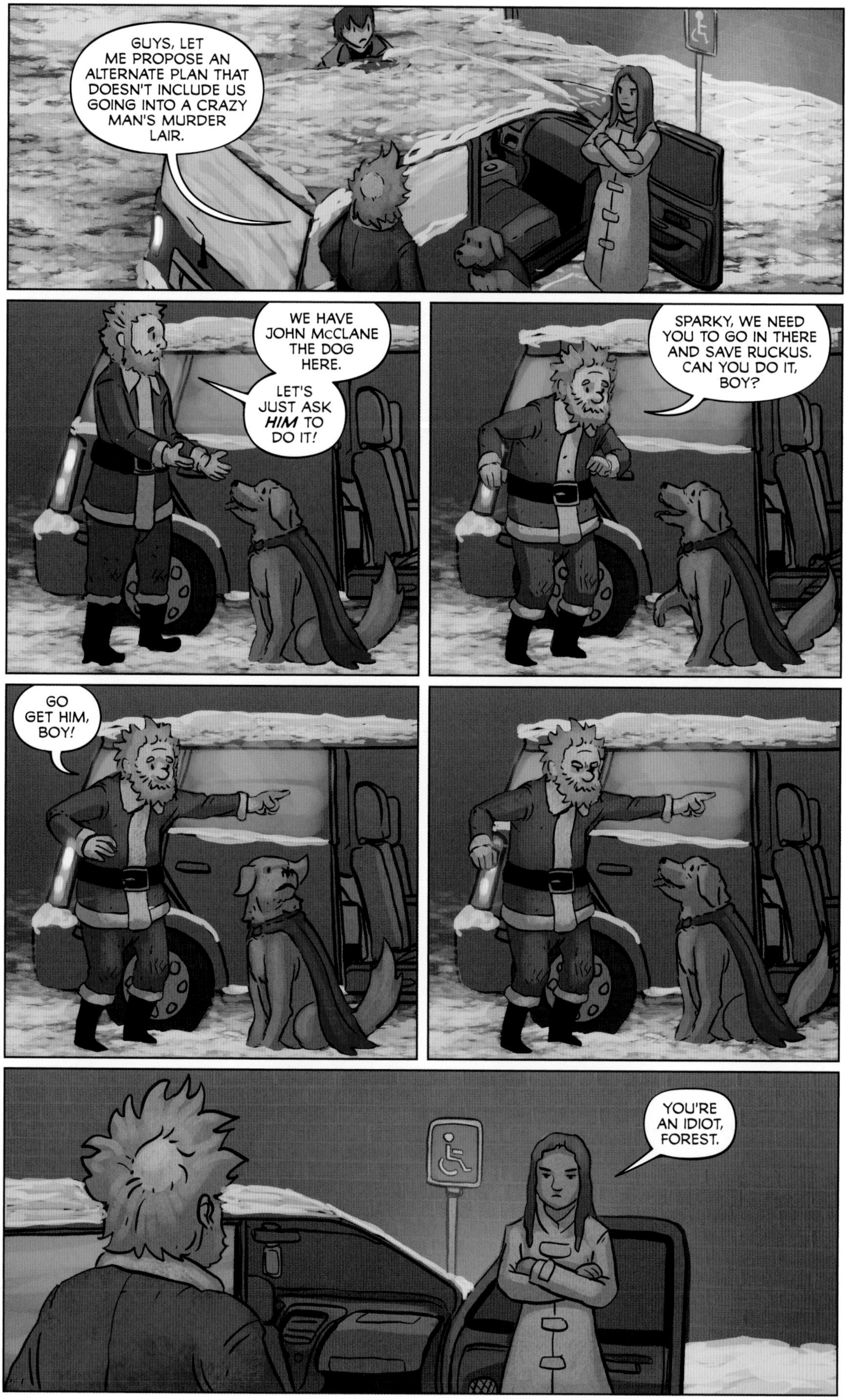
GUYS, LET ME PROPOSE AN ALTERNATE PLAN THAT DOESN'T INCLUDE US GOING INTO A CRAZY MAN'S MURDER LAIR.
WE HAVE JOHN McCLANE THE DOG HERE.
LET'S JUST ASK *HIM* TO DO IT!
SPARKY, WE NEED YOU TO GO IN THERE AND SAVE RUCKUS. CAN YOU DO IT, BOY?
GO GET HIM, BOY!
YOU'RE AN IDIOT, FOREST.

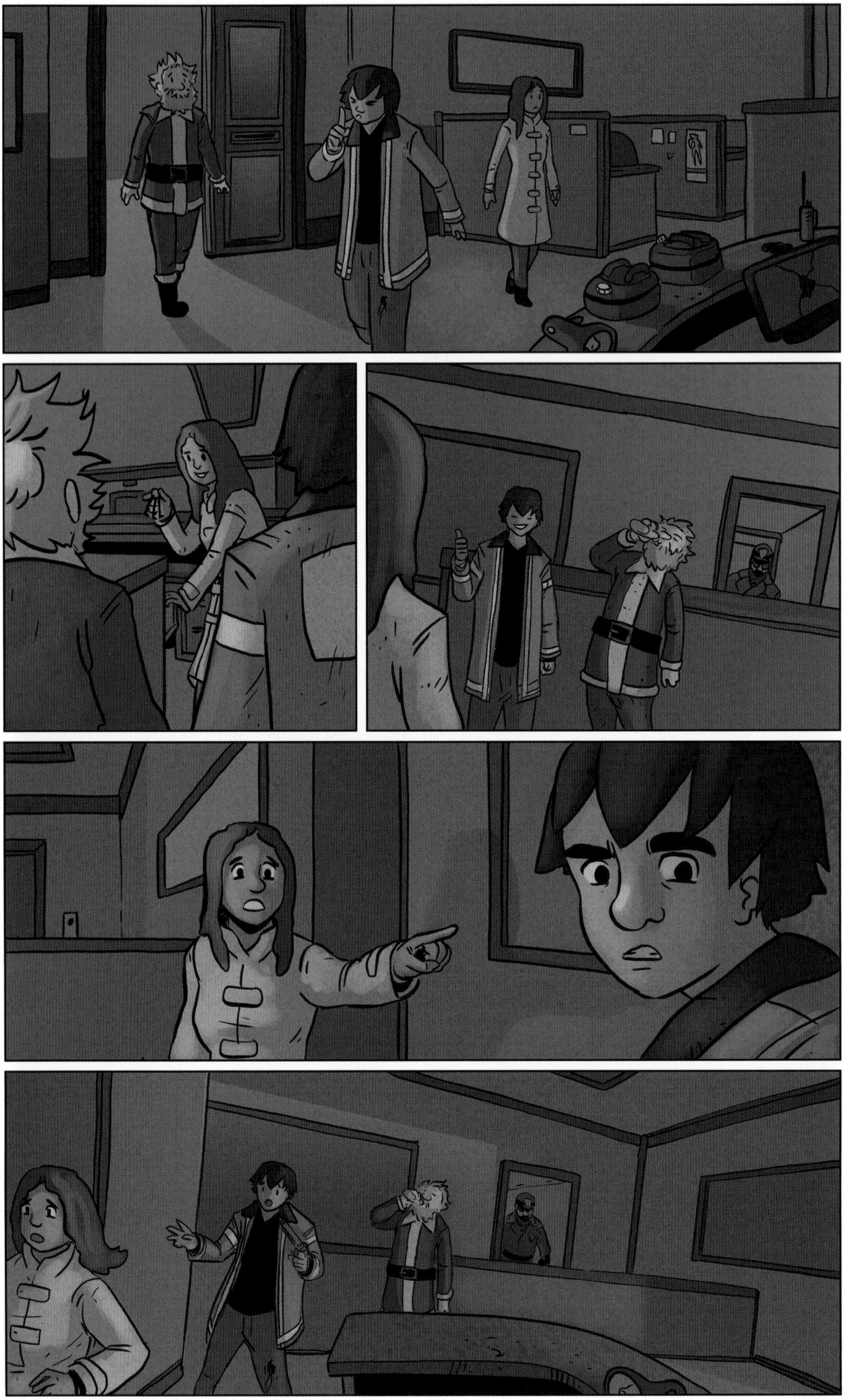

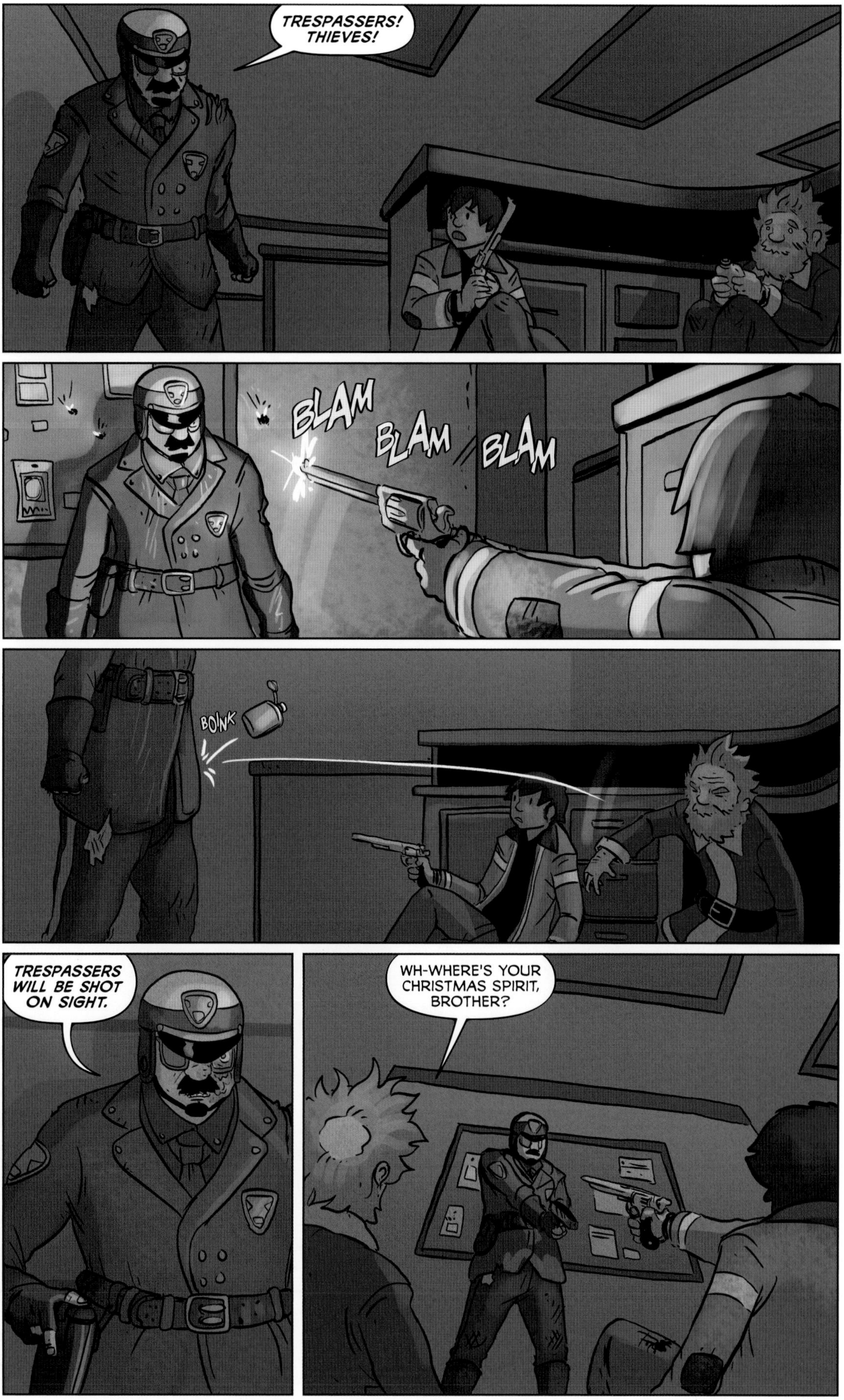
TRESPASSERS! THIEVES!
BLAM
BLAM
BLAM
BOINK
TRESPASSERS WILL BE SHOT ON SIGHT.
WH-WHERE'S YOUR CHRISTMAS SPIRIT, BROTHER?

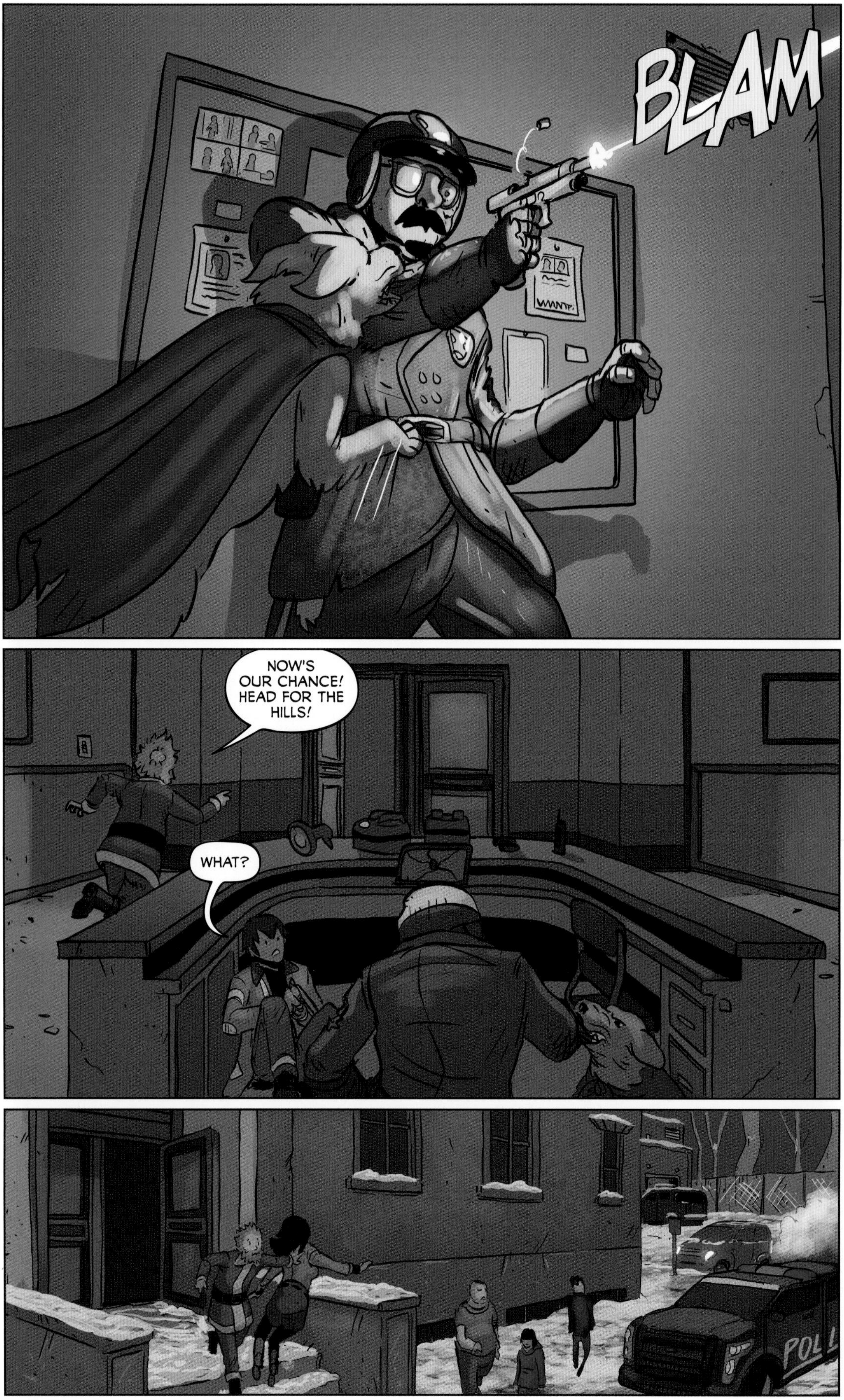
BLAM
NOW'S OUR CHANCE! HEAD FOR THE HILLS!
WHAT?
POLI

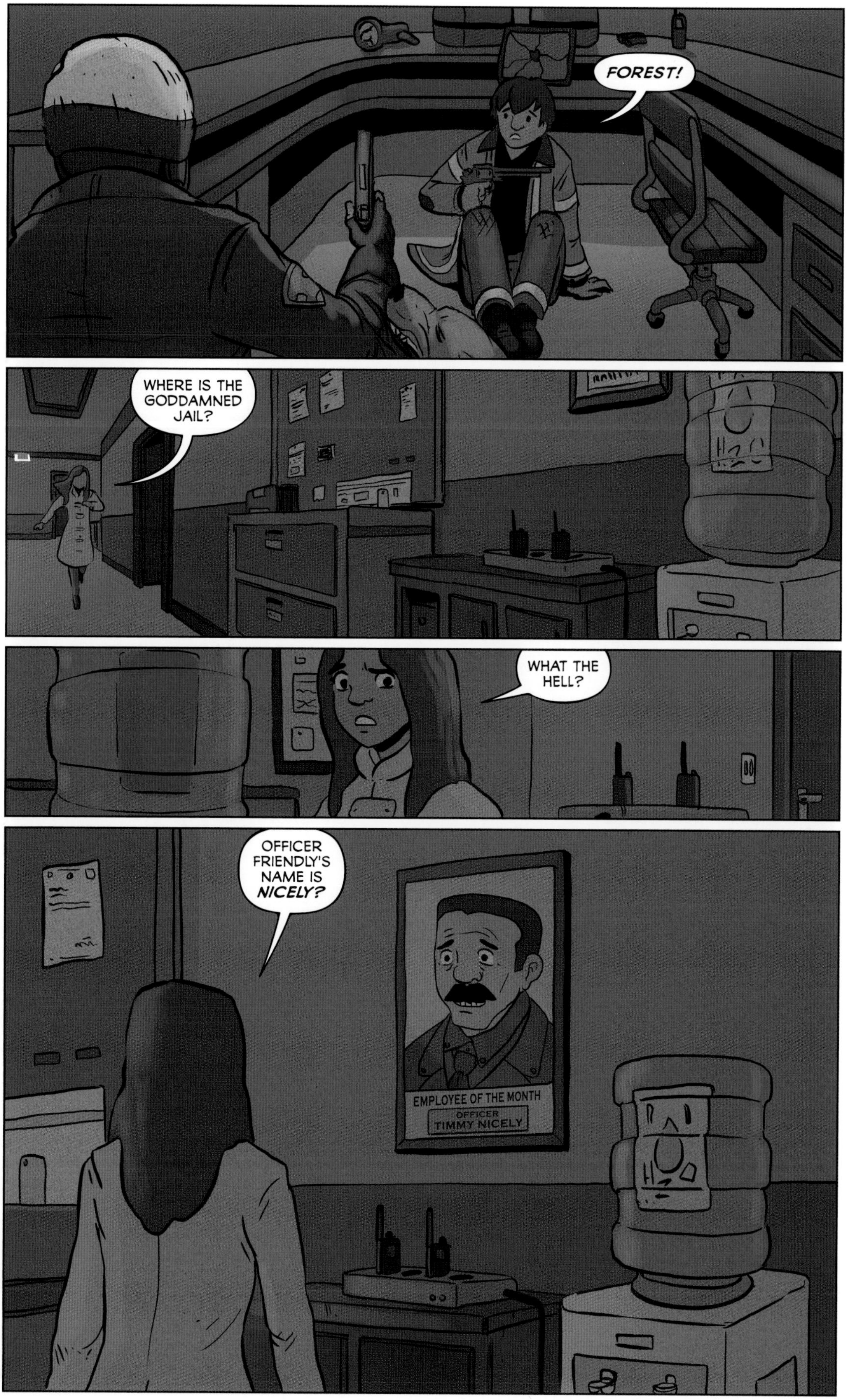
FOREST!
WHERE IS THE GODDAMNED JAIL?
WHAT THE HELL?
OFFICER FRIENDLY'S NAME IS *NICELY?*
EMPLOYEE OF THE MONTH
OFFICER TIMMY NICELY

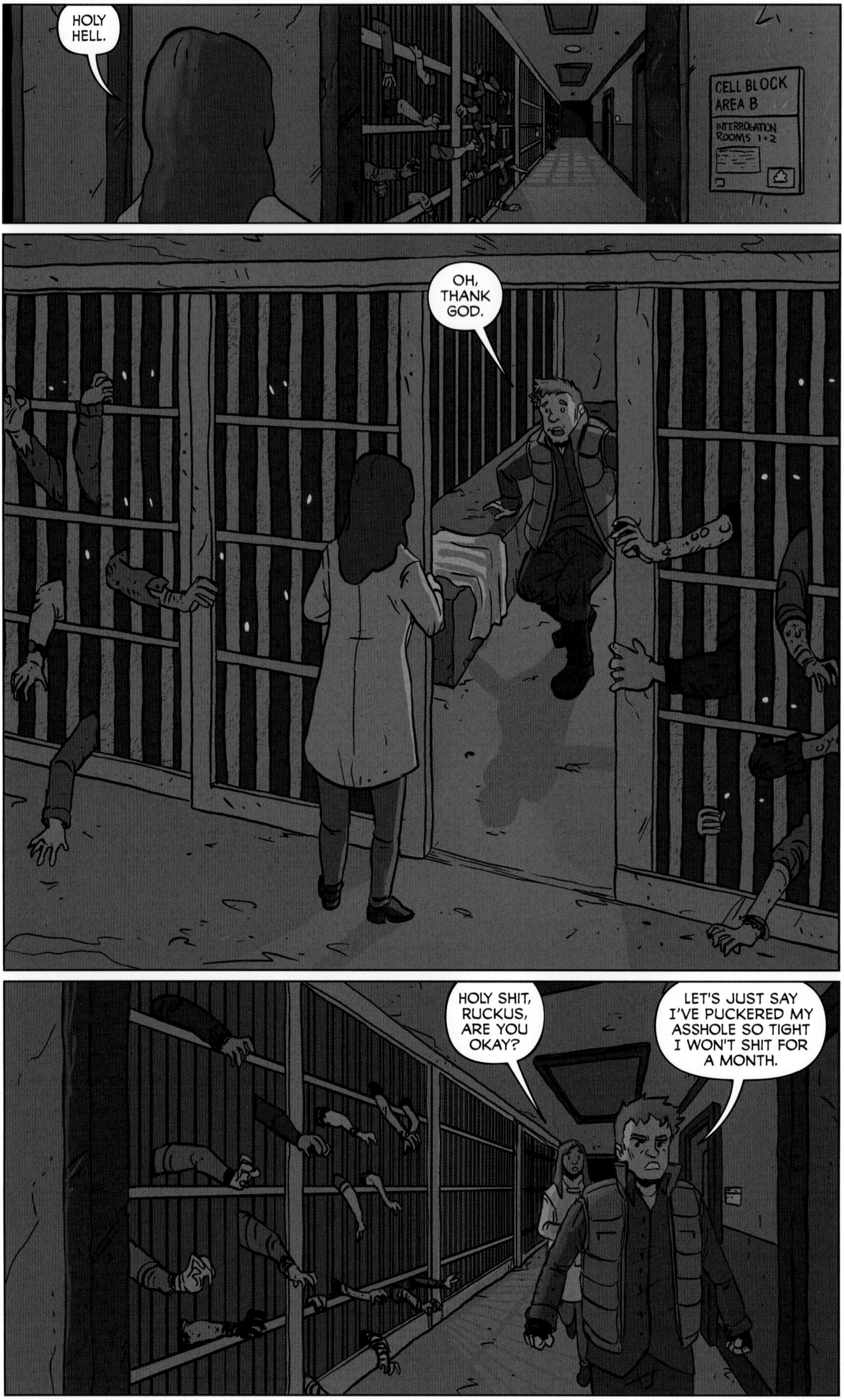
HOLY HELL.
CELL BLOCK AREA B
INTERROGATION ROOMS 1+2
OH, THANK GOD.
HOLY SHIT, RUCKUS, ARE YOU OKAY?
LET'S JUST SAY I'VE PUCKERED MY ASSHOLE SO TIGHT I WON'T SHIT FOR A MONTH.

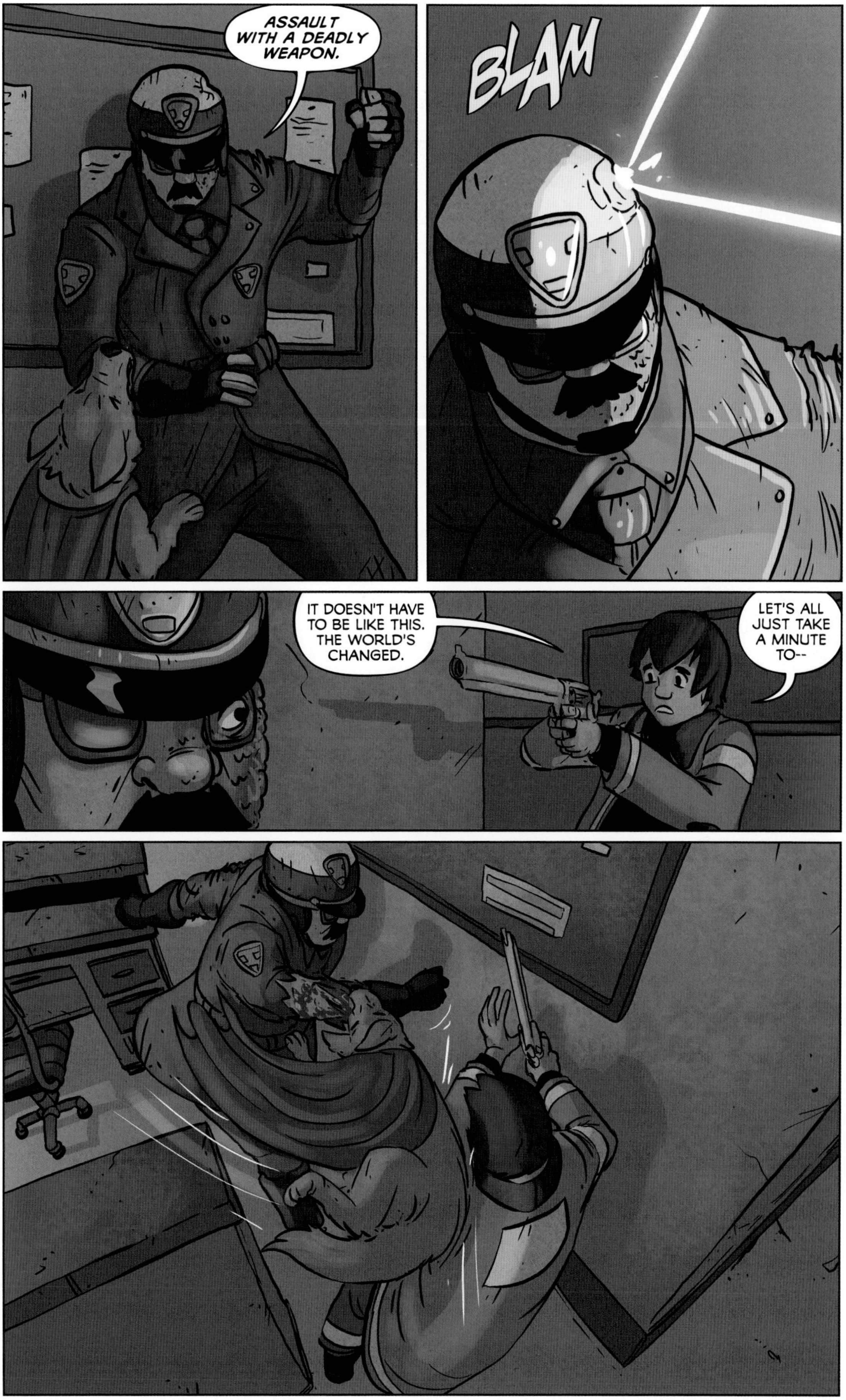
ASSAULT WITH A DEADLY WEAPON.
BLAM
IT DOESN'T HAVE TO BE LIKE THIS. THE WORLD'S CHANGED.
LET'S ALL JUST TAKE A MINUTE TO--

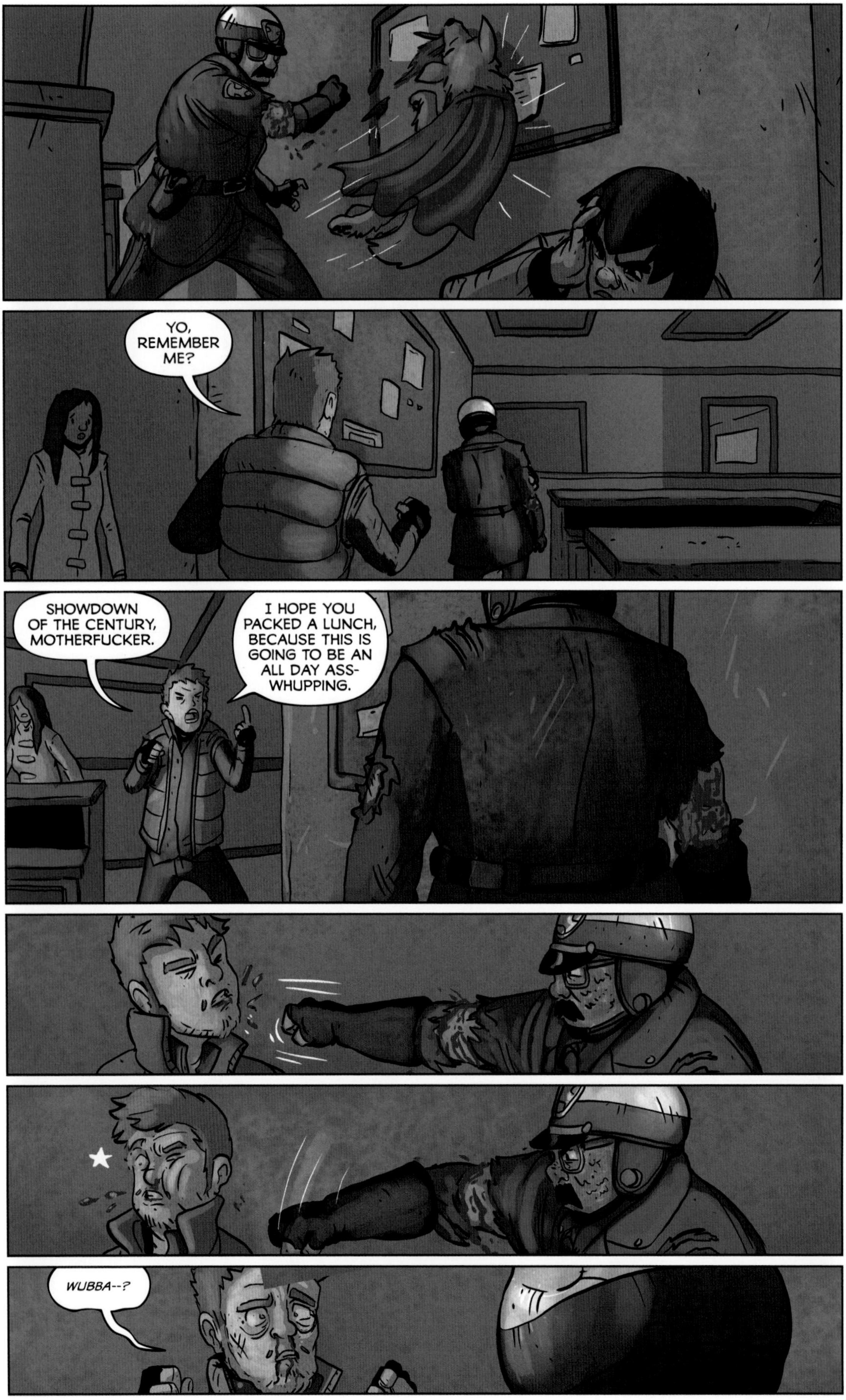
YO, REMEMBER ME?
SHOWDOWN OF THE CENTURY, MOTHERFUCKER.
I HOPE YOU PACKED A LUNCH, BECAUSE THIS IS GOING TO BE AN ALL DAY ASS-WHUPPING.
WUBBA--?

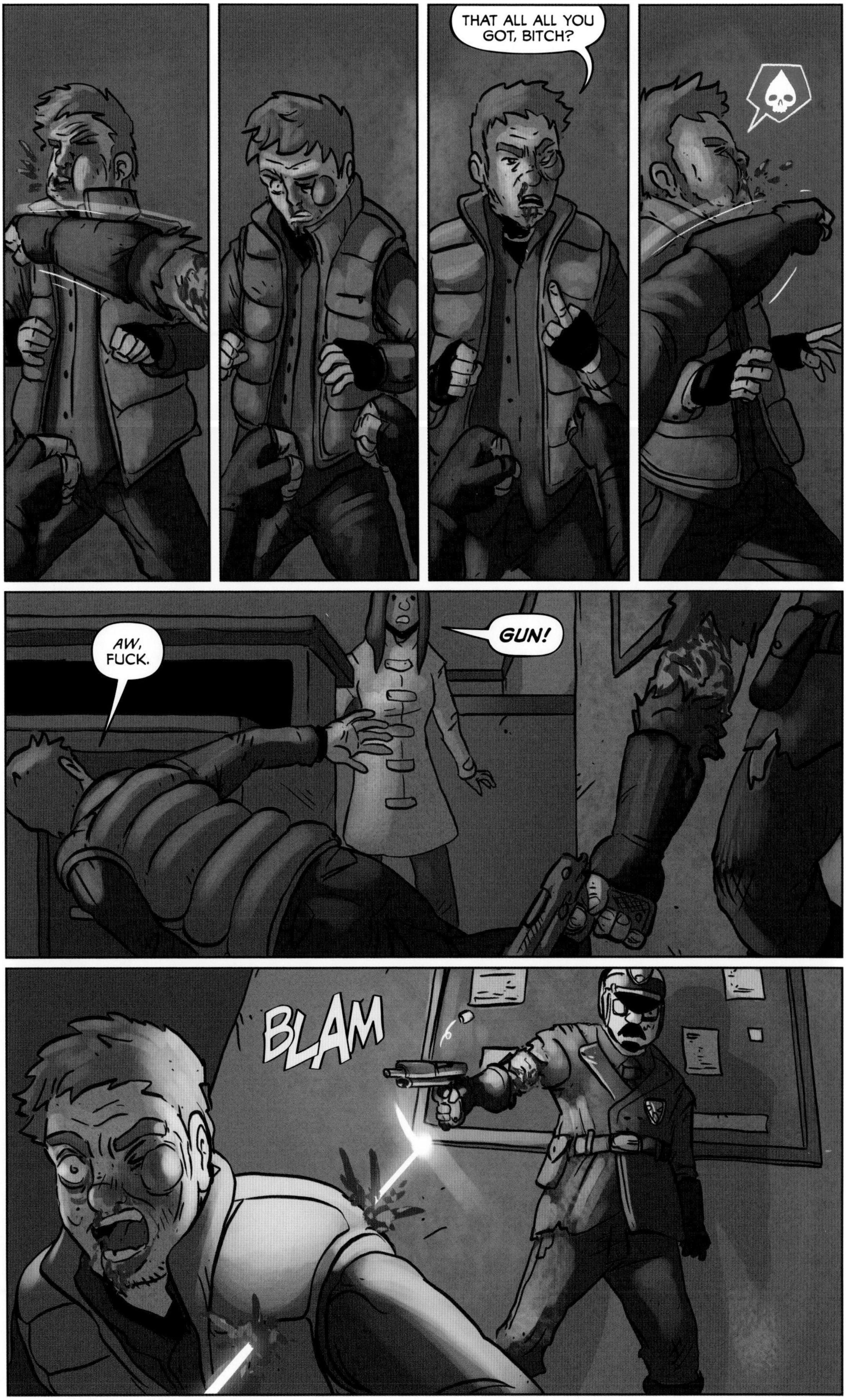
THAT ALL ALL YOU GOT, BITCH?
AW, FUCK.
GUN!
BLAM

BLAM

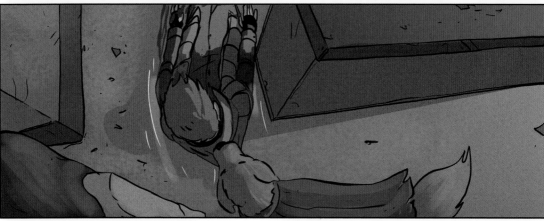

REAL FUCKHOLE OF A DAY, *HUH*, SPARK?

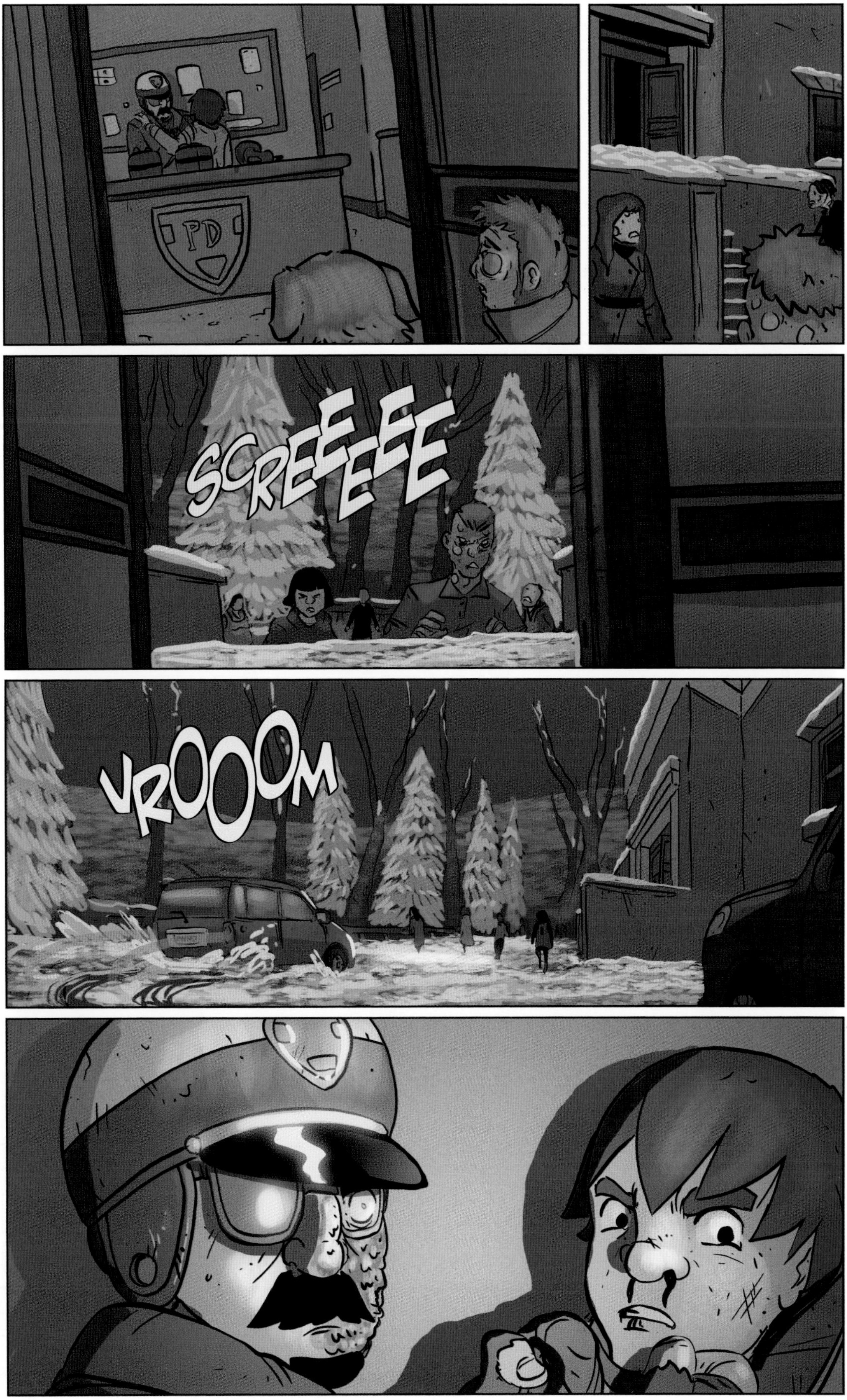
PD
SCREEEEEE
VROOOM

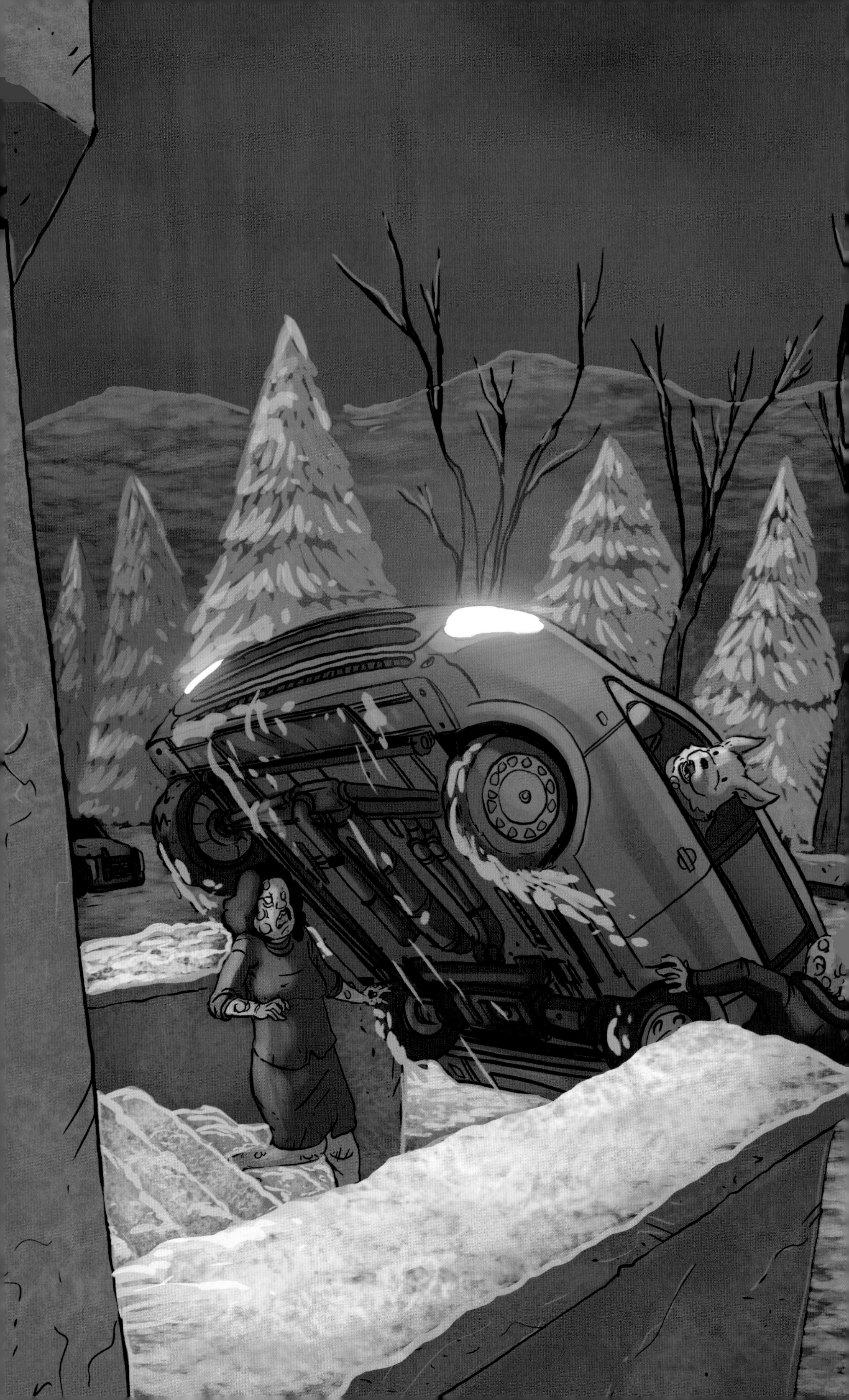

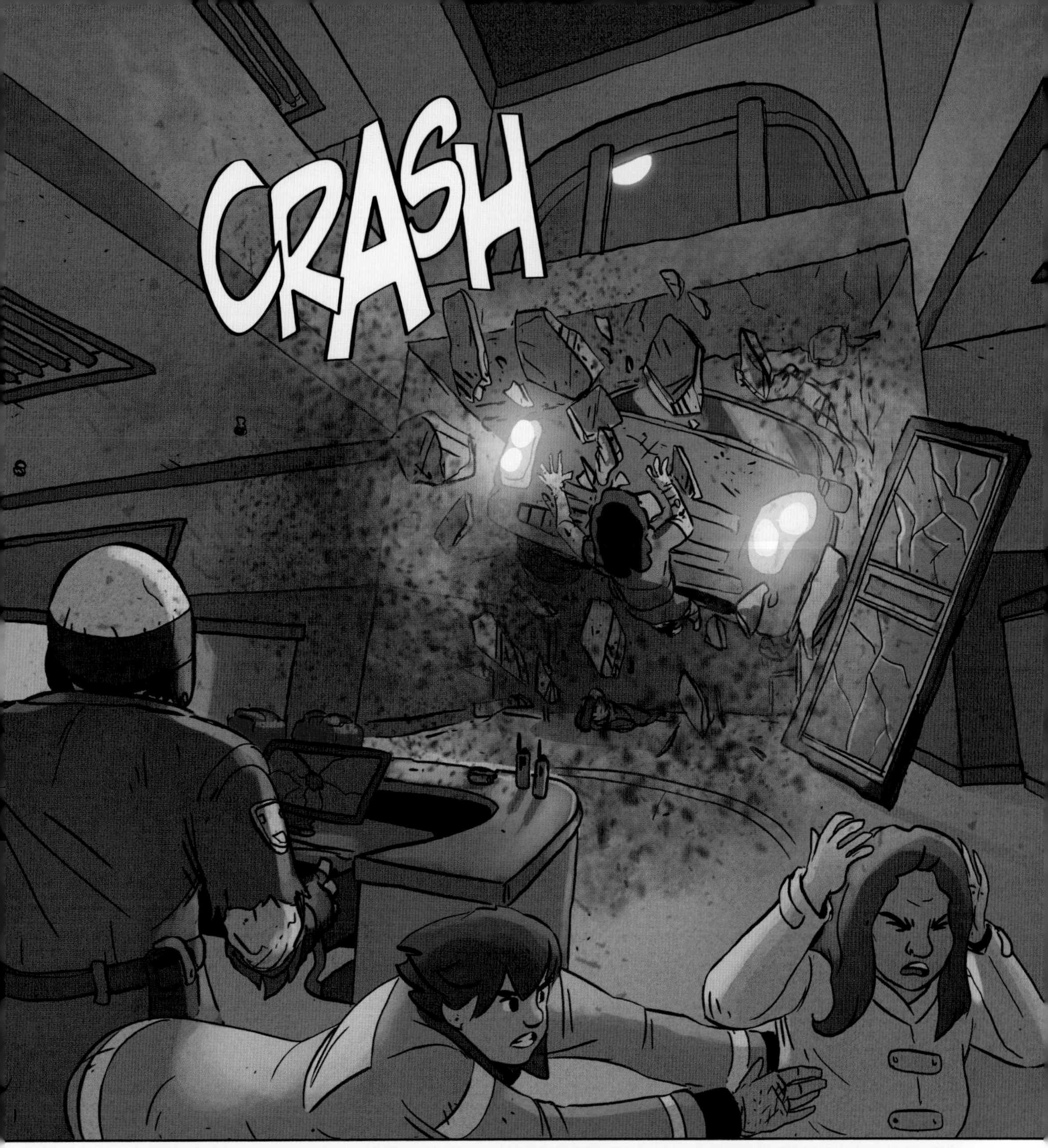
CRASH

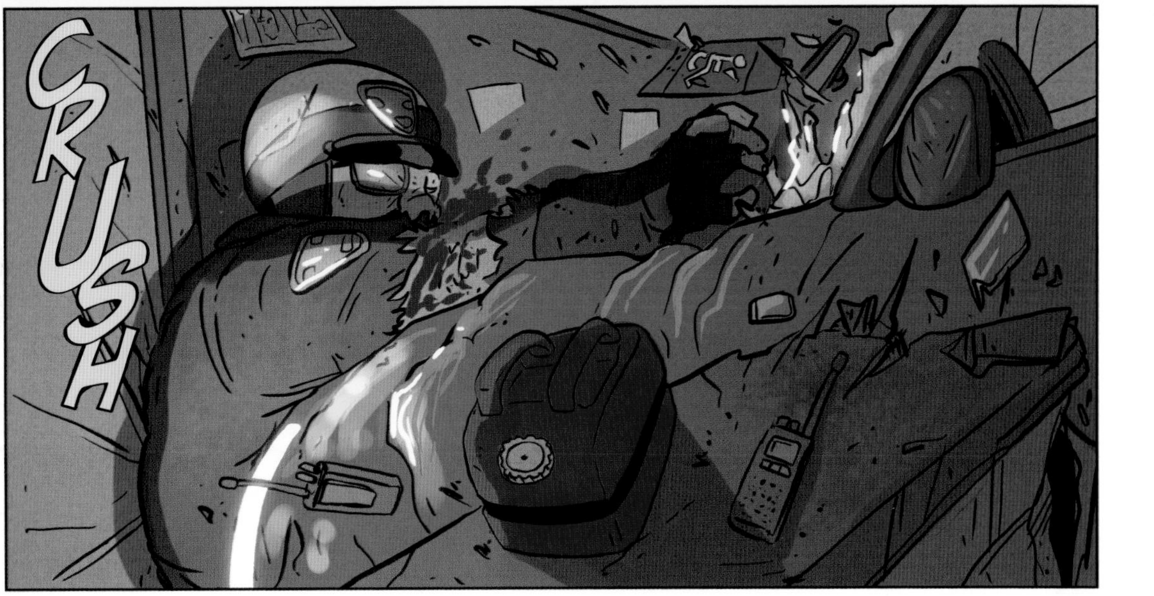
CRUSH

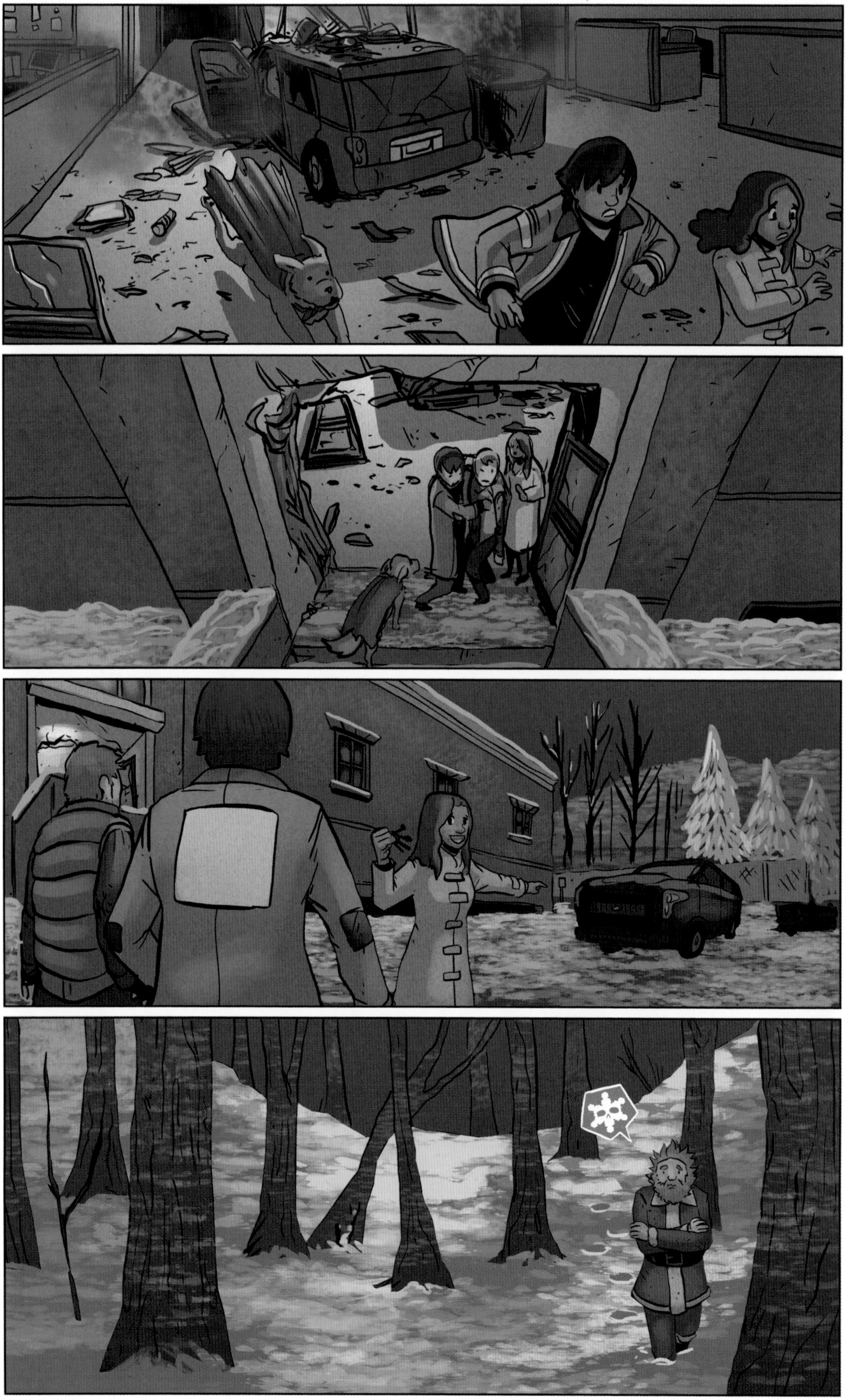

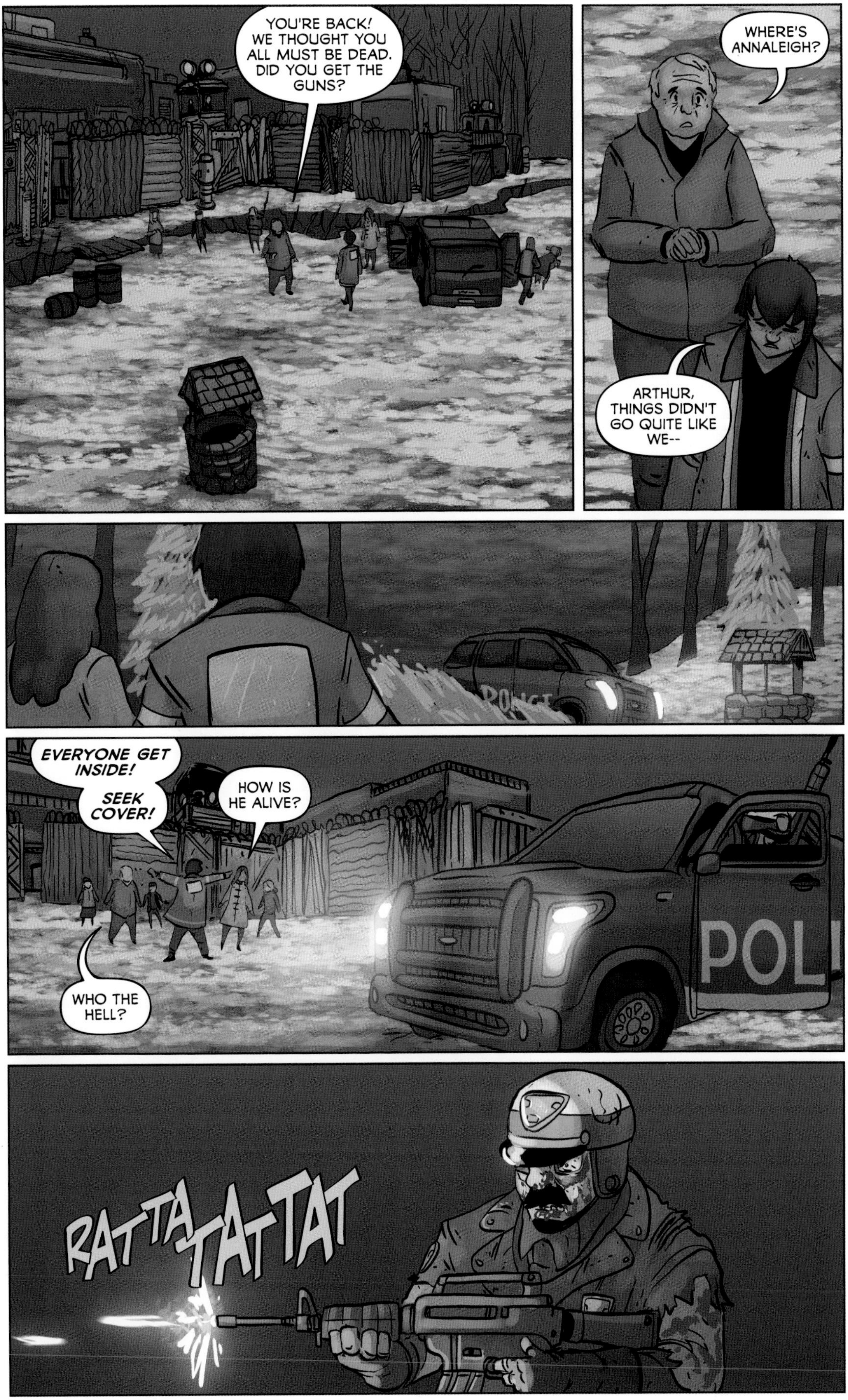
YOU'RE BACK! WE THOUGHT YOU ALL MUST BE DEAD. DID YOU GET THE GUNS?
WHERE'S ANNALEIGH?
ARTHUR, THINGS DIDN'T GO QUITE LIKE WE--
POLI
EVERYONE GET INSIDE!
SEEK COVER!
HOW IS HE ALIVE?
WHO THE HELL?
POLI
RATTATATTAT

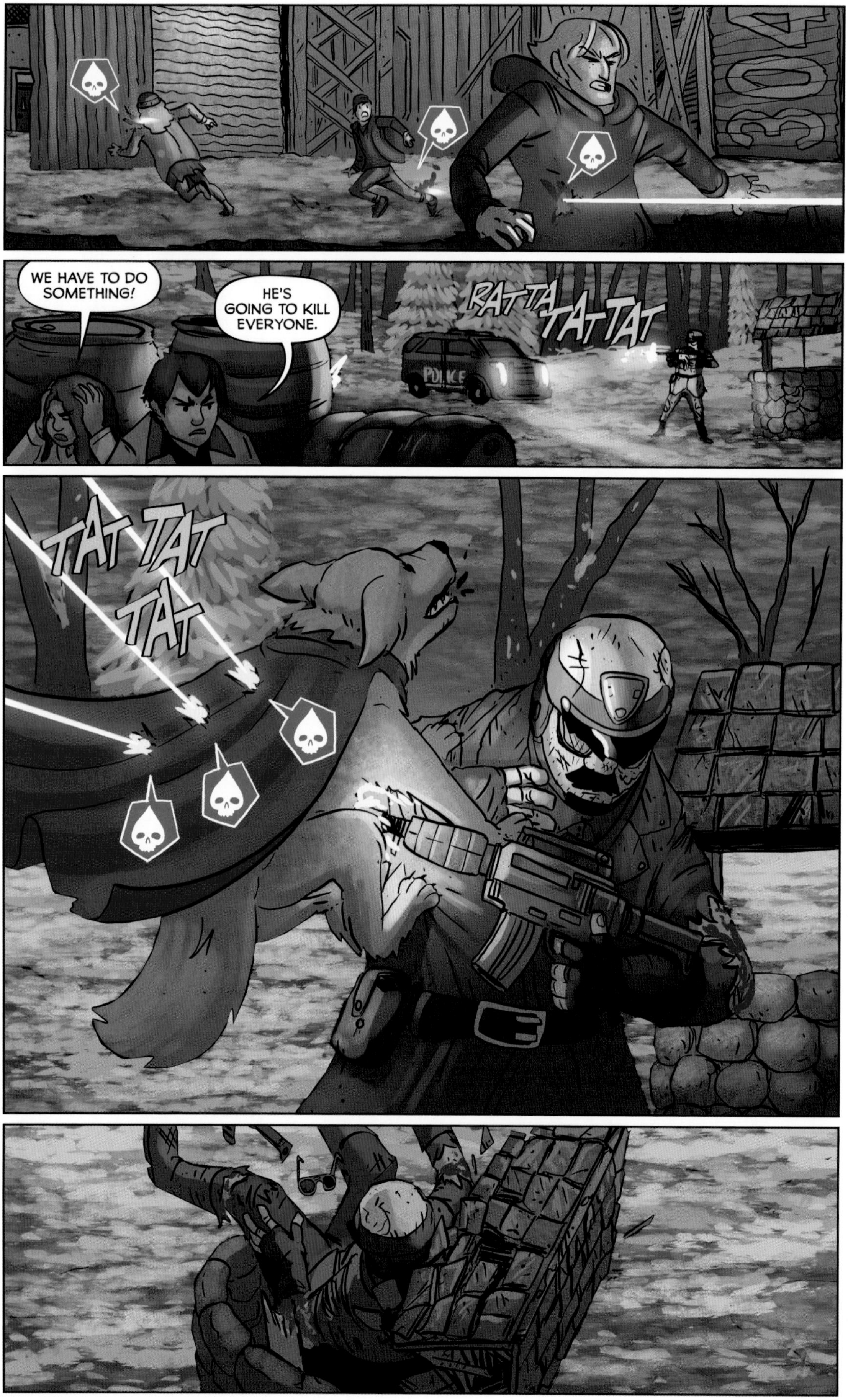
WE HAVE TO DO SOMETHING!
HE'S GOING TO KILL EVERYONE.
RATTA TAT TAT TAT
POLICE
TAT TAT TAT

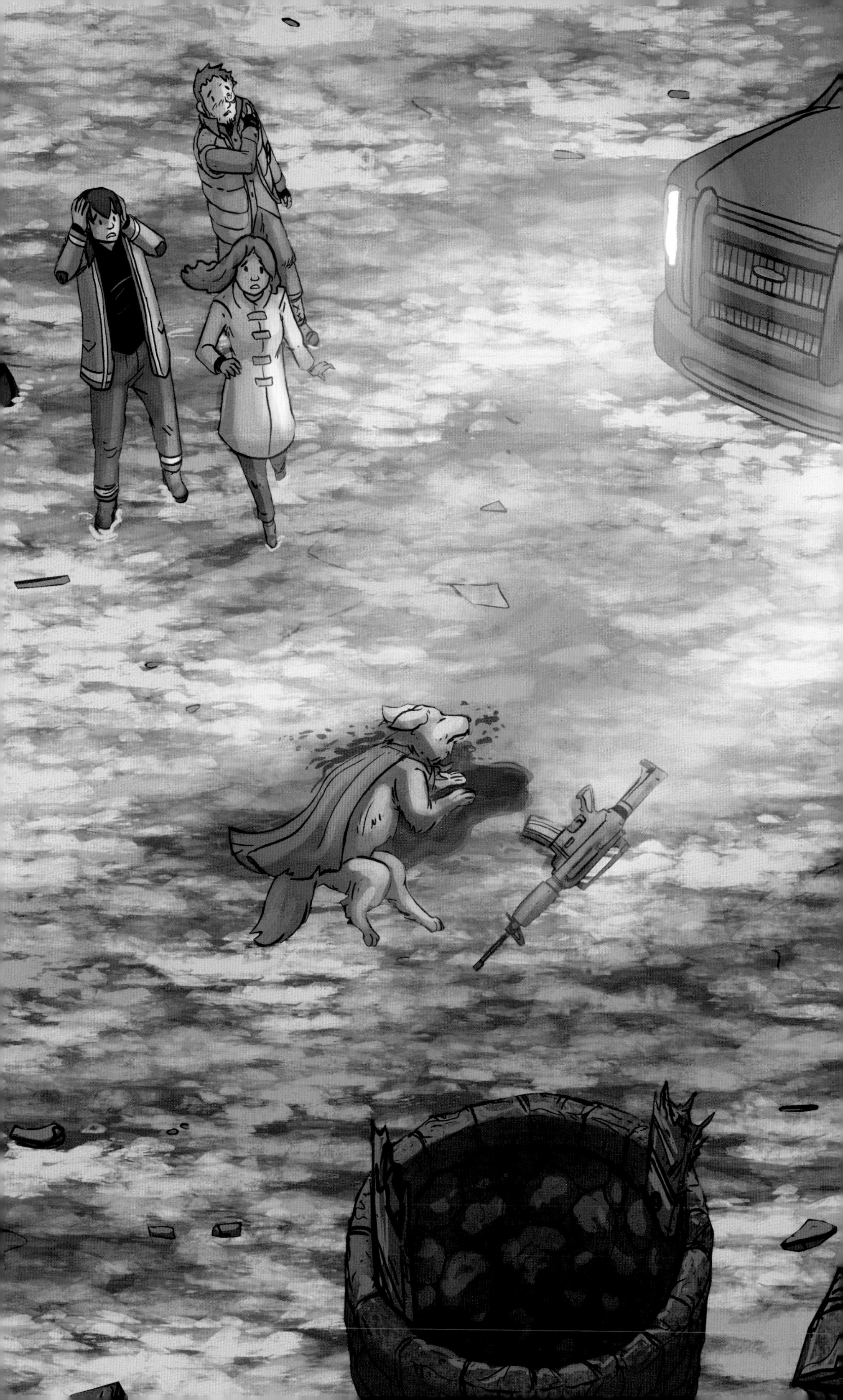

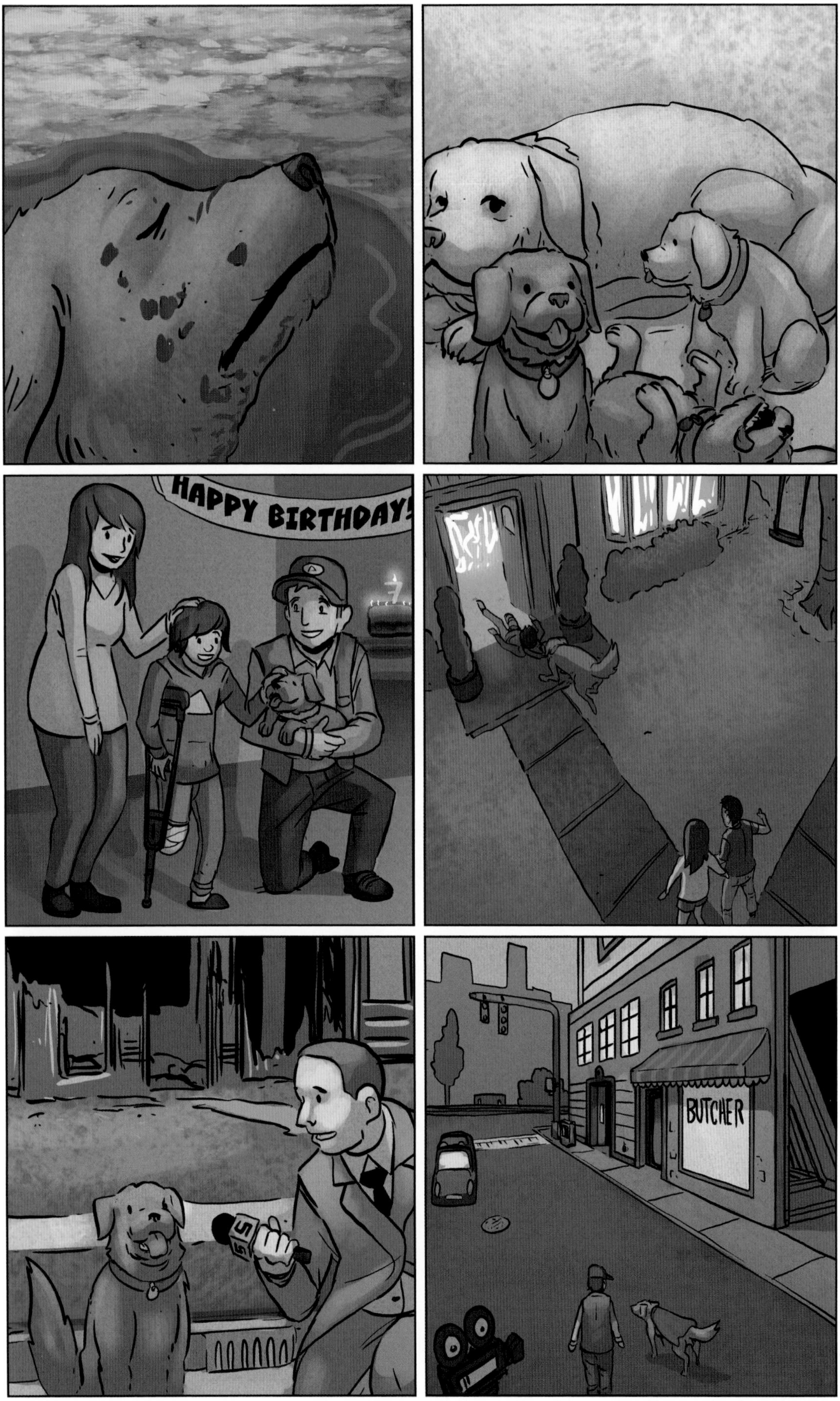
HAPPY BIRTHDAY!
BUTCHER

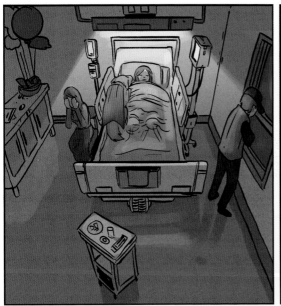

SPARKY

DON'T LEAVE US, SPARKY.

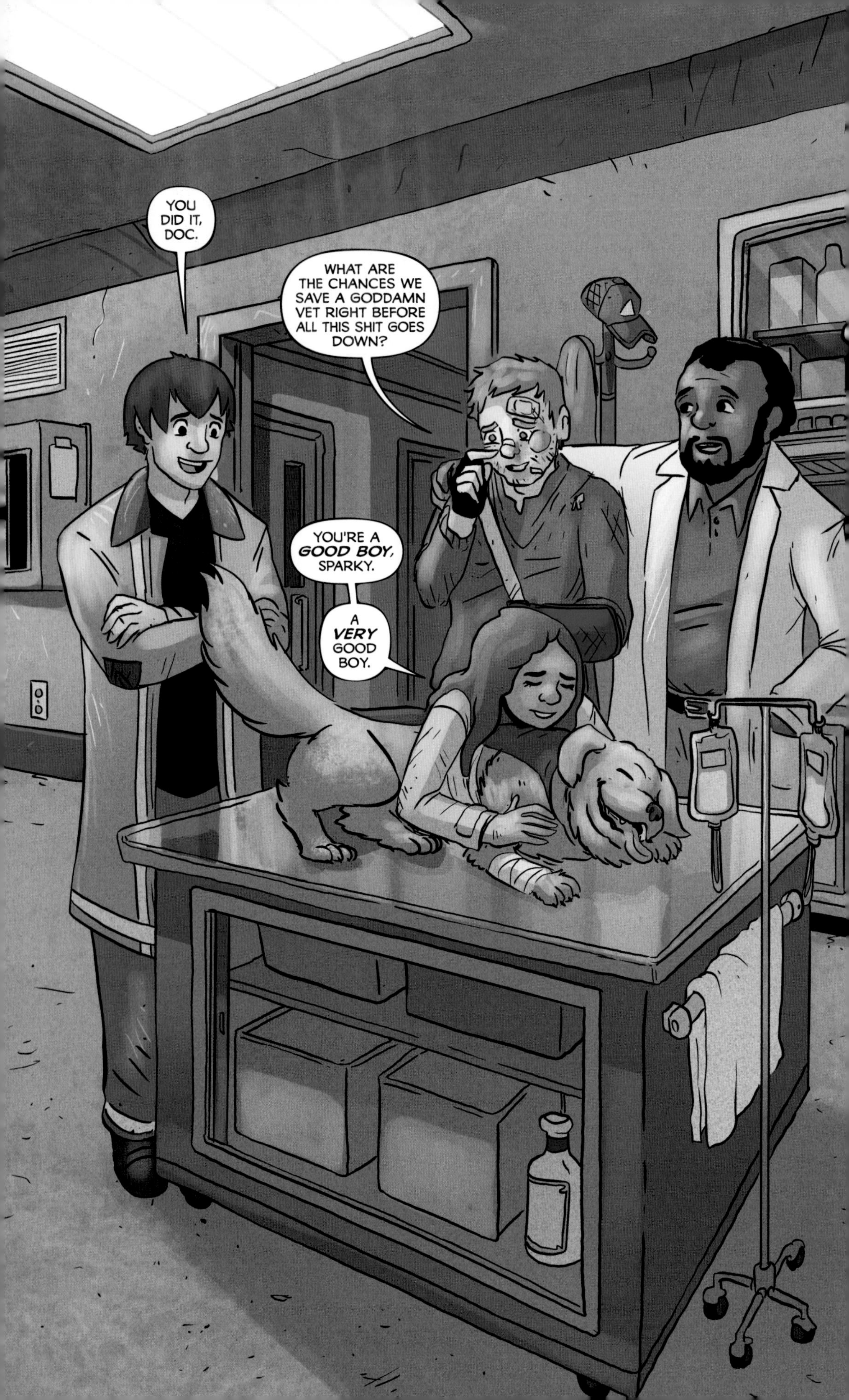
YOU DID IT, DOC.
WHAT ARE THE CHANCES WE SAVE A GODDAMN VET RIGHT BEFORE ALL THIS SHIT GOES DOWN?
YOU'RE A ***GOOD BOY,*** SPARKY.
A ***VERY*** GOOD BOY.

COVER
GALLERY

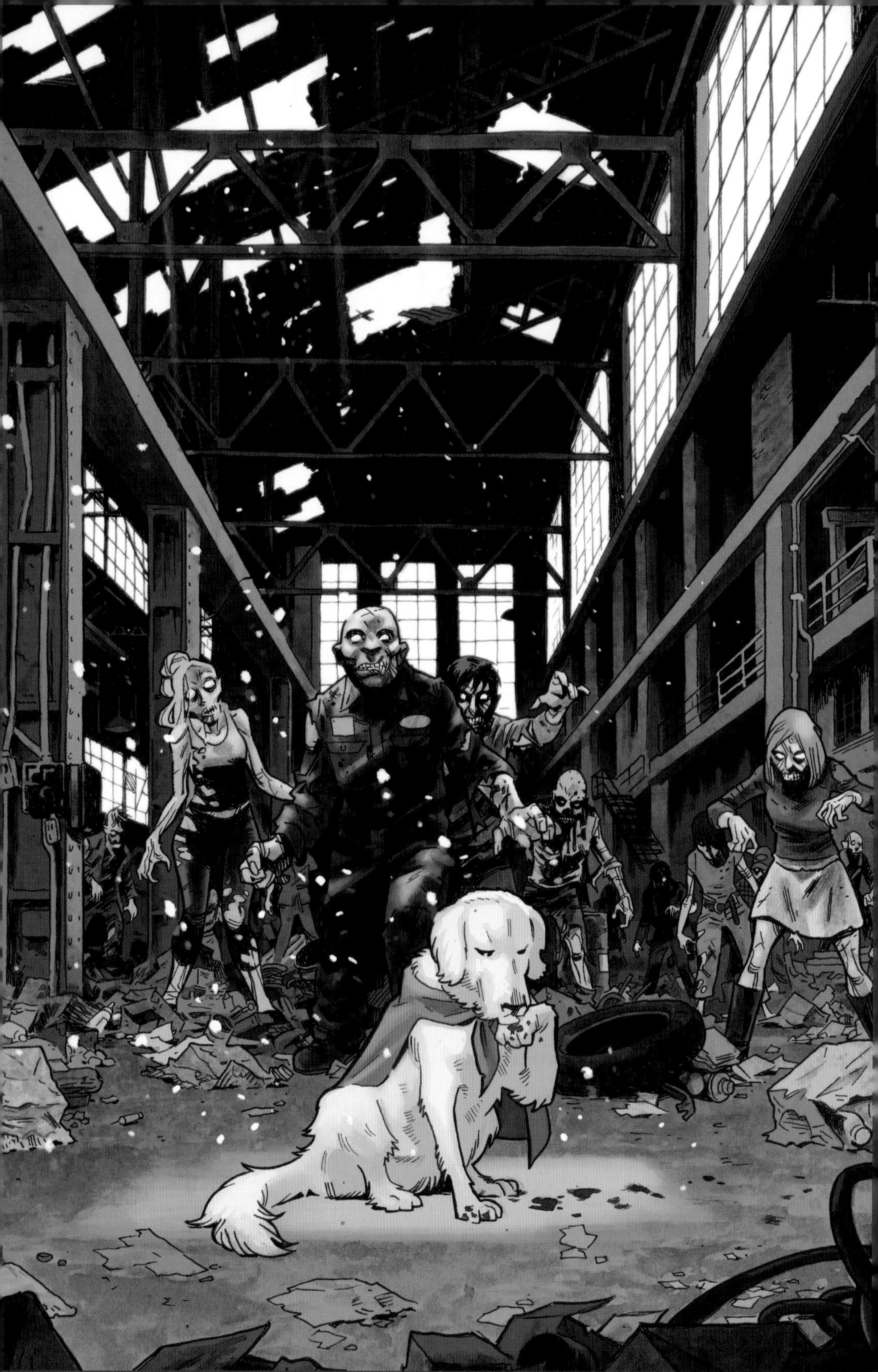

Issue #1 retail and comic shop trade paperback cover illustrated by Brian Hurtt and colored by Bill Crabtree

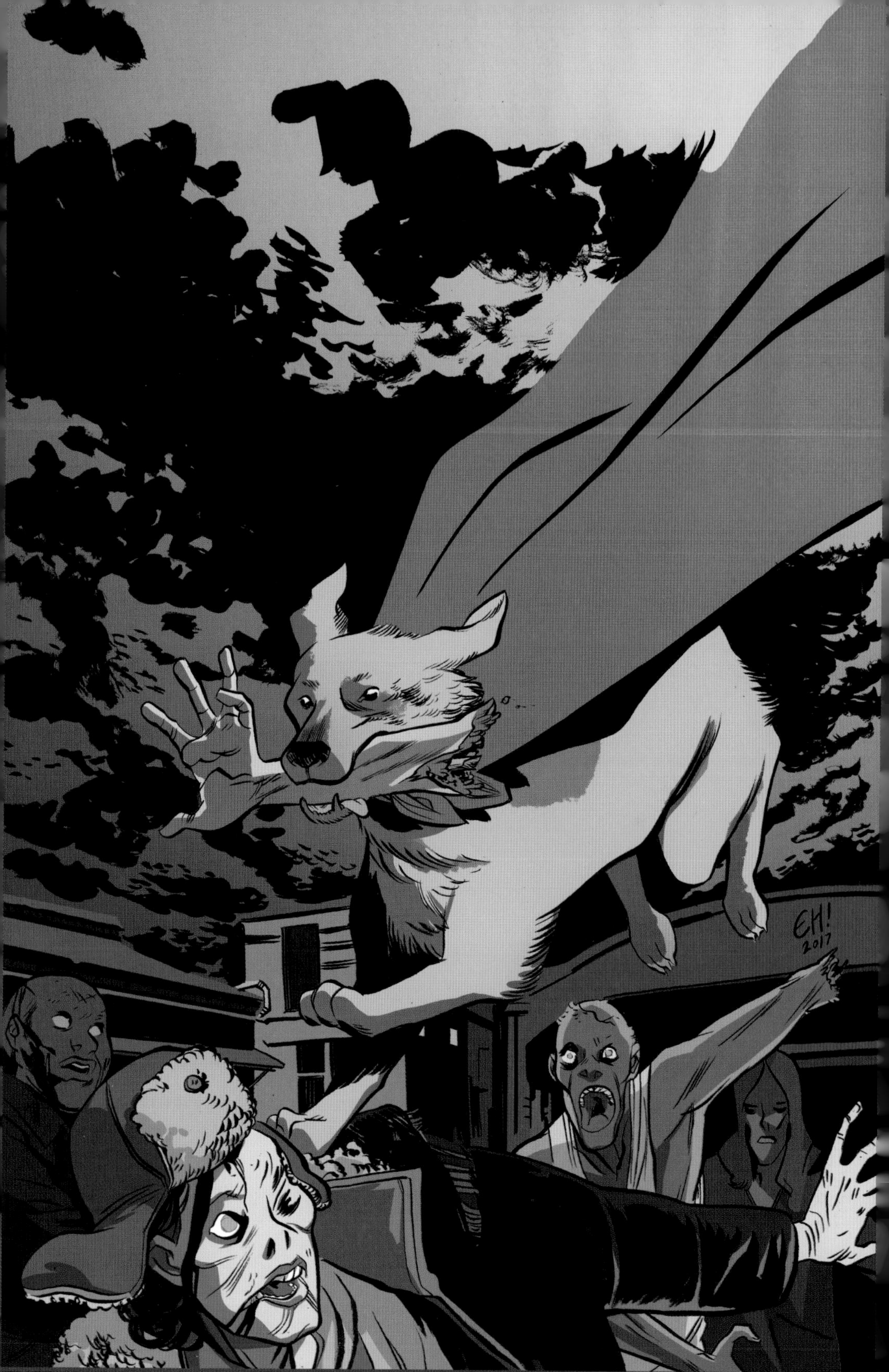
EH!
2017

Issue #1 retail variant cover by Erica Henderson

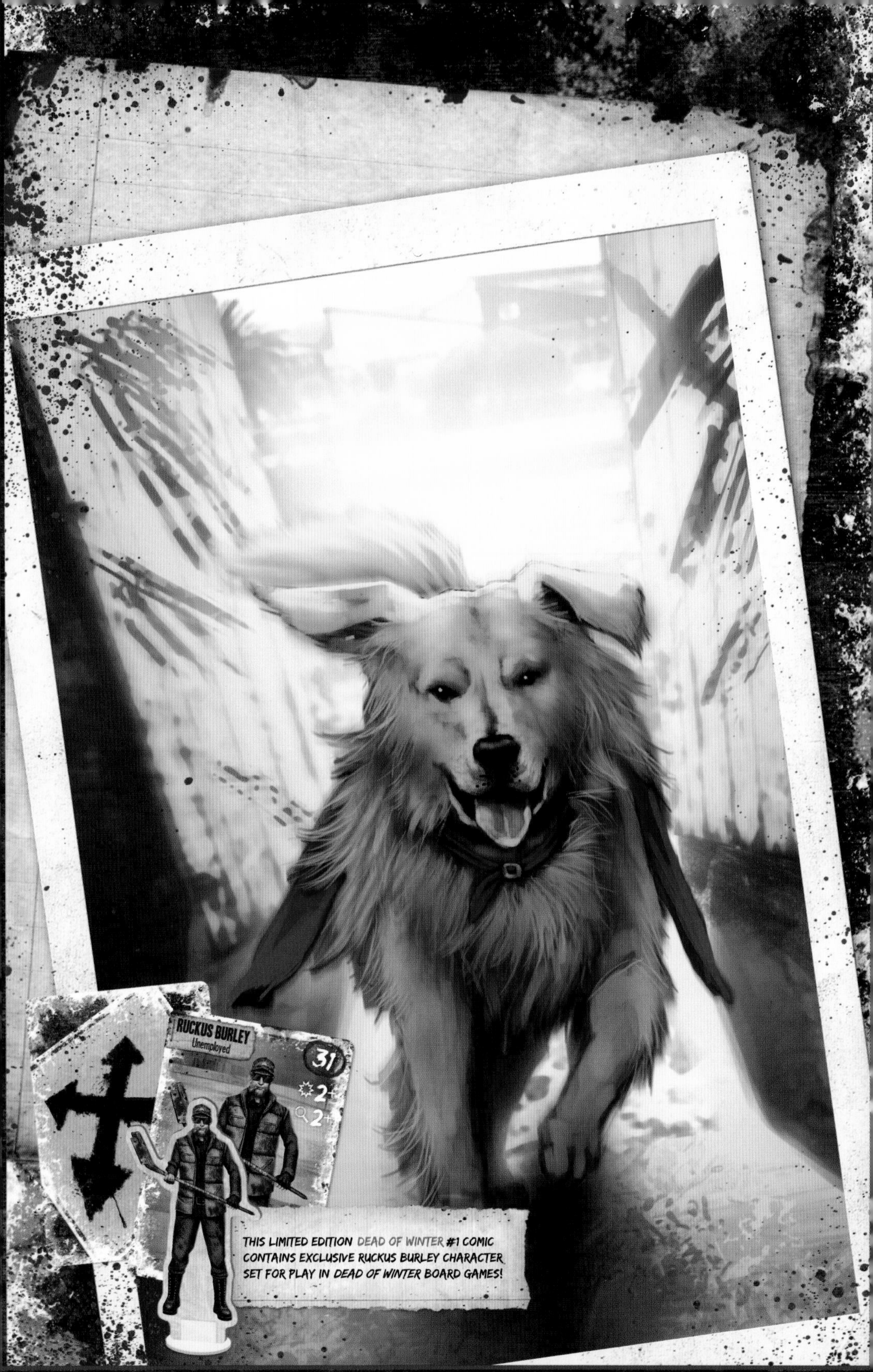
RUCKUS BURLEY
Unemployed
31
THIS LIMITED EDITION DEAD OF WINTER #1 COMIC CONTAINS EXCLUSIVE RUCKUS BURLEY CHARACTER SET FOR PLAY IN DEAD OF WINTER BOARD GAMES!

Issue #1 and trade paperback exclusive cover by Fernanda Suarez

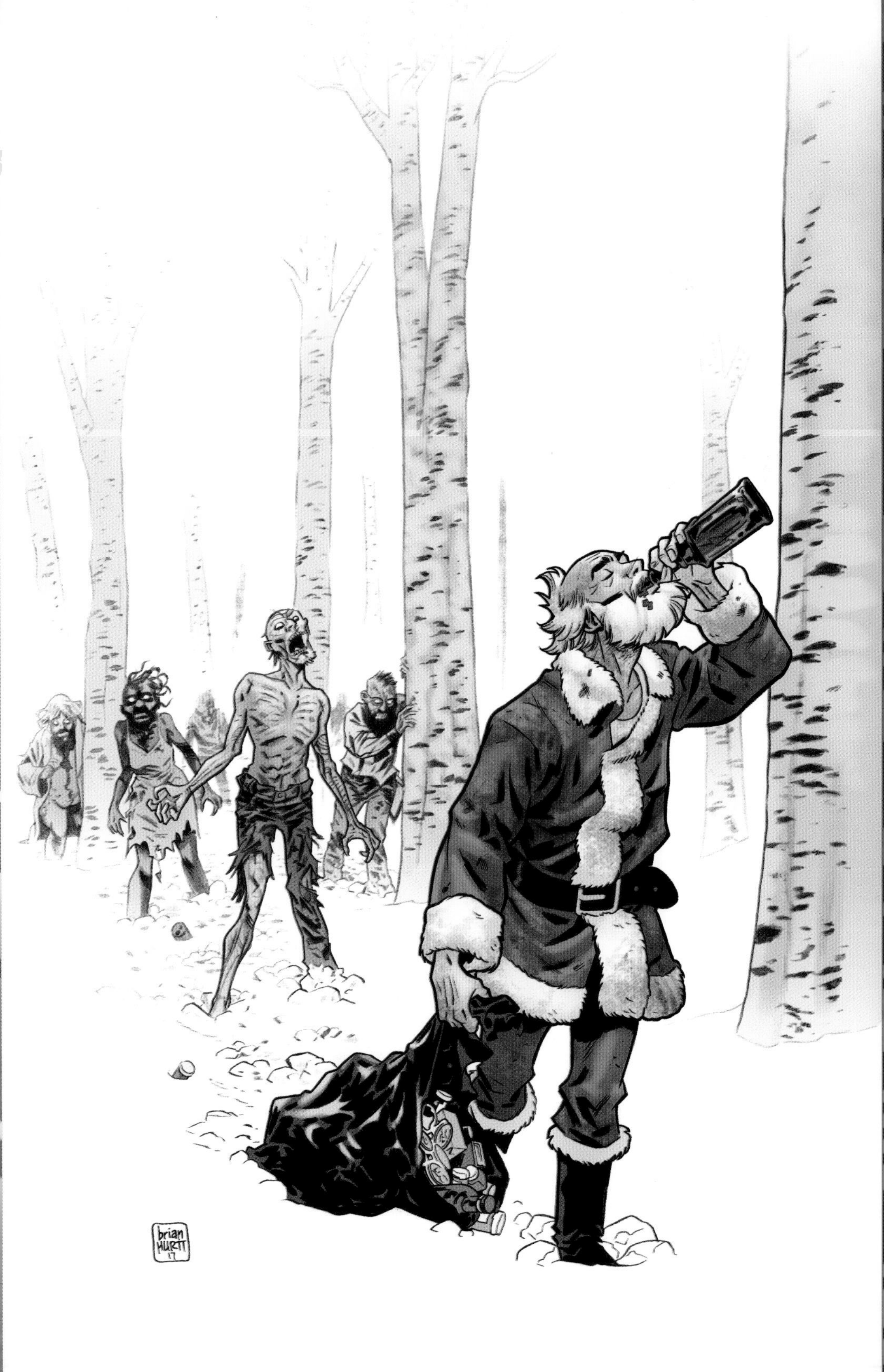
brian
HURTT
17

Issue #2 cover illustrated by Brian Hurtt and colored by Bill Crabtree

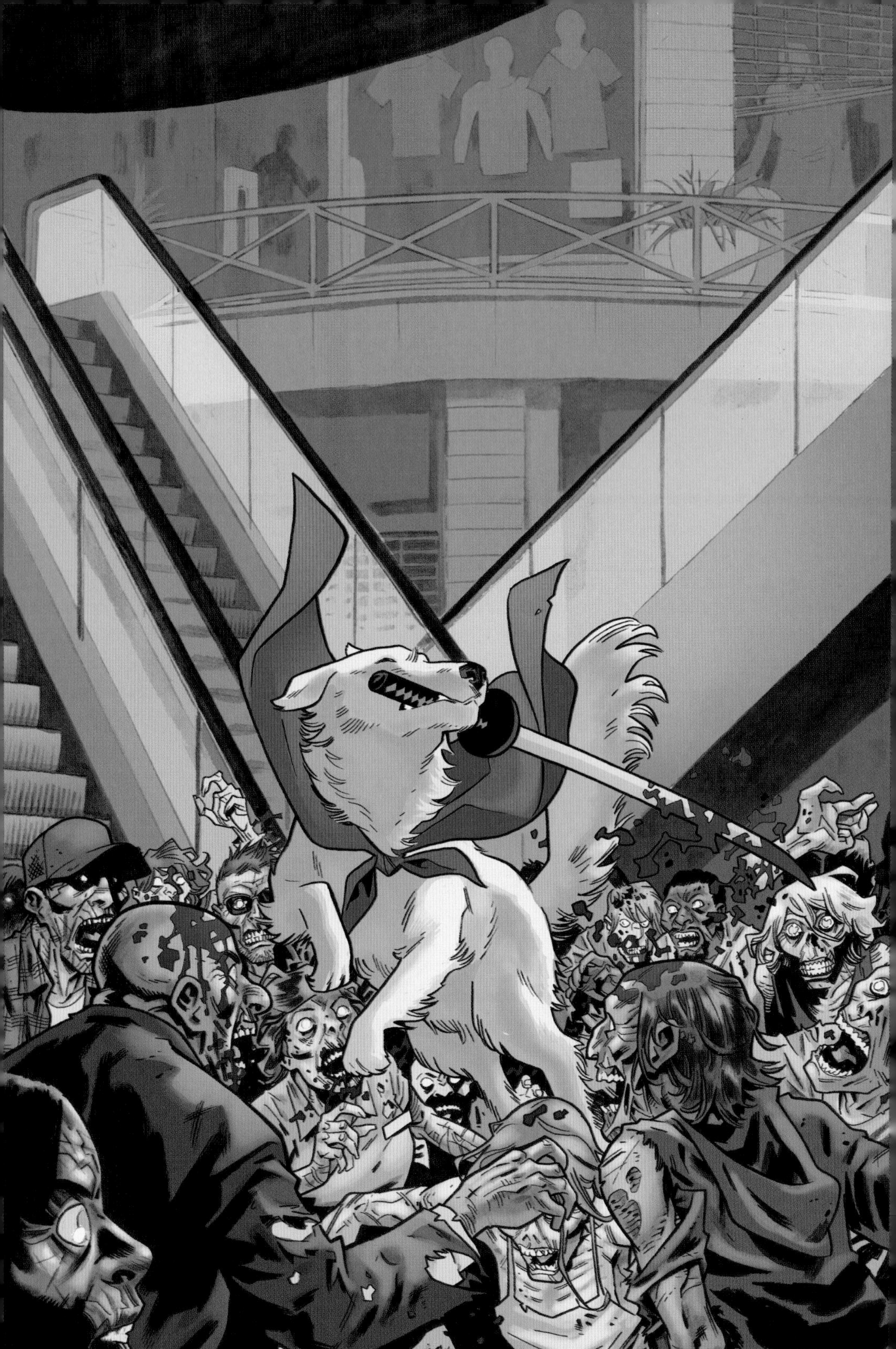

Issue #3 cover illustrated by Brian Hurtt and colored by Bill Crabtree

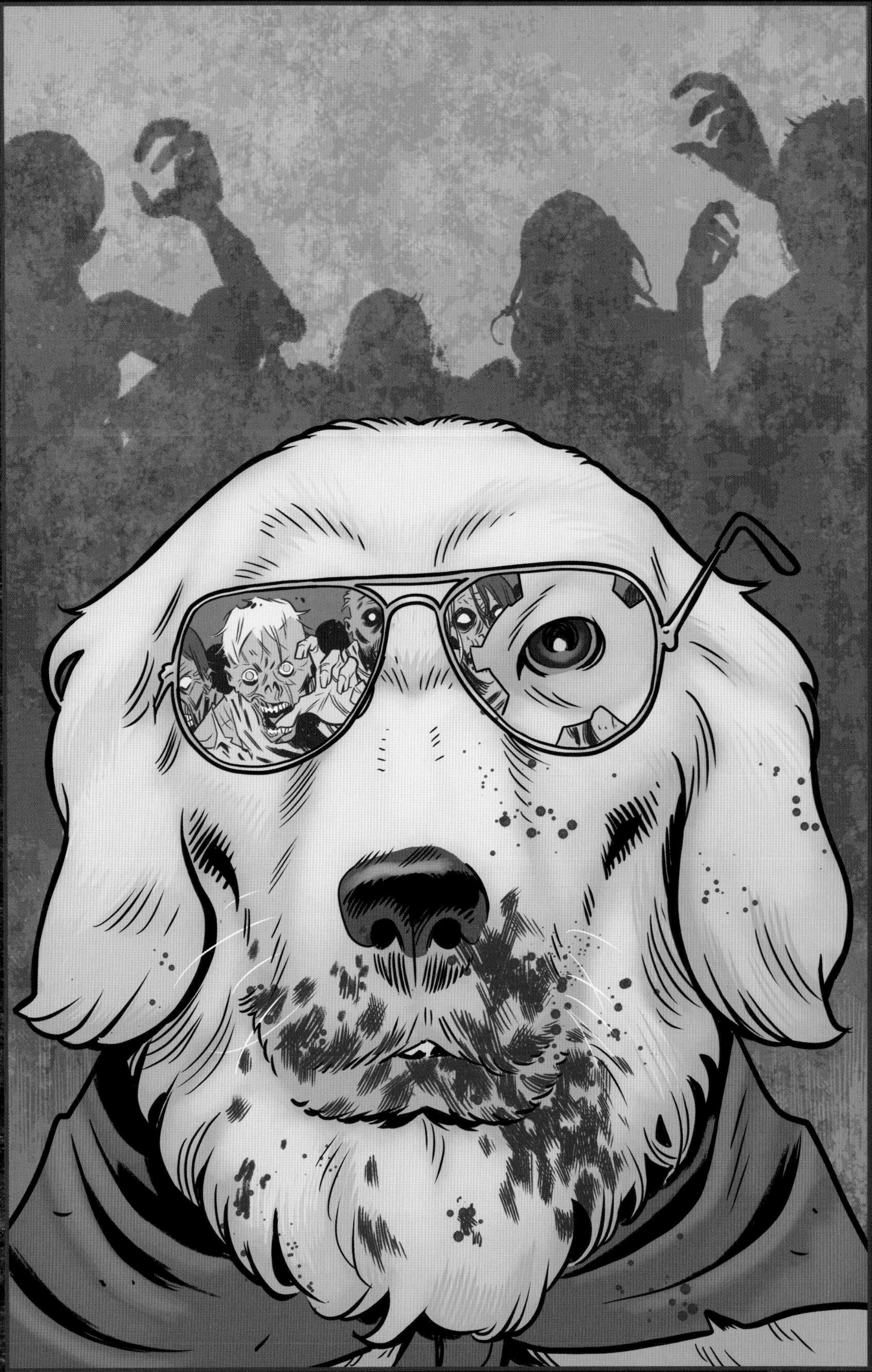

Issue #4 cover illustrated by Brian Hurtt and colored by Bill Crabtree

GABO

If player is in super market and Gabo is not in play: You hear a rustling and turn to see a man, completely obtuse to your appearance, rummaging through the shelves. "Hey is that Russ Manning Promising Newcomer Award nominee GABO?" "Who is GABO?" "He draws dope ass comics, man." GABO looks up, finally acknowledging you, "Hey do you guys have any batteries?" He shakes a drained Gameboy at you.

OPTION 1

Add GABO to your group.

OPTION 2

Add GABO to your group. Why wouldn't you? He's great.

GABO
Artist

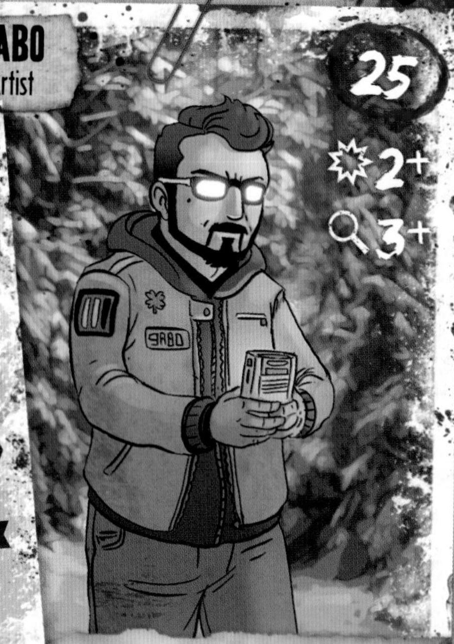

25
2+
3+

ANYWHERE: If Gabo can discard two cards, increase Morale by 1.

KYLE STARKS
Writer

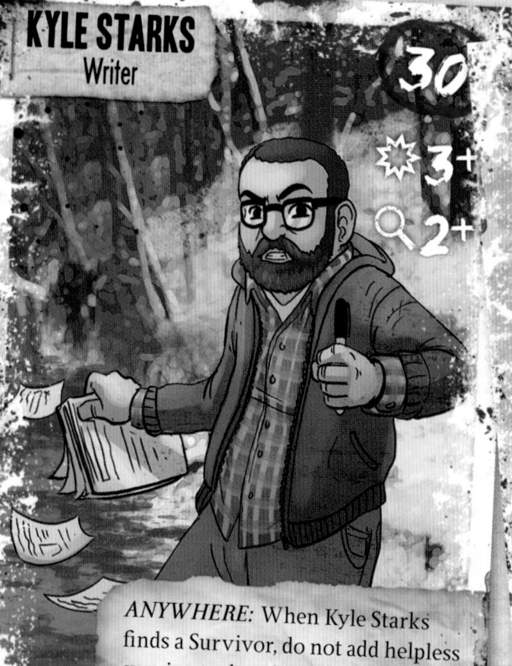

30
3+
2+

ANYWHERE: When Kyle Starks finds a Survivor, do not add helpless survivors—but the user can spend no more actions this round.

KYLE STARKS

If you're in the library and Kyle Starks is not in play: "Hey, my dudes, what are you doing here?" says the clearly unhinged man with an excellent beard. "Are you looking for some books to read? Because I'm going to recommend all these Kyle Starks comic books." In his arms are several comic collections: *Dead of Winter, Kill Them All, Rock Candy Mountain, Sexcastle.* "Please?" he whines.

OPTION 1

Kyle Starks? What are the odds? Such an amazing storyteller! Add Kyle Starks to your hand and increase moral by 3! Yay!

OPTION 2

You use the books for firewood and the lowly comic creator for food. Times are desperate. Add three food to the pantry. Put Kyle Starks in the graveyard.

MORE BOOKS FROM ONI PRESS...

Rick and Morty
VOLUME FOUR
STARKS CANNON ELLERBY HILL FARINA CRANK!

RICK AND MORTY, VOL. 4
By Kyle Starks, CJ Cannon, Marc Ellerby, and more

128 pages, softcover, full color
ISBN 978-1-62010-377-7

THE LIFE AFTER
JOSHUA HALE FIALKOV • GABO
1
$10
10/10

THE LIFE AFTER, VOL. 1
SQUARE ONE EDITION
By Joshua Hale Fialkov and Gabo

136 pages, softcover, full color
ISBN 978-1-62010-389-0

AN EX-COP. HIS PARTNER. A DEADLY ASSASSIN.
A MURDEROUS TEAM-UP AS THEY FIGHT FROM THE LOBBY TO THE PENTHOUSE IN SEARCH OF BLOODY VENGEANCE.
KILL THEM ALL
A GRAPHIC NOVEL BY KYLE STARKS
THE DUDE WHO BROUGHT YOU SEXCASTLE

KILL THEM ALL
By Kyle Starks

184 pages, softcover, full color
ISBN 978-1-62010-434-7

THE DAMNED
VOLUME 1, "THREE DAYS DEAD"
— by —
Cullen Bunn
and
Brian Hurtt
with
Bill Crabtree
ONLY $9.99 U.S.

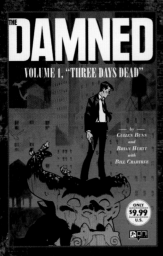

THE DAMNED, VOL. 1: THREE DAYS DEAD
By Cullen Bunn, Brian Hurtt, and Bill Crabtree

152 pages, softcover, full color
ISBN 978-1-62010-385-2

HELHEIM

HELHEIM, VOL. 1: THE WITCH WAR
By Cullen Bunn, Joëlle Jones, and Nick Filardi

160 pages, softcover, full color
ISBN 978-1-62010-014-1

$10
LETTER 44
01

LETTER 44, VOL. 1: ESCAPE VELOCITY
SQUARE ONE EDITION
By Charles Soule, Alberto Jiménez Alburquerque, Guy Major, and Dan Jackson

160 pages, softcover, full color
ISBN 978-1-62010-388-3